Gustave J. Stoeckel

The College Hymn Book

Gustave J. Stoeckel

The College Hymn Book

ISBN/EAN: 9783337372156

Printed in Europe, USA, Canada, Australia, Japan

Cover: Foto ©Thomas Meinert / pixelio.de

More available books at **www.hansebooks.com**

THE

COLLEGE HYMN BOOK

FOR USE IN THE BATTELL CHAPEL

AT

YALE COLLEGE.

WITH TUNES SELECTED AND ARRANGED FOR

MALE VOICES

BY

GUSTAVE J. STOECKEL, Mus. D.

INSTRUCTOR IN MUSIC AT YALE COLLEGE

———

NEW YORK
WM. A. POND & CO.
1886

PREFACE.

This work stands alone as a collection of English hymns, with tunes arranged for male voices.

The tunes have been selected with especial reference to the singing of a large choir or congregation; very few of them have the sentimental character or the musical form which would adapt them solely to the use of a few trained singers.

No tune has been intentionally omitted of all those which have stood the test of use in our churches, and have proved themselves the most appropriate musical expression for the hymns with which they are connected. On the other hand, only a few tunes have been admitted for their cherished associations rather than for their intrinsic worth. No pains have been spared to present tunes not only ecclesiastical, — devotional, "redolent of the incense of worship and adoration," — but also of such character that their melody, harmony, and movement are all fitted to please the musically untrained, and to satisfy trained musicians. The preferences of many college-generations of students have had great weight in making this selection. A few tunes have been omitted as unsuited to arrangement for male voices.

The Index of Tunes shows the presence of a large number of German chorals, and of arrangements from Beethoven, Händel, Haydn, and Mendelssohn. Many tunes also have been taken from the works of modern English composers of church music, — from Barnby, Dykes, Hopkins, and others. Some of these tunes are here published for the first time in this country.

The tunes are arranged for "male voices," such as are found in a College community, where the majority are barytones, with a decided numerical preponderance of voices for the lower notes. The setting of some tunes may be found rather high for the tenors, and others rather low for the basses; but in most cases that key has been selected which long experience has shown to be generally best. Transpositions into higher or lower keys may be desirable for choirs of maturer voices. The key should be adapted to the voices, not the voices to the key. Many tunes have been so set as to facilitate transposition into neighboring keys, with a more simple signature.

(III)

Church Music arranged for male voices is most effective when sung without instrumental accompaniment, provided that the voices are of good quality and well trained. If organ accompaniment is used, the following rules are suggested:

1. If 8-foot stops are used, the Tenor parts should be played an octave lower than they are written.

2. If 16-foot stops are drawn, the Bass parts should be played an octave higher.

3. If the tunes are used for Soprano and Alto voices only (for which many of the tunes are well fitted), with only 8-foot stops, the lower parts should be played an octave higher.

The hymns of this collection have in general the same form and the same topical arrangment as in the *College Hymnal*, published by H. Holt & Co., N. Y. A large number of these hymns are by Watts, Wesley, Newton, Montgomery, Doddridge, Steele, Heber, and Cowper; but the collection contains also the most lyric and devotional hymns and translations of Neale, Newman, Faber, Bonar, Thring, and others, of more recent times.

YALE COLLEGE, *Jan. 1st,* 1886.

TABLE OF SUBJECTS.

College Hymn Book.

For the Lord's Day.

OLD HUNDRED. L. M.

MIXED VOICES.

Praise God, from whom all blessings flow, Praise Him, all crea-tures here be-low;

Praise Him a-bove, ye heavenly host, Praise Fa-ther, Son, and Ho-ly Ghost.

OLD HUNDRED. L. M.

MALE VOICES. 1ST TENOR.

2ND TENOR.

Praise God, from whom all blessings flow, Praise Him, all crea-tures here be-low;

1ST BASS.

2ND BASS.

Praise Him a-bove, ye heavenly host, Praise Father, Son, and Ho-ly Ghost.

1

"O praise the Lord, all ye nations."

FROM all that dwell below the skies,
Let the Creator's praise arise ;
Let the Redeemer's name be sung
Through every land by every tongue.

2 Eternal are Thy mercies, Lord,
Eternal truth attends Thy word ;
Thy praise shall sound from shore to shore,
Till suns shall rise and set no more.

ISAAC WATTS.

2. HOMAGE. L. M.

With one con-sent, let all the earth To God their cheer-ful voi-ces raise;

Glad hom-age pay, with aw-ful mirth, And sing be-fore Him songs of praise.

2
"Enter into His gates with thanksgiving."

WITH one consent, let all the earth
To God their cheerful voices raise ;
Glad homage pay, with awful mirth,
And sing before Him songs of praise :—

2 Convinced that He is God alone,
From whom both we and all proceed ;
We, whom He chooses for His own,
The flock that He vouchsafes to feed.

3 O enter then His temple gate,
Thence to His courts devoutly press :
And still your grateful hymns repeat,
And still His name with praises bless.

4 For He's the Lord—supremely good,
His mercy is forever sure ;
His truth, which always firmly stood,
To endless ages shall endure.
TATE AND BRADY.

EFFEN. L. M.

God, in the gospel of His Son, Makes His eternal counsels known ;'Tis here His richest mercy shines, And truth is drawn in fairest lines.

3
"The law of the Lord is perfect, converting the soul."

GOD, in the gospel of His Son,
Makes His eternal counsels known ;
'Tis here His richest mercy shines,
And truth is drawn in fairest lines.

2 Here sinners of a humble frame
May taste His grace and learn His name ;
May read in characters of blood,
The wisdom, power, and grace of God.

3 Here faith reveals to mortal eyes
A brighter world beyond the skies ;
Here shines the light which guides our
way
From earth to realms of endless day.

4. O grant us grace, Almighty Lord.
To read and mark Thy holy word ;
Its truth with meekness to receive,
And by its holy precepts live.
BENJAMIN BEDDOME.

EXCELSIS. L. M.

1. Ho - san-na to the liv - ing Lord! Ho-san - na to th' in-carnate Word! To Christ, Creator,

Saviour, King, Let earth, let heaven, Hosanna sing. Ho-san-na Lord! Ho-san-na in the high-est.

4 *"Blessed is He that cometh in the name of the Lord."*
HOSANNA to the living Lord !
Hosanna to the incarnate Word !
To Christ, Creator, Saviour, King,
Let earth, let heaven, Hosanna sing.

2 Hosanna, Lord ! Thine angels cry ;
Hosanna, Lord ! Thy saints reply :
Above, beneath us, and around,
The dead and living swell the sound.

3 O Saviour ! with protecting care,
Return to this Thy house of prayer :

Assembled in Thy sacred name,
Here we Thy parting promise claim.

4 But, chiefest, in our cleansed breast,
Eternal ! bid Thy Spirit rest,
And make our secret soul to be
A temple pure, and worthy Thee !

5 So, in the last and dreadful day,
When earth and heaven shall melt away,
Thy flock, redeemed from sinful stain,
Shall swell the sound of praise again.
REGINALD HEBER.

ST. THOMAS. S. M.

How charming is the place Where my Re -deem-er, God, En -vails the beau-ty of His face, And sheds His love a-broad ! :

5 *"The place where Thine Honor dwelleth."*
How charming is the place
Where my Redeemer, God,
Unvails the beauty of His face,
And sheds His love abroad !

2 Not the fair palaces,
To which the great resort,
Are once to be compared with this,
Where Jesus holds His court.

3 Here on the mercy-seat,
With radiant glory crowned,
Our joyful eyes behold Him sit
And smile on all around.

4 Give me, O Lord, a place
Within Thy blest abode,
Among the children of Thy grace,
The servants of my God.
SAMUEL STENNETT.

HOCHGESANG. L. M.

Lord of the Sab-bath! hear our vows, On this Thy day, in this Thy house;

And own as grate-ful sac - ri - fice   The songs which from the de - sert rise.

6   *"There remaineth a rest to the people of God."*

LORD of the Sabbath! hear our vows,
On this Thy day, in this Thy house;
And own as grateful sacrifice
The songs which from the desert rise.

2 Thine earthly Sabbaths, Lord, we love ;
But there's a nobler rest above ;
To that our laboring souls aspire
With ardent pangs of strong desire.

3 No more fatigue, no more distress,
Nor sin nor hell shall reach the place ;

No groans to mingle with the songs
Which warble from immortal tongues.

4 No rude alarms of raging foes ;
No cares to break the long repose ;
No midnight shade, no clouded sun,
But sacred, high, eternal noon.

5 O long-expected day, begin !
Dawn on these realms of woe and sin !
Fain would we leave this weary road,
And sleep in death, to rest with God !

PHILIP DODDRIDGE.

DARMSTADT. C. M.

Praise waits in Zi -on, Lord, for Thee ; There shall our vows be paid : Thou hast an ear when sinners pray ; All flesh shall seek Thine aid.

7   *"O Thou that hearest prayer, unto Thee shall all flesh come."*

PRAISE waits in Zion, Lord, for Thee ;
There shall our vows be paid :
Thou hast an ear when sinners pray ;
All flesh shall seek Thine aid.

2 Lord, our iniquities prevail,
But pardoning grace is Thine,
And Thou wilt grant us power and skill
To conquer every sin.

3 In answering what Thy church requests
Thy truth and terror shine ;
And works of dreadful righteousness
Fulfill Thy kind design.

4 Thus shall the wondering nations see
The Lord is good and just ;
And distant islands fly to Thee,
And make Thy name their trust.

ISAAC WATTS.

RETREAT. L. M.

Je - sus, wher - e'er Thy peo - ple meet, There they be - hold Thy mer - cy-seat;

Wher-e'er they seek Thee, Thou art found, And ev - ery place is hal-lowed ground.

8   *"Every one that asketh, receiveth."*

JESUS, where'er Thy people meet,
There they behold Thy mercy-seat;
Where'er they seek Thee, Thou art found,
And every place is hallowed ground.

2 For Thou, within no walls confined,
Inhabitest the humble mind;
Such ever bring Thee where they come,
And going take Thee to their home.

3 Dear Shepherd of Thy chosen few,
Thy former mercies here renew;
Here to our waiting hearts proclaim
The sweetness of Thy saving Name.

4 Here may we prove the power of prayer
To strengthen faith and sweeten care,
To teach our faint desires to rise.
And bring all Heaven before our eyes.

       WILLIAM COWPER.

ST. AGNES. C. M.

Early, my God, without de-lay, I haste to seek Thy face; My thirsty Spi - rit faints away, Without Thy cheering grace.

9   *"My soul thirsteth for Thee."*

EARLY, my God, without delay,
I haste to seek Thy face;
My thirsty spirit faints away,
Without Thy cheering grace.

2 So pilgrims on the scorching sand,
Beneath a burning sky,
Long for a cooling stream at hand,
And they must drink or die.

3 I've seen Thy glory and Thy power
Through all Thy temple shine:
My God, repeat that heavenly hour,
That vision so divine.

4 Not all the blessings of a feast
Can please my soul so well,
As when Thy richer grace I taste,
And in Thy presence dwell.

5 Not life itself, with all its joys,
Can my best passions move,
Or raise so high my cheerful voice,
As Thy forgiving love.

6 Thus till my last expiring day,
I'll bless my God and King;
Thus will I lift my hands to pray,
And tune my lips to sing.

       ISAAC WATTS.

SCHUMANN. L. M.

Sweet is the work, my God, my King! To praise Thy name, give thanks, and sing; To

show Thy love by morn-ing light, And talk of all Thy truth at night.

10 *"It is a good thing to give thanks unto the Lord."*

SWEET is the work, my God, my King !
To praise Thy name, give thanks, and sing ;
To show Thy love by morning light,
And talk of all Thy truth at night.

2 Sweet is the day of sacred rest ;
No mortal cares shall seize my breast ;
Oh ! may my heart in tune be found,
Like David's harp of solemn sound !

3 My heart shall triumph in my Lord,
And bless His works, and bless His word ;
Thy works of grace, how bright they shine !
How deep Thy counsels ! how divine !

4 Lord, I shall share a glorious part,
When grace hath well refined my heart,
And fresh supplies of joy are shed
Like holy oil to cheer my head.

5 Then shall I see, and hear, and know,
All I desired or wished below ;

And every power find sweet employ
In that eternal world of joy.

ISAAC WATTS.

11 *"This is the day which the Lord hath made."*

THIS day at Thy creating word
First o'er the earth the light was poured :
O Lord, this day upon us shine,
And fill our souls with light divine.

2 This day the Lord, for sinners slain,
In might victorious rose again :
O Jesus, may we raised be
From death of sin to life in Thee.

3 This day the Holy Spirit came
With fiery tongues of cloven flame :
O Spirit, fill our hearts this day
With grace to hear, and grace to pray.

4 O day of light, and life, and grace,
From earthly toils sweet resting-place !
Thy hallowed hours, best gift of love,
Give we again to God above.

WILLIAM WALSHAM HOW.

ZEPHYR. L. M.

Great God, attend, while Zion sings The joy that from Thy presence springs; To spend one day with Thee on earth, Exceeds a thousand days of mirth.

MIGDOL. L. M.

An-oth-er six days' work is done, An-oth-er Sab-bath is be-gun;

Re-turn, my soul! en-joy thy rest: Im-prove the day thy God hath blest.

12 *"Remember the Sabbath Day."*
ANOTHER six days' work is done,
Another Sabbath is begun ;
Return, my soul! enjoy thy rest :
Improve the day thy God hath blest.

2 Oh, that our tho'ts and thanks may rise,
As grateful incense to the skies :
And draw from heaven that sweet repose,
Which none but he that feels it knows.

3 This heavenly calm within the breast,
Is the dear pledge of glorious rest,
Which for the church of God remains —
The end of cares, the end of pains.

4 In holy duties, let the day,
In holy pleasures, pass away ;
How sweet a Sabbath thus to spend,
In hope of one that ne'er shall end.
JOSEPH STENNETT.

13 *"They that wait upon the Lord shall renew their strength."*
How pleasant, how divinely fair,
O Lord of hosts, Thy dwellings are!
With long desire my spirit faints
To meet the assemblies of Thy saints.

14 *"O Lord God of hosts hear my prayer."*
GREAT God, attend, while Zion sings
The joy that from Thy presence springs ;
To spend one day with Thee on earth
Exceeds a thousand days of mirth.

2 Might I enjoy the meanest place
Within Thy house, O God of grace,
Not tents of ease, nor thrones of power,
Should tempt my feet to leave Thy door.

3 God is our sun — He makes our day ;
God is our shield — He guards our way

2 My flesh would rest in Thine abode,
My panting heart cries out for God ;
My God, my King, why should I be
So far from all my joys and Thee !

3 Blest are the saints who sit on high
Around Thy throne of majesty ;
Thy brightest glories shine above,
And all their work is praise and love.

4 Blest are the souls that find a place
Within the temple of Thy grace ;
There they behold Thy gentler rays,
And seek Thy face, and learn Thy praise.

5 Blest are the men whose hearts are set
To find the way to Zion's gate :
God is their strength ; and thro' the road
They lean upon their helper, God.

6 Cheerful they walk with growing strength,
Till all shall meet in heaven at length ;
Till all before Thy face appear,
And join in nobler worship there.
ISAAC WATTS.

From all th' assaults of hell and sin,
From foes without, and foes within.

4 All needful grace will God bestow,
And crown that grace with glory too ;
He gives us all things, and witholds
No real good from upright souls.

5 O God our King, Thy sovereign sway
The glorious hosts of heaven obey.
Display Thy grace, exert Thy power,
Till all on earth Thy name adore.
ISAAC WATTS.

For the Lord's Day.

BURNEY. L. M.

1. O Thou, to whom, in an-cient time, The lyre of He-brew bards was strung,

Whom kings a-dored in song sub-lime, And pro-phets praised with glow-ing tongue!

15 *"This is the generation of them that seek Him."*

O Thou, to whom, in ancient time,
 The lyre of Hebrew bards was strung,
Whom kings adored in song sublime,
And prophets praised with glowing tongue!

2 Not now on Zion's height alone
 The favored worshipper may dwell,
Nor where, at sultry noon, Thy Son
 Sat weary by the patriarch's well.

3 From every place below the skies,
 The grateful song, the fervent prayer,
The incense of the heart, may rise
 To heaven, and find acceptance there.

4 O Thou, to whom, in ancient time,
 The lyre of prophet bards was strung,
To Thee, at last, in every clime,
 Shall temples rise, and praise be sung.

JOHN PIERPONT.

GLUCK. C. M.

The Spi-rit breaths upon the word, And brings the truth to sight, Precepts and prom-i-ses af-ford A sanc-ti-fy-ing light.

16 *"The entrance of Thy words giveth light."*

THE Spirit breathes upon the word,
 And brings the truth to sight;
Precepts and promises afford
 A sanctifying light.

2 A glory gilds the sacred page,
 Majestic, like the sun;
It gives a light to every age,
 It gives, but borrows none.

3 The hand that gave it, still supplies
 The gracious light and heat;

Its truths upon the nations rise,
 They rise but never set.

4 Let everlasting thanks be Thine,
 For such a bright display,
As makes a world of darkness shine
 With beams of heavenly day.

5 My soul rejoices to pursue
 The steps of Him I love,
Till glory breaks upon my view
 In brighter worlds above.

WILLIAM COWPER.

WARWICK. C. M.

Lord, in the morn-ing Thou shalt hear My voice as-cend-ing high;

To Thee will I di-rect my prayer, To Thee lift up mine eye.

17 *"In Thy fear will I worship toward Thy holy temple."*

LORD, in the morning Thou shalt hear
My voice ascending high ;
To Thee will I direct my prayer,
To Thee lift up mine eye :—

2 Up to the hills where Christ is gone,
To plead for all His saints,
Presenting at His Father's throne
Our songs and our complaints.

3 Thou art a God, before whose sight
The wicked shall not stand ;

Sinners shall ne'er be Thy delight,
Nor dwell at Thy right hand.

4 But to Thy house will I resort,
To taste Thy mercies there ;
I will frequent Thy holy court,
And worship in Thy fear.

5 O may Thy Spirit guide my feet
In ways of righteousness !
Make every path of duty straight,
And plain before my face.

ISAAC WATTS.

CAPERNAUM. 7s.

To Thy temple 'we repair—Lord, we love to worship there, When with-in the veil we meet Thee up-on the mercy-seat.

18 *"Lord, I have loved the habitation of Thy house."*

To Thy temple we repair—
Lord, we love to worship there,
When within the vail we meet
Thee upon the mercy-seat.

2 While Thy glorious name is sung,
Tune our lips—unloose our tongue ;
Then our joyful souls shall bless
Thee, the Lord our righteousness.

3 While to Thee our prayers ascend,
Let Thine ear in love attend ;

Hear us, for Thy Spirit pleads—
Hear, for Jesus intercedes.

4 While Thy word is heard with awe,
While we tremble at Thy law,
Let Thy gospel's wondrous love
Every doubt and fear remove.

5 From Thy house when we return,
Let our hearts within us burn,
That at evening we may say—
"We have walked with God to-day."

JAMES MONTGOMERY.

LATOUR. C. M.

Spir-it of truth! on this Thy day, To Thee for help we cry, To guide us

thro' the drear-y way Of dark mor-tal-i-ty, Of dark mor-tal-i-ty.

19   *"The gift of the Holy Ghost."*

Spirit of truth! on this Thy day,
  To Thee for help we cry,
To guide us through the dreary way
  Of dark mortality.

2 We ask not, Lord, Thy cloven flame,
  Or tongues of various tone;
But long Thy praises to proclaim
  With fervor in our own.

3 No heavenly harpings soothe our ear,
  No mystic dreams we share;
Yet hope to feel Thy comfort near,
  And hear Thee in our prayer.

4 When tongues shall cease, and power
  And knowledge empty prove, [decay,
Do Thou Thy trembling servants stay,
  With faith, with hope, with love.
                  REGINALD HEBER.

20   *"The Lord loveth the gates of Zion."*

Arise, O King of grace! arise,
  And enter to Thy rest;
Lo! Thy church waits with longing eyes,
  Thus to be owned and blest.

2 Enter with all Thy glorious train,
  Thy Spirit and Thy word;
All that the ark did once contain
  Could no such grace afford.

3 Here, mighty God! accept our vows,
  Here let Thy praise be spread;
Bless the provisions of Thy house,
  And fill Thy poor with bread.

4 Here let the Son of David reign,
  Let God's Anointed shine;
Justice and truth His court maintain,
  With love and power divine.
                  ISAAC WATTS.

AVON. C. M.

The God of peace, who from the dead Brought up again our Lord, And, thro' the cov'nant of His blood, Our souls to peace restor'd.

21   *"Make you perfect in every good work."*

The God of peace, who from the dead
  Brought up again our Lord,
And, thro' the covenant of His blood,
  Our souls to peace restored:—

2 Confirm our hearts in each good work,
  To do His perfect will;

That, made well pleasing in His sight,
  Our course with joy we fill.

3 So shall we, in His heavenly courts,
  Hereafter, ever live;
And to His name, thro' Jesus Christ,
  Eternal glory give.
             ELEAZAR THOMPSON FITCH.

ST. GEORGE'S.   C. M.

This is the day the Lord hath made, He calls the hours His own;

Let heaven re-joice, let earth be glad, And praise sur - round the throne.

22 *"The Lord is my strength and song, and is become my salvation."*

This is the day the Lord hath made,
He calls the hours His own ;
Let heaven rejoice, let earth be glad,
And praise surround the throne.

2 To-day He rose and left the dead,
And Satan's empire fell ;
To-day the saints His triumph spread,
And all His wonders tell.

3 Hosanna to the anointed King,
To David's holy Son ;

Help us, O Lord ; descend, and bring
Salvation from Thy throne.

4 Blest be the Lord, who comes to men
With messages of grace ;
Who comes, in God His Father's name,
To save our sinful race.

5 Hosanna in the highest strains
The church on earth can raise ;
The highest heavens in which he reigns,
Shall give Him nobler praise.

ISAAC WATTS.

WOODSTOCK. C. M.

O God, by whom the seed is given, By whom the har- vest blest, Whose word, like manna showered from heaven, is planted in our breast.

23 *"Herein is my Father glorified, that ye bear much fruit."*

O God ! by whom the seed is given,
By whom the harvest blest ;   [heaven,
Whose word, like manna showered from
Is planted in our breast.

2 Preserve it from the passing feet,
And plunderers of the air,

The sultry sun's intenser heat,
And thorns of worldly care.

3 Though buried deep, or thinly strown,
Do Thou Thy grace supply ;
The hope in earthly furrows sown
Shall ripen in the sky !

REGINALD HEBER.

LISBON. S. M.

Welcome, sweet day of rest, That saw the Lord a - rise! Wel - come to this re-viv-ing breast, And these re-joic-ing eyes!

24   *"A day in Thy courts is better than a thousand."*

WELCOME, sweet day of rest,
   That saw the Lord arise!
Welcome to this reviving breast,
   And these rejoicing eyes!

2 The King Himself comes near,
   And feasts His saints to-day;
Here may we sit and see Him here,
   And love, and praise, and pray.

3 One day, amid the place
   Where my dear Lord hath been,
Is sweeter than ten thousand days
   Within the tents of sin.

4 My willing soul would stay
   In such a frame as this,
And sit and sing herself away
   To everlasting bliss.
             ISAAC WATTS.

25   *"In the Spirit on the Lord's day."*

THIS is the day of light:
   Let there be light to-day:

O Day-spring, rise upon our night,
   And chase its gloom away.

2 This is the day of rest:
   Our failing strength renew;
On weary brain and troubled breast
   Shed Thou Thy freshening dew.

3 This is the day of peace:
   Thy peace our spirits fill;
Bid Thou the blasts of discord cease,
   The waves of strife be still.

4 This is the day of prayer;
   Let earth to heaven draw near;
Lift up our hearts to seek Thee there,
   Come down to meet us here.

5 This is the first of days:
   Send forth Thy quickening breath,
And wake dead souls to love and praise,
   O Vanquisher of death!
             JOHN ELLERTON.

MENDELSSOHN. C. M.

Come, Thou de - sire of all Thy saints, Our hum-ble strains at · tend,

While with our prais - es and com-plaints, Low at Thy feet we bend.

HENDON. 7s.

Lord, we come before Thee now, At Thy feet we humbly bow; Oh, do not our

suit disdain! Shall we seek Thee, Lord, in vain? Shall we seek Thee, Lord, in vain?

26 *"Thy face we seek."*

LORD, we come before Thee now,
At Thy feet we humbly bow;
Oh, do not our suit disdain!
Shall we seek Thee, Lord, in vain?

2 Lord, on Thee our souls depend,
In compassion now descend;
Fill our hearts with Thy rich grace,
Tune our lips to sing Thy praise.

3 In Thine own appointed way,
Now we seek thee; here we stay;

Lord, we know not how to go,
Till a blessing Thou bestow.

4 Send some message from Thy word,
That may joy and peace afford;
Let Thy Spirit now impart
Full salvation to each heart.

5 Comfort those who weep and mourn:
Let the time of joy return;
Those that are cast down lift up;
Make them strong in faith and hope.

WILLIAM HAMMOND.

27 *"In Thee, O Lord, do I hope."* [MENDELSSOHN.

COME, Thou desire of all Thy saints,
Our humble strains attend,
While, with our praises and complaints,
Low at Thy feet we bend.

2 How should our songs, like those above,
With warm devotion rise!
How should our souls, on wings of love,
Mount upward to the skies!

3 Come, Lord, Thy love alone can raise
In us the heavenly flame;
Then shall our lips resound Thy praise,
Our hearts adore Thy name.

4 Dear Saviour, let Thy glory shine,
And fill Thy dwellings here,
Till life, and love, and joy divine
A heaven on earth appear.

5 Then shall our hearts enraptured say,—
Come, great Redeemer, come,

And bring the bright, the glorious day,
That calls Thy children home.

ANNE STEELE.

28 *"A day in Thy courts is better than a thousand."*

BLEST day of God, most calm, most bright,
The first and best of days,
The laborer's rest, the saints delight,
A day of joy and praise!

2 My Saviour's face did make thee shine,
His rising did thee raise:
This made thee heavenly and divine
Beyond the common days.

3 The first-fruits oft a blessing prove
To all the sheaves behind:
And they the day of Christ that love
A happy week shall find.

4 This day I must with God appear,
For, Lord, the day is Thine;
O help me spend it in Thy fear,
Then shall the day be mine.

JOHN MASON.

St. BERNARD. 7s. D.

Christ the Lord is risen to-day, Sons of men and angels say; Raise your joys and triumphs high, Sing, ye heavens, and earth reply.

love's re- deem-ing work is done, Fought the fight, the battle won: Lo! our Sun's eclipse is o'er; Lo! He sets in blood no more.

29   *"The Lord is risen indeed."*

CHRIST the Lord is risen to-day,
  Sons of men and angels say ;
Raise your joys and triumphs high,
  Sing, ye heavens, and earth reply.
Love's redeeming work is done,
  Fought the fight, the battle won :
Lo ! our Sun's eclipse is o'er ;
  Lo ! He sets in blood no more.

2 Vain the stone, the watch, the seal ;
  Christ hath burst the gates of hell !
Death in vain forbids His rise ;
  Christ hath opened Paradise !
Lives again our glorious King :
  Where, O Death, is now thy sting ?
Once He died. our souls to save :
  Where thy victory, O Grave ?

3 Soar we now where Christ has led,
  Following our exalted Head ;
Made like Him, like Him we rise ;
  Ours the cross, the grave, the skies.
Love's redeeming work is done,
  Fought the fight, the battle won :
Lo ! our Sun's eclipse is o'er ;
  Lo ! He sets in blood no more.
              CHARLES WESLEY.

30   *" Whosoever abideth in Him sinneth not."*

LIGHT of light, seraphic fire,
  Love divine, Thyself impart ;
Every fainting soul inspire,
  Shine in every drooping heart ;

Every mournful sinner cheer,
  Scatter all our guilty gloom,
Holy Ghost, appear, appear ;
  To Thy human temple come.

2 Come in this accepted hour,
  Bring Thy heavenly kingdom in ;
Fill us with Thy glorious power,
  Rooting out the seeds of sin :
Nothing more can we require,
  We will covet nothing less ;
Be Thou all our hearts desire,
  Joy and peace and holiness.
              CHARLES WESLEY.

31   *"Praise Him for His mighty acts: praise Him according to His excellent greatness."*

PRAISE the Lord, His glories show,
Saints within His courts below,
Angels round His throne above,
All that see and share His love.
Earth to heaven, and heaven to earth,
Tell His wonders, sing His worth ;
Age to age, and shore to shore,
Praise Him, praise Him, evermore !

2 Praise the Lord, His mercies trace,
Praise His providence and grace,
All that He for man hath done,
All He sends us through His Son :
Strings and voices, hands and hearts,
In the concert bear your parts ;
All that breathe, your Lord adore,
Praise Him, praise Him. evermore !
              HENRY FRANCIS LYTE.

LISCHER. H. M.

Welcome, delightful morn, Thou day of sacred rest!
I hail thy kind return, Lord, make these moments blest: } From the low train of mortal toys, I

soar to reach im-mor-tal joys, I   soar   to   reach   im - mor-tal   joys.
I soar to reach

---

32   *"Quicken us and we will call upon Thy name."*

WELCOME, delightful morn,
   Thou day of sacred rest !
I hail thy kind return ;—
   Lord, make these moments blest :
From the low train of mortal toys,
I soar to reach immortal joys.

2 Now may the King descend
   And fill His throne of grace ;
Thy scepter, Lord, extend,
   While saints address Thy face :
Let sinners feel Thy quickening word,
And learn to know and fear the Lord.

3 Descend, celestial Dove,
   With all Thy quickening powers ;
Disclose a Saviour's love,
   And bless these sacred hours :
Then shall my soul new life obtain,
Nor Sabbaths be enjoyed in vain.
            HAYWARD.

33   *"How amiable are Thy tabernacles, O Lord of Hosts."*

LORD of the worlds above,
   How pleasant and how fair
The dwellings of Thy love,
   Thine earthly temples are !
To Thine abode | With warm desires
My heart aspires, | To see my God.

2 O happy souls, that pray
   Where God appoints to hear !

O happy men, that pay
   Their constant service there !
They praise Thee still ; | That love the way
And happy they | To Zion's hill.

3 They go from strength to strength,
   Through this dark vale of tears,
Till each arrives at length,
   Till each in heaven appears.
O glorious seat, | Shall thither bring
When God our King | Our willing feet !
            ISAAC WATTS.

34   *"To Whom be glory forever."*

WE give immortal praise
   To God the Father's love,
For all our comforts here,
   And all our hopes above ;
He sent His own Eternal Son
To die for sins that man had done.

2 To God the Son belongs
   Immortal glory too,
Who saved us by His blood
   From everlasting woe :
And now He lives, and now He reigns
And sees the fruit of all His pains.

3 To God the Spirit, praise
   And endless worship give,
Whose new-creating power
   Makes the dead sinner live :
His work completes the great design,
And fills the soul with joy divine.
            ISAAC WATTS.

HAMDEN. 8s, 7s, 4s.

In Thy name, O Lord, as-sem-bling, We,Thy,peo-ple,now draw near;
Teach us to rejoice with trembling; Speak,and let Thy ser-vants hear,— Hear with meekness,—Hear Thy word with god-ly fear.

35 *"He will fulfill the desire of them that fear Him."*

In Thy name, O Lord! assembling,
  We, Thy people, now draw near ;
Teach us to rejoice with trembling ;
  Speak, and let Thy servants hear,—
    Hear with meekness,—
Hear Thy word with godly fear.

2 While our days on earth are lengthened,
  May we give them, Lord! to Thee ;
Cheered by hope, and daily strengthened,

May we run, nor weary be,
  Till Thy glory
Without cloud in heaven we see.

3 There, in worship purer, sweeter,
  All Thy people shall adore ;
Tasting of enjoyment greater
  Than they could conceive before ;
    Full enjoyment,
Full and pure for evermore.

THOMAS KELLY.

FERRIER. 7s.

On this day, the first of days, God the Fa-ther's name we praise ;
Who, cre - a - tion's Lord and Spring, Did the world from dark - ness bring.

36 *"And God said, Let there be light: and there was light."*

On this day, the first of days,
God the Father's name we praise ;
Who, creation's Lord and Spring,
Did the world from darkness bring.

2 On this day the Eternal Son
Over death His triumph won ;
On this day the Spirit came
With His gifts of living flame.

3 O that fervent love to-day
May in every heart have sway,
Teaching us to praise aright
God the Source of life and light.

4 Father, who did fashion me
Image of Thyself to be,
Fill me with Thy love divine,
Let my every thought be Thine.

5 Holy Jesus, may I be
Dead and buried here with Thee ;
And, by love inflamed, arise
Unto Thee a sacrifice.

6 Thou who dost all gifts impart,
Shine, sweet Spirit, in my heart ;
Best of gifts Thyself bestow ;
Make me burn Thy love to know.

SIR HENRY WILLIAMS BAKER.

INNOCENTS. 7s.

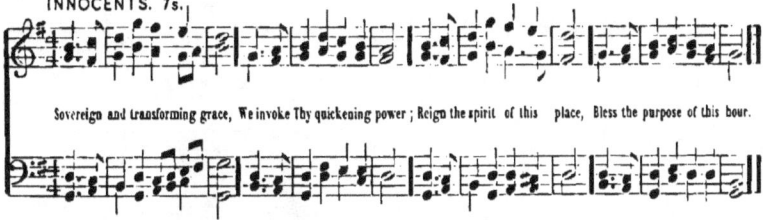

Sovereign and transforming grace, We invoke Thy quickening power ; Reign the spirit of this place, Bless the purpose of this hour.

37 *"The grace of God that bringeth salvation."*

SOVEREIGN and transforming Grace,
   We invoke Thy quickening power ;
Reign the spirit of this place,
   Bless the purpose of this hour.

2 To the anxious soul impart
   Hope all other hopes above :
Stir the dull and hardened heart
   With a longing and a love.

3 Give the struggling peace for strife ;
   Give the doubting light for gloom ;
Speed the living into life ;
   Warn the dying of their doom.

4 Work in all, in all renew,
   Day by day, the life divine ;
All our wills to Thee subdue,
   All our hearts to Thee incline.

FREDERIC HENRY HEDGE.

38 *"In Thy light shall we see light."*

MORN of morns, and day of days !
   Beauteous were thy new-born rays :

Brighter yet from death's dark prison,
   Christ, the Light of lights, is risen.

2 He commanded, and His word
   Death and the dread chaos heard ;
O shall we, more deaf than they,
   In the chains of darkness stay ?

3 Unto hearts in slumber weak,
   Let the heavenly trumpet speak ;
And a newer walk express
   Their new life to righteousness.

4 Grant us this, and with us be,
   O Thou Fount of charity,
Thou who dost the Spirit give,
   Bidding the dead letter live.

5 Glory to the Father, Son,
   And to Thee, O Holy One,
By whose quickening breath divine
   Our dull spirits burn and shine.

ISAAC WILLIAMS.

PLEYEL'S HYMN. 7s.

Now may He who from the dead Bro't the Shepherd of the sheep, Jesus Christ, our King and Head, All our souls in safety keep.

39 *"He that keepeth thee will not slumber."*

Now may He who from the dead
   Brought the Shepherd of the sheep,
Jesus Christ, our King and Head,
   All our souls in safety keep.

2 May He teach us to fulfill
   What is pleasing in His sight ;
Perfect us in all His will,
   And preserve us day and night.

JOHN NEWTON.

MENDEBRAS. 7s, 6s. Double.

O   day of   rest and glad-ness,   O   day of joy   and light, ⎫
O   balm of care and sad- ness,   Most beau-ti-ful, most bright; ⎰ On thee the high and

low-ly, Thro' a-ges joined in tune, Sing, Ho-ly, Ho-ly, Ho- ly, To the great God Tri - une.

40   *"Return unto thy rest, O my soul."*

O DAY of rest and gladness,
   O day of joy and light,
O balm of care and sadness,
   Most beautiful, most bright ;
On thee the high and lowly,
   Through ages joined in tune,
Sing, Holy, Holy, Holy,
   To the great God Triune.

2 On thee, at the creation,
   The light first had its birth ;
On thee for our salvation
   Christ rose from depths of earth ;
On thee our Lord victorious
   The Spirit sent from heaven ;
And thus on thee most glorious
   A triple light was given.

3 To-day on weary nations
   The heavenly manna falls ;
To holy convocations
   The silver trumpet calls.
Where gospel-light is glowing,
   With pure and radiant beams,
And living water flowing
   With soul-refreshing streams.

4 New graces ever gaining
   From this our day of rest,
We reach the rest remaining
   To spirits of the blest ;
To Holy Ghost be praises,
   To Father and to Son ;
The church her voice upraises
   To Thee, blest Three in One.

CHRISTOPHER WORDSWORTH.

TOURS.   7s, 6s, Double.

The day of resurrection! Earth, tell it out abroad! The Passover of gladness! The Passover of God!

From death to life e - ter-nal, From this world to the sky, Our Christ hath brought us over, With hymns of vic - to - ry.

SABBATH. 7s. 6 lines.

Safely through another week, God has brought us on our way; let us now a blessing seek, Waiting in His courts to-day:

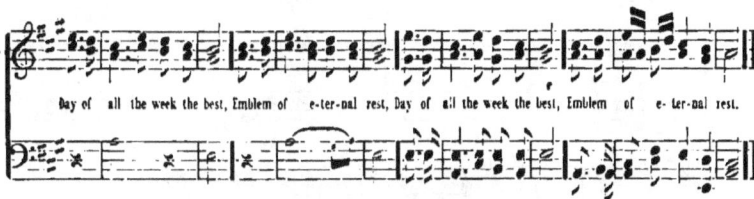

Day of all the week the best, Emblem of e-ter-nal rest, Day of all the week the best, Emblem of e- ter-nal rest.

---

41 *"Thou wilt keep him in perfect peace, whose mind is stayed on Thee."*

SAFELY through another week,
  God has brought us on our way ;
Let us now a blessing seek,
  Waiting in His courts to-day :
Day of all the week the best,
Emblem of eternal rest.

2 While we pray for pardoning grace,
  Through the dear Redeemer's name,
Show Thy reconciled face—
  Shine away our sin and shame ;
From our worldly care set free,
May we rest this day in Thee.

3 Here we come Thy name to praise ;
  May we feel Thy presence near :
May Thy glory meet our eyes,
  While we in Thy house appear :
Here afford us, Lord, a taste
Of our everlasting rest.

4 May the gospel's joyful sound
  Wake our minds to raptures new ;
Let Thy victories abound,—
  Unrepenting souls subdue ;
Thus may all our Sabbaths prove,
Till we rest in Thee above.

          JOHN NEWTON.

---

42 *"Now is Christ risen from the dead."*

THE day of resurrection !
  Earth, tell it out abroad !
The Passover of gladness !
  The Passover of God !
From death to life eternal,
  From this world to the sky,
Our Christ hath brought us over,
  With hymns of victory.

2 Our hearts be pure from evil,
  That we may see aright
The Lord in rays eternal
  Of resurrection-light :

And, listening to His accents,
  May hear, so calm and plain,
His own All Hail.—and hearing,
  May raise the victor strain !

3 Now let the heavens be joyful !
  Let earth her song begin !
Let the round world keep triumph,
  And all that is therein :
Invisible and visible
  Their notes let all things blend,
For Christ the Lord hath risen,—
  Our Joy that hath no end.

          JOHN MASON NEALE.

UNION. L. P. M.

I love the vol-ume of Thy word; What light and joy those leaves af-ford

To souls benighted and distrest! Thy precepts guide my doubtful way, Thy fear forbids my

feet to stray, Thy promise leads my heart to rest, Thy promise leads my heart to rest.

43 *"If ye know these things, happy are ye if ye do them."*

I LOVE the volume of Thy word ;
What light and joy those leaves afford
  To souls benighted and distrest !
Thy precepts guide my doubtful way,
Thy fear forbids my feet to stray,
Thy promise leads my heart to rest.
              [eyes,
2 Thy threatenings wake my slumbering
And warn me where my danger lies ;
  But 'tis Thy blessed gospel, Lord,

That makes my guilty conscience clean,
Converts my soul, subdues my sin,
  And gives a free but large reward.

3 Who knows the errors of his thoughts?
My God, forgive my secret faults,
  And from presumptuous sins restrain :
Accept my poor attempts of praise,
That I have read Thy book of grace,
  And book of nature, not in vain.

ISAAC WATTS.

TRUST. 8s, 7s.

May the grace of Christ our Saviour, And the Father's boundless love, With the Holy Spirit's fa-vor, Rest up-on us from a-bove!

44   *"Go in peace."*

MAY the grace of Christ our Saviour,
  And the Father's boundless love,
With the Holy Spirit's favor,
  Rest upon us from above !

2 Thus may we abide in union
  With each other and the Lord ;
And possess in sweet communion,
  Joys which earth cannot afford.

JOHN NEWTON.

JESU MEIN LEBEN. 8s, 7s, 6l.

Christ is made the sure foundation, Christ the Head and Corner-stone, Chosen of the Lord, and precious,

Bind-ing all the church in one, Ho-ly Zi-on's Help for ev-er, And her Con-fi-dence a - lone.

45 *"The foundation of God standeth sure."*

CHRIST is made the sure foundation,
Christ the Head and Corner-stone,
Chosen of the Lord, and precious,
Binding all the church in one,
Holy Zion's Help for ever,
And her Confidence alone.

2 To this temple, where we call Thee,
Come, O Lord of hosts, to-day:
With Thy wonted loving-kindness,
Hear Thy servants as they pray;
And Thy fullest benediction
Shed within its walls alway.

3 Here vouchsafe to all Thy servants
What they ask of Thee to gain,
What they gain from Thee for ever
With the blessed to retain,
And hereafter in Thy glory
Evermore with Thee to reign.

JOHN MASON NEALE.

SCOTT. S. M.

Once more, be-fore we part, Oh, bless the Saviour's name! Let every tongue and every heart Adore and praise the same.

46 *"God, even our own God, shall give us His blessing."*

ONCE more, before we part,
Oh, bless the Saviour's name!
Let every tongue and every heart
Adore and praise the same.

2 Lord, in Thy grace we came,
That blessing still impart;
We met in Jesus' sacred name,
In Jesus' name we part.

3 Still on Thy holy word,
Help us to feed, and grow,
Still to go on to know the Lord,
And practice what we know.

4 Now, Lord, before we part,
Help us to bless Thy name:
Let every tongue and every heart
Adore and praise the same.

JOSEPH HART.

CHORAL. C. M.

A - gain the Lord of   Life and Light A - wakes the kind - ling   ray,

Un - seals the eye - lids   of   the morn, And pours in - creas - ing   day.

47   *"Walk as children of light."*

AGAIN the Lord of Life and Light
  Awakes the kindling ray,
Unseals the eyelids of the morn,
  And pours increasing day.

2 O what a night was that which wrapt
  The heathen world in gloom !
O what a sun, which broke this day
  Triumphant from the tomb !

3 This day be grateful homage paid,
  And loud hosannas sung ;
Let gladness dwell in every heart,
  And praise on every tongue.

4 Ten thousand differing lips shall join
  To hail this welcome morn,

Which scatters blessings from its wings
  To nations yet unborn.

5 The powers of darkness leagued in vain
  To bind His soul in death ;
He shook their kingdom, when He fell,
  With His expiring breath.

6 And now His conquering chariot-wheels
  Ascend the lofty skies ;
While broke beneath His powerful cross
  Death's iron scepter lies.

7 To Thee, my Saviour and my King,
  Glad homage let me give ;
And stand prepared like Thee to die,
  With Thee that I may live !
                 ANNA LÆTITIA BARBAULD.

BOYLSTON. S. M.

Lord, at this clos-ing hour, Es - tab-lish ev-ery heart Up - on Thy word of truth and power, To keep us when we part.

48   *"Thy kingdom come; Thy will be done."*

LORD, at this closing hour,
  Establish every heart
Upon Thy word of truth and power,
  To keep us when we part.

2 Peace to our brethren give ;
  Fill all our hearts with love ;
In faith and patience may we live,
  And seek our rest above.

3 Through changes, bright or drear,
  We would Thy will pursue ;
And toil to spread Thy kingdom here,
  Till we its glory view.

4 To God, the Only Wise,
  In every age adored,
Let glory from the church arise
  Through Jesus Christ our Lord.
             ELEAZAR THOMPSON FITCH.

O SANCTISSIMA. 8s, 7s, 4s.

Lord, dis - miss us with Thy bless-ing, Fill our hearts with joy and peace ; }
Let us each, Thy love pos - sess-ing, Tri- umph in re - deem - ing grace ; }

O re - fresh us, O re fresh us, Travel-ing through this wil - der - ness.

49 "While He blessed them, He was parted from them."

Lord, dismiss us with Thy blessing,
Fill our hearts with joy and peace ;
Let us each, Thy love possessing,
Triumph in redeeming grace ;
O refresh us,
Traveling through this wilderness.

2 Thanks we give, and adoration,
For Thy gospel's joyful sound ;
May the fruits of Thy salvation
In our hearts and lives abound ;
May Thy presence
With us evermore be found.

3 So, whene'er the signal's given
Us from earth to call away,
Borne on angels' wings to heaven,
Glad the summons to obey,
May we ever
Reign with Christ in endless day.
WALTER SHIRLEY.

ERNAN. L. M.

Dis-miss us with Thy bless-ing, Lord ; Help us to feed up - on Thy word ;

All that has been a - miss for - give, And let Thy truth with - in us live.

50 "The Lord will bless His people with peace."

Dismiss us with Thy blessing, Lord,
Help us to feed upon Thy word ;
All that has been amiss forgive,
And let Thy truth within us live.

2 Though we are guilty, Thou art good ;
Wash all our works in Jesus' blood ;
Give every fettered soul release,
And bid us all depart in peace.
JOSEPH HART.

ASHFORD. L. M.

The peace which God a - lone re-veals, And by His word of grace imparts,

Which on - ly the be - liev - er feels, Di - rect, and keep, and cheer our hearts!

51   *"The blessing of peace."*

The peace which God alone reveals,
  And by His word of grace imparts,
Which only the believer feels,
  Direct, and keep, and cheer our hearts!

2 And may the holy Three in One,
  The Father, Word, and Comforter,

Pour an abundant blessing down
  On every soul assembled here!

3 Praise God, from whom all blessings flow;
  Praise Him, all creatures here below;
Praise Him above, ye heavenly host!
  Praise Father, Son, and Holy Ghost.
                   JOHN NEWTON.

DENNIS. S. M.

To God the on - ly wise, Who keeps us by His word,

Be glo - ry now and ev - er - more, Through Je - sus Christ our Lord.

52   *"That we may glory in Thy praise."*

To God the only wise,
  Who keeps us by His word,
Be glory now and evermore,
  Through Jesus Christ our Lord.

2 Hosanna to the Word,
  Who from the Father came;

Ascribe salvation to the Lord,
  And ever bless His name.

3 The grace of Christ our Lord,
  The Father's boundless love,
The Spirit's blest communion, too,
  Be with us from above.
                   ISAAC WATTS.

ALL SAINTS. L. M.

Forth in Thy Name, O Lord, I go, My dai - ly la - bor to pur-sue,

Thee, on - ly Thee, re-solved to know In all I think, or speak, or do.

53 *"I have set the Lord always before me."*

FORTH in Thy Name, O Lord, I go,
 My daily labor to pursue,
Thee, only Thee, resolved to know
 In all I think, or speak, or do.

2 The task Thy wisdom hath assigned
 O let me cheerfully fulfill ;
In all my works Thy presence find,
 And prove Thine acceptable will.

3 Thee may I set at my right hand,
 Whose eyes mine inmost substance see,
And labor on at Thy command,
 And offer all my works to Thee.

4 Give me to bear Thy easy yoke,
 And every moment watch and pray ;
And still to things eternal look,
 And hasten to Thy glorious day ;

5 For Thee delightfully employ [given,
 Whate'er Thy bounteous grace hath
And run my course with even joy,
 And closely walk with Thee to heaven.
 CHARLES WESLEY.

54 *"I will go in the strength of the Lord God."*

AGAIN the daylight fills the sky ;
We lift our hearts to God on high,
That He, in all we do or say,
Would keep us free from harm to-day ;

2 Would guard our hearts and tongues
 from strife ;
Would shield from anger's din our life ;

From all ill sights would turn our eyes,
And close our ears from vanities ;

3 Would keep our inmost conscience pure ;
Our souls from folly would secure ;
Would bid us check the pride of sense
With due and holy abstinence.

4 So we, when this new day is gone,
And shades of night are drawing on,
With conscience by the world unstained
Shall praise His name for victory gained.

5 All praise to God the Father be ;
All praise, eternal Son, to Thee ;
Whom with the Spirit we adore
For ever and for evermore.
 JOHN MASON NEALE.

55 *"All my springs are in Thee."*

O GOD of truth, O Lord of might,
Who orderest time and change aright,
Brightening the morn with golden gleams,
Kindling the noon-day's fiery beams ;

2 Quench Thou in us the flames of strife,
From passion's heat preserve our life,
Our bodies keep from perils free,
And give our souls true peace in Thee.

3 Almighty Father, hear our cry,
Through Jesus Christ our Lord most high,
Who with the Holy Ghost and Thee
Doth live and reign eternally !
 JOHN MASON NEALE.

For Morning and Evening.

BURNEY. L. M.

My God, how end-less is Thy love! Thy gifts are ev-ery eve-ning new;

And morn-ing mer-cies from a - bove Gen-tly dis-till like ear-ly dew.

---

56 *"The Lord is my portion."*

My God, how endless is Thy love!
 Thy gifts are every evening new;
And morning mercies from above
Gently distill like early dew.

2 Thou spread'st the curtains of the night,
 Great Guardian of my sleeping hours;
Thy sovereign word restores the light,
 And quickens all my drowsy powers.

3 I yield my powers to Thy command;
 To Thee I consecrate my days;
Perpetual blessings from Thine hand
Demand perpetual songs of praise.
 ISAAC WATTS.

57 *"My voice shalt Thou hear in the morning, O Lord."*

Awake, my soul, and with the sun
Thy daily stage of duty run;
Shake off dull sloth, and joyful rise
To pay thy morning sacrifice.

2 Thy precious time misspent redeem;
Each present day thy last esteem;
Improve thy talent with due care;
For the great day thyself prepare.

3 In conversation be sincere;
Keep conscience as the noontide clear;
Think how All-seeing God thy ways
And all thy secret thoughts surveys.

4 By influence of the light divine
Let thy own light to others shine;
Reflect all heaven's propitious rays,
In ardent love and cheerful praise.

5 Wake and lift up thyself, my heart,
And with the angels bear thy part,
Who, all night long, unwearied sing
High praise to the Eternal King.

6 Lord, I my vows to Thee renew;
Disperse my sins as morning dew;
Guard my first springs of thought and will,
And with Thyself my spirit fill.

7 Direct, control, suggest, this day,
All I design, or do, or say,
That all my powers, with all their might,
In Thy sole glory may unite.

8 Praise God, from whom all blessings flow;
Praise Him, all creatures here below!
Praise Him above, ye heavenly host;
Praise Father, Son, and Holy Ghost!
 THOMAS KEN.

58 *"He that keepeth thee will not slumber."*

Up to the hills I lift mine eyes,
The eternal hills beyond the skies;
Thence all her help my soul derives,
There my Almighty Refuge lives.

2 He lives, the Everlasting God,
That built the world, that spread the flood;
The heavens with all their hosts He made,
And the dark regions of the dead.

3 He guides our feet, He guards our way;
His morning smiles bless all the day;
He spreads the evening veil, and keeps
The silent hours while Israel sleeps.
 ISAAC WATTS.

STELLA. L. M. 6 lines.

When, streaming from the east-ern skies, The morn-ing light sa - lutes mine eyes, O Sun of righteous-ness divine,

On me with beams of mer-cy shine! O chase the clouds of guilt a way, And turn my darkness in - to day.

59 *"Ask, and it shall be given you."*

WHEN, streaming from the eastern skies,
The morning light salutes mine eyes,
O Sun of righteousness divine,
On me with beams or mercy shine!
O chase the clouds of guilt away,
And turn my darkness into day.

2 When to heaven's great and gloriousKing,
My morning sacrifice I bring,
And, mourning o'er my guilt and shame,
Ask mercy, in my Saviour's name;
Then, Jesus, sprinkle with Thy blood,
And be my advocate with God.

3 When each day's scenes and labors close,
And wearied nature seeks repose,
With pardoning mercy, richly blest,
Guard me, my Saviour, while I rest:
And as each morning sun shall rise,
O lead me onward to the skies!

4 And at my life's last setting sun,
My conflicts o'er, my labors done,
Jesus, Thy heavenly radiance shed,
To cheer and bless my dying bed;
And from death's gloom my spirit raise,
To see Thy face, and sing Thy praise.
WILLIAM SHRUBSOLE.

MORNINGTON. S. M.

Behold the morning sun Be - gins his glo-rious way; His beams through all the nations run, And life and light con-vey.

60 *"Christ shall give thee light."*

BEHOLD the morning sun
Begins his glorious way;
His beams through all the nations run,
And life and light convey.

2 But where the gospel comes
It spreads diviner light;
It calls dead sinners from their tombs,
And gives the blind their sight.

3 How perfect is Thy word!
And all Thy judgments just!
For ever sure Thy promise, Lord,
And men securely trust.

4 While with my heart and tongue
I spread Thy praise abroad,
Accept the worship and the song,
My Saviour and my God.
ISAAC WATTS.

OVERBERG. L. M.

O Christ! with each re - turn- ing morn Thine im - age to our hearts be borne;

And may we ev - er clear-ly see Our God and Sav - iour, Lord, in Thee!

61 *"My soul from death, my feet from falling."*

O Christ! with each returning morn
Thine image to our hearts be borne;
And may we ever clearly see
Our God and Saviour, Lord, in Thee!

2 All hallowed be our walk this day;
May meekness form our early ray,
And faithful love our noontide light,
And hope our sunset, calm and bright.

3 May grace each idle thought control,
And sanctify our wayward soul;
May guile depart, and malice cease,
And all within be joy and peace.

4 Our daily course, O Jesus, bless;
Make plain the way of holiness:
From sudden falls our feet defend,
And cheer at last our journey's end.

JOHN CHANDLER.

ERNAN. L. M.

Lord God of morn-ing and of night, We thank Thee for Thy gift of light;

As in the dawn the sha - dows fly, We seem to find Thee now more nigh.

62 *"Until the day dawn, and the Day Star arise in your hearts."*

Lord God of morning and of night,
We thank Thee for Thy gift of light;
As in the dawn the shadows fly,
We seem to find Thee now more nigh.

2 Yet whilst Thy will we would pursue,
Oft what we would we cannot do;
The sun may stand in zenith skies,
But on the soul thick midnight lies.

3 O Lord of lights! 'tis Thou alone
Canst make our darkened hearts Thine own;
Though this new day with joy we see,
Great Dawn of God! we cry for Thee!

4 Praise God, our Maker and our Friend!
Praise Him thro' time, till time shall end!
Till psalm and song His Name adore
Through Heaven's great day of Evermore!

FRANCIS TURNER PALGRAVE.

MATIN. P. M.

When morn-ing gilds the skies . . My heart a-wak-ing cries,

May Je-sus Christ be praised: A-like at work and prayer,

To Je-sus I re-pair; May Je - sus Christ . . be praised.

63 *"Rejoice in the Lord alway."*

WHEN morning gilds the skies
My heart awaking cries,
   May Jesus Christ be praised :
Alike at work and prayer,
To Jesus I repair ;
   May Jesus Christ be praised.

2 To Thee, O God, above,
I cry with glowing love,
   May Jesus Christ be praised :
This song of sacred joy,
It never seems to cloy :
   May Jesus Christ be praised.

3 Does sadness fill my mind
A solace here I find,
   May Jesus Christ be praised :
Or fades my earthly bliss
My comfort still is this,
   May Jesus Christ be praised.

4 When evil thoughts molest,
With this I shield my breast,
   May Jesus Christ be praised :
The powers of darkness fear,
When this sweet chant I hear :
   May Jesus Christ be praised.

5 When sleep her balm denies,
My silent spirit sighs,
   May Jesus Christ be praised :
The night becomes as day,
When from the heart we say,
   May Jesus Christ be praised.

6 Be this, while life is mine,
My canticle divine,
   May Jesus Christ be praised :
Be this the eternal song,
Through all the ages on, .
   May Jesus Christ be praised.
EDWARD CASWALL.

KELSO. 7s. 6 lines.

Ev-ery morning mercies new Fall as fresh as morning dew; Ev-ery morning let us pay

Tribute with the ear-ly day ; For Thy mercies, Lord, are sure ; Thy compassion doth en-dure.

64   *"His compassions fail not; they are new every morning."*

EVERY morning mercies new
Fall as fresh as morning dew ;
Every morning let us pay
Tribute with the early day ;
For Thy mercies, Lord, are sure ;
Thy compassion doth endure.

2 Still the greatness of Thy love
Daily doth our sins remove ;
Daily, far as east from west,
Lifts the burden from the breast :
Gives unbought to those who pray
Strength to stand in evil day.

3 Let our prayers each morn prevail,
That these gifts may never fail ;
And, as we confess the sin
And the tempter's power within,
Feed us with the Bread of Life ;
Fit us for our daily strife.

4 As the morning light returns,
As the sun with splendor burns,
Teach us still to turn to Thee,
Ever blessed Trinity,
With our hands our hearts to raise,
In unfailing prayer and praise.

HORATIUS BONAR.

PARK ST. L. M.

God of the morning, at whose voice The cheerful sun makes haste to rise, And like a

gi - ant doth re-joice To run his journey thro' the skies: To run his journey thro' the skies:

REMEMBRANCE. C. M.

Now that the day-star glim-mers bright We sup-pli-ant-ly pray

That He, the un-cre-a-ted Light, May guide us on our way.

65   *"Order my steps in Thy word."*

Now that the day-star glimmers bright
We suppliantly pray
That He, the uncreated Light,
May guide us on our way.

2 No sinful word, nor deed of wrong,
Nor thoughts that idly rove;
But simple truth be on our tongue,
And in our hearts be love.

3 And, while the hours in order flow,
O Christ, securely fence
Our gates, beleaguered by the foe,—
The gate of every sense.

4 And grant that to Thine honor, Lord,
Our daily toil may tend;
That we begin it at Thy word,
And in Thy favor end.

5 To God the Father glory be,
And to His Only Son,
And to the Spirit, One and Three,
While endless ages run.
JOHN HENRY NEWMAN.

66   *"The Lord shall preserve thy going out and thy coming in."*

SHINE on our souls, Eternal God,
With rays of beauty shine!
O let Thy favor crown our days,
And all their round be Thine!

2 Did we not raise our hands to Thee,
Our hands might toil in vain;
Small joy success itself could give,
If Thou Thy love restrain.

3 With Thee let every week begin,
With Thee each day be spent;
For Thee each fleeting hour improved,
Since each by Thee is lent.

4 Thus cheer us through this desert road,
Till all our labors cease,
And heaven refresh our weary souls
With everlasting peace!
PHILIP DODDRIDGE.

67   *"Thou shalt guide me with Thy counsel, and afterward receive me to glory."*

GOD of the morning, at whose voice
The cheerful sun makes haste to rise,
And like a giant doth rejoice
To run his journey through the skies:

2 O, like the sun, may I fulfill
The appointed duties of the day,
With ready mind and active will,
March on, and keep my heavenly way.

3 But I shall rove and lose the race,
If God, my Sun, shall disappear,
And leave me in the world's wide maze
To follow every wandering star.

4 Give me Thy counsel for my guide,
And then receive me to Thy bliss;
All my desires and hopes beside
Are faint and cold, compared with this.
ISAAC WATTS.

DEDICATION. L. M.

Sun of my soul, Thou Saviour dear, It is not night if Thou be near; O! may no earth-born cloud a - rise

To hide Thee from Thy servant's eyes! O! may no earth-born cloud a - rise To hide Thee from Thy servant's eyes!

68   *" Thy sun shall no more go down."*

Sun of my soul, Thou Saviour dear,
It is not night if Thou be near ;
O! may no earth-born cloud arise
To hide Thee from Thy servant's eyes !

2 When the soft dews of kindly sleep
My wearied eyelids gently steep,
Be my last thought, how sweet to rest
For ever on my Saviour's breast.

3 Abide with me from morn till eve,
For without Thee I cannot live !
Abide with me when night is nigh,
For without Thee I dare not die !

4 If some poor wandering child of Thine
Have spurned, to-day, the voice divine,
Now, Lord, the gracious work begin ;
Let him no more lie down in sin !

5 Watch by the sick, enrich the poor
With blessings from Thy boundless store !
Be every mourner's sleep to-night
Like infants' slumbers, pure and light !

6 Come near and bless us when we wake,
Ere through the world our way we take ;
Till in the ocean of Thy love
We lose ourselves in heaven above.
JOHN KEBLE.

69 *" His compassions fail not: they are new every morning."*
O TIMELY happy, timely wise,
Hearts that with rising morn arise !

Eyes that the beam celestial view,
Which evermore makes all things new !

2 New every morning is the love
Our wakening and uprising prove,
Through sleep and darkness safely brought,
Restored to life, and power, and thought.

3 New mercies, each returning day,
Hover around us while we pray ;
New perils past, new sins forgiven,
New thoughts of God, new hopes of heaven.

4 If, on our daily course, our mind
Be set to hallow all we find,
New treasures still, of countless price,
God will provide for sacrifice.

5 The trivial round, the common task,
Will furnish all we ought to ask ;
Room to deny ourselves ; a road
To bring us, daily, nearer God.

6 Seek we no more : content with these,
Let present rapture, comfort, ease,
As Heaven shall bid them, come and go ;
The secret this of rest below.

7 Only, O Lord, in Thy dear love
Fit us for perfect rest above ;
And help us, this and every day,
To live more nearly as we pray !
JOHN KEBLE.

ROSEFIELD. 7s, 6 lines.

Christ, whose glory fills the skies, Christ, the true, the on-ly light, } Son of Righteousness, a- rise, Triumph o'er the shades of night; } Day-spring from on high, be near, Day-star in my heart appear.

70 "Unto you that fear my name, shall the Sun of Righteousness arise."

CHRIST, whose glory fills the skies,
  Christ, the true, the only light,
Sun of Righteousness, arise,
  Triumph o'er the shades of night;
Day-spring from on high, be near,
Day-star in my heart appear.

2 Dark and cheerless is the morn,
  If Thy light is hid from me;
Joyless is the day's return,

Till Thy mercy's beams I see—
Till they inward light impart,
Warmth and gladness to my heart.

3 Visit, then, this soul of mine,
  Pierce the gloom of sin and grief;
Fill me, radiant Sun divine!
  Scatter all my unbelief;
More and more Thyself display,
Shining to the perfect day.

CHARLES WESLEY.

MORNING PRAYER. 7s.

As the sun doth dai-ly rise, Brightening all the morn-ing skies,

So to Thee with one ac-cord Lift we up our hearts, O Lord!

71 "In all thy ways acknowledge Him."

As the sun doth daily rise,
Brightening all the morning skies,
So to Thee with one accord
Lift we up our hearts, O Lord!

2 Thou by whom all things are fed,
Give us for the day our bread;
Strength unto our souls afford
From the Bread of Heaven, O Lord!

3 Be our Guard in sin and strife;
Be the Leader of our life;

While we daily search Thy word,
Wisdom true impart, O Lord!

4 When the hours are dark and drear,
When the tempter lurketh near,
By Thy strengthening grace outpoured
Save the tempted ones, O Lord!

5 Praise we with the heavenly host
Father, Son, and Holy Ghost:
Thee would we with one accord
Praise and magnify, O Lord!

HORATIO, EARL NELSON.

ZOELLNER. C. M. D.

Hail tran-quil hour of clos-ing day! Be-gone dis-turb-ing care!

And look, my soul, from earth a-way To Him who hear-eth prayer.

How sweet the tear of pen-i-tence, Be-fore His throne of grace, While,

How sweet

to the con-trite spirit's sense, He shows His smiling face, He shows His smiling face.

72   *"The Lord will bless His people with peace."*

HAIL tranquil hour of closing day!
  Begone disturbing care!
And look, my soul, from earth away
  To Him who heareth prayer.
How sweet the tear of penitence,
  Before His throne of grace,
While, to the contrite spirit's sense,
  He shows His smiling face.

2 How sweet, through long-remembered [years,
  His mercies to recall,
And, pressed with wants and griefs and [fears,
  To trust His love for all.
How sweet to look, in thoughtful hope,
  Beyond this fading sky,
And hear Him call His children up
  To His fair home on high.

(From *S.*)
3 Calmly the day forsakes our heaven,
  To dawn beyond the west;
So let my soul, in life's last even,
  Retire to glorious rest.

LEONARD BACON.

ANNA. P. M.

God, that madest earth and heaven, Darkness and light; Who the day for toil hast given, For rest the night;

May Thine an-gel- guards defend us, Slumber sweet Thy mercy send us, Holy dreams and hopes attend us, This livelong night.

73 *"Whether we wake or sleep, we should live together with Him."*

God, that madest earth and heaven,
Darkness and light ;
Who the day for toil hast given,
For rest the night ;
May Thine angel-guards defend us,
Slumber sweet Thy mercy send us,
Holy dreams and hopes attend us,
This livelong night.

2 Guard us waking, guard us sleeping:
And when we die,
May we in Thy mighty keeping
All peaceful lie ;
When the last dread call shall wake us,
Do not Thou, O God, forsake us,
But to reign in glory take us
With Thee on high.—

REGINALD HEBER. (2nd verse RICHARD WHATELY.)

SEYMOUR. 7s.

Softly, now, the light of day Fades upon my sight a-way; Free from care, from labor free, Lord! I would commune with Thee.

74 *"Let the lifting up of my hands be an evening sacrifice."*

Softly, now, the light of day
Fades upon my sight away ;
Free from care, from labor free,
Lord ! I would commune with Thee.

2 Thou, whose all-pervading eye
Naught escapes, without, within,
Pardon each infirmity,
Open fault, and secret sin.

3 Soon, for me, the light of day
Shall for ever pass away ;
Then, from sin and sorrow free,
Take me, Lord ! to dwell with Thee.

4 Thou who, sinless, yet hast known
All of man's infirmity ;
Then, from Thine eternal throne,
Jesus, look with pitying eye.

GEORGE WASHINGTON DOANE.

EVENTIDE. 10s.

Abide with me! fast falls the even-tide; The darkness deepens; Lord, with me abide!

When other helpers fail, and comforts flee, Help of the helpless, O abide with me!

75 *"Abide with us."*

Abide with me! fast falls the even-tide;
The darkness deepens; Lord, with me
abide!
When other helpers fail, and comforts
flee,
Help of the helpless, O abide with me!

2 Swift to its close ebbs out life's little day;
Earth's joys grow dim; its glories pass
away;
Change and decay in all around I see;
O Thou, who changest not, abide with me!

3 Not a brief glance I beg, a passing word;
But, as Thou dwelt'st with Thy disciples,
Lord,
Familiar, condescending. patient, free,
Come, not to sojourn, but abide, with
me!

4 Come not in terrors, as the King of kings;
But kind and good, with healing in Thy
wings;
Tears for all woes, a heart for every plea;
Come, Friend of sinners, and thus 'bide
with me!

5 I need Thy presence every passing hour;
What but Thy grace can foil the tempter's
power?
Who like Thyself my guide and stay can be?
Thro' cloud and sunshine, O abide with me!

6 Hold Thou Thy cross before my closing
eyes;
Shine thro' the gloom, and point me to the
skies;
Heaven's morning breaks, and earth's vain
shadows flee;
In life, in death, O Lord, abide with me!
HENRY FRANCIS LYTE.

STOCKWELL. 8s. 7s.

Saviour! breathe an evening blessing, Ere repose our eyelids seal: Sin and want we come confessing; Thou canst save, and Thou canst heal.

76 *"He that keepeth thee will not slumber."*

Saviour! breathe an evening blessing,
Ere repose our eyelids seal:
Sin and want we come confessing;
Thou canst save, and Thou canst heal.

2 Though destruction walk around us,
Though the arrows past us fly,
Angel-guards from Thee surround us;
We are safe, if Thou art nigh.

3 Though the night be dark and dreary,
Darkness cannot hide from Thee:
Thou art He who, never weary,
Watcheth where Thy people be.

4 Should swift death this night o'ertake us,
And our couch become our tomb,
May the morn in heaven awake us,
Clad in bright and deathless bloom.
JAMES EDMESTON.

YORK. L. M.

All praise to Thee, my God, this night, For all the blessings of the light;

Keep me, O keep me, King of kings, Be-neath Thine own al - mighty wings!

77 *"Under His wings shalt thou trust."*

ALL praise to Thee, my God, this night,
For all the blessings of the light;
Keep me, O keep me, King of kings,
Beneath Thine own almighty wings!

2 Forgive me, Lord, for Thy dear Son,
The ill that I this day have done;
That with the world, myself, and Thee,
I, ere I sleep, at peace may be.

3 Teach me to live, that I may dread
The grave as little as my bed!
To die, that this vile body may
Rise glorious at the awful day!

4 O may my soul on Thee repose;
And may sweet sleep mine eyelids close;
Sleep, that may me more vigorous make
To serve my God when I awake!

5 When in the night I sleepless lie,
My soul with heavenly thoughts supply!
Let no ill dreams disturb my rest,
No powers of darkness me molest!

6 Praise God, from whom all blessings flow;
Praise Him, all creatures here below!
Praise Him above, ye heavenly host;
Praise Father, Son, and Holy Ghost!
THOMAS KEN.

HEBRON. L. M.

Thus far the Lord has led me on; Thus far His power prolongs my days; And every evening shall make known Some fresh memorial of His grace.

78 *"The Lord redeemeth the soul of His servants."*

THUS far the Lord has led me on;
Thus far His power prolongs my days;
And every evening shall make known
Some fresh memorial of His grace.

2 Much of my time has run to waste,
And I, perhaps, am near my home;
But He forgives my follies past,
And gives me strength for days to come.

3 Faith in His name forbids my fear:
O may Thy presence ne'er depart!
And in the morning make me hear
The love and kindness of Thy heart.

4 Thus, when the night of death shall come,
My flesh shall rest beneath the ground,
And wait Thy voice to rouse my tomb,
With sweet salvation in the sound.
ISAAC WATTS.

SOLITUDE. 7s.

Lord, for-ev-er at Thy side Let my place and por-tion be;

Strip me of my robe of pride, Clothe me with hu-mi-li-ty.

79   *"O Lord my Strength and my Refuge."*

Lord, for ever at Thy side
Let my place and portion be ;
Strip me of my robe of pride,
Clothe me with humility.

2 Meekly may my soul receive
All Thy Spirit hath revealed ;
Thou hast spoken — I believe.
Though the oracles be sealed.

3 Humble as a little child
Weaned from the mother's breast,
By no subtleties beguiled,
On Thy faithful word I rest.

4 Israel. now and evermore
In the Lord Jehovah trust;
Him in all His ways adore,
Wise and wonderful and just.

JAMES MONTGOMERY.

WOODSTOCK. C. M.

I love to steal a-while a-way from every cum-bering care, And spend the hours of setting day in hum-ble, grateful prayer.

80   *"Thy Father which seeth in secret."*

I love to steal awhile away
From every cumbering care.
And spend the hours of setting day
In humble, grateful prayer.

2 I love in solitude to shed
The penitential tear,
And all His promises to plead.
Where none but God can hear.

3 I love to think on mercies past,
And future good implore,

And all my cares and sorrows cast
On Him whom I adore.

4 I love by faith to take a view,
Of brighter scenes in heaven ;
The prospect doth my strength renew,
While here by tempests driven.

5 Thus, when life's toilsome day is o'er,
May its departing ray
Be calm as this impressive hour,
And lead to endless day.

PHEBE H. BROWN.

God the Creator.

ELDRIDGE. 10s.

Blessing,and hon - or,and glo-ry, and power, Wisdom,and rich-es,and strength,ever-more,

Give ye to Him who our battle hath won, Whose are the kingdom,the crown,and the throne.

81 *"Thou hast led captivity captive."*

Blessing, and honor, and glory, and power,
Wisdom, and riches, and strength, evermore,
Give ye to Him who our battle hath won,
Whose are the kingdom, the crown, and
the throne.

2 Dwelleth the light of the glory with Him,
Light of a glory that cannot grow dim,
Light in its silence and beauty and calm,
Light in its gladness and brightness and
balm.

3 Ever ascendeth the song and the joy,
Ever descendeth the love from on high,
Blessing, and honor, and glory, and praise,
This is the theme of the hymns that we
raise.

4 Life of all life,and true Light of all light,
Star of the dawning, unchangingly bright,
Sun of the Salem whose lamp is the Lamb,
Theme of the ever-new, ever-glad psalm!

5 Give we the glory and praise to the Lamb,
Take we the robe and the harp and the palm,
Sing we the song of the Lamb that was
slain,
Dying in weakness, but rising to reign.

HORATIUS BONAR.

82 *"Thine is the kingdom, O Lord, and Thou reignest over all."*

Honor and glory, thanksgiving and praise,
Maker of all things, to Thee we upraise;
God the Almighty, the Father, the Lord;
God by the angels obeyed and adored.

2 Thou art the Father of heaven and earth;
Worlds uncreated to Thee owe their birth;
All the creation, Thy voice when it heard,
Started to light and to life at Thy word.

3 Onward the sun and the moon on their
march
Span with the rainbow the firmament's arch;
Stars yet unknown, and whose light is to
come,
Find in creation their place and a home.

4 Earth with the mountain, the river, the
plain,
Sky with the dew-drop, the wind, and the
rain,
Beast of the forest, wild bird of the air,
All are Thy creatures,and all are Thy care.

5 Ocean the restless, and waters that swell,
Lightnings that flash over flood, over fell,
Own Thee the Master Almighty, and call
Thee the Creator, the Father of all.

6 Yea,Thou art Father of all,and Thy love
Pity for man that is fallen doth move;
Sharing our nature, tho' sinless, Thy Son
Came to redeem us, by Satan undone.

EDWARD ARTHUR DAYMAN.

ST. ALBAN. L. M.

Sing to the Lord a joyful song; Lift up your hearts, your voices raise; To us His gracious gifts belong, To Him our songs of love and praise.

83   *"Praise the Lord for His goodness."*

Sing to the Lord a joyful song ;
  Lift up your hearts, your voices raise ;
To us His gracious gifts belong,
  To Him our songs of love and praise.

2 For life and love, for rest and food,
  For daily help and nightly care,
Sing to the Lord, for He is good,
  And praise His name, for it is fair :—

3 For strength to those who on Him wait,
  His truth to prove, His will to do,

Praise ye our God, for He is great,
  Trust in His name, for it is true : —

4 For joys untold that daily move
  Round those who love His sweet employ,
Sing to our God, for He is love,
  Exalt His name, for it is joy :—

5 For life below, with all its bliss,
  And for that life, more ,pure and high,
That inner life, which over this
  Shall ever shine, and never die.

                       JOHN SAMUEL BEWLEY MONSELL.

NICAEA. P. M.

Ho-ly, ho-ly, ho - ly, Lord God Al-migh - ty! Ear - ly in the morn-ing our song shall rise to Thee;

Ho-ly, ho-ly, ho - ly! merciful and mighty! God in three persons, blessèd Trini - ty!

84   *"They rest not day nor night, saying, Holy, holy, holy, Lord God Almighty."*

Holy, holy, holy, Lord God Almighty !
  Early in the morning our song shall rise
    to Thee ;
Holy, holy, holy ! merciful and mighty !
  God in three persons, blessèd Trinity !

2 Holy, holy, holy ! all the saints adore
    Thee,   [the glassy sea :
Casting down their golden crowns around
Cherubim and seraphim falling down before
    Thee,   ·[be.
Which wert, and art, and evermore shalt

3 Holy, holy, holy ! though the darkness
  hide Thee,   [may not see ;
Though the eye of sinful man Thy glory
Only Thou art holy, there is none beside
  Thee,
Perfect in power, in love. and purity.

4 Holy, holy, holy ! Lord God Almighty !
All Thy works shall praise Thy name,
  in earth, and sky, and sea ;
Holy, holy, holy ! merciful and mighty !
God in three persons, blessèd Trinity !

                  REGINALD HEBER.

GLORIA. L. M.

Lord of all being! throned a - far, Thy glory flames from sun and star; Center and soul of every sphere, Yet to each loving heart how near!

85 *"Who hath called you out of darkness into His marvelous light."*

Lord of all being! throned afar,
Thy glory flames from sun and star;
Center and soul of every sphere,
Yet to each loving heart how near!

2 Sun of our life, Thy quickening ray
Sheds on our path the glow of day;
Star of our hope, Thy softened light
Cheers the long watches of the night.

3 Our midnight is Thy smile withdrawn;
Our noontide is Thy gracious dawn;

Our rainbow arch Thy mercy's sign;
All, save the clouds of sin, are Thine!

4 Lord of all life, below, above,
Whose light is truth, whose warmth is love,
Before Thy ever-blazing throne
We ask no luster of our own.

5 Grant us Thy truth, to make us free,
And kindling hearts that burn for Thee,
Till all Thy living altars claim
One holy light, one heavenly flame!

OLIVER WENDELL HOLMES.

HOCHGESANG. L. M.

High in the heavens, E - ter - nal God, Thy goodness in full glo - ry shines;

Thy truth shall break through every cloud That veils and dark - ens Thy de - signs.

86 *"With Thee is the fountain of life."*

High in the heavens, Eternal God,
Thy goodness in full glory shines;
Thy truth shall break through every cloud
That veils and darkens Thy designs.

2 For ever firm Thy justice stands,
As mountains their foundations keep;
Wise are the wonders of Thy hands;
Thy judgments are a mighty deep.

3 My God! how excellent Thy grace,
Whence all our hope and comfort springs!

The sons of Adam, in distress,
Fly to the shadow of Thy wings.

4 From the provisions of Thy house
We shall be fed with sweet repast:
There mercy like a river flows,
And brings salvation to our taste.

5 Life, like a fountain rich and free,
Springs from the presence of my Lord;
And in Thy light our souls shall see
The glories promised in Thy word.

ISAAC WATTS.

GERMAN TE DEUM. L. M.

Lord God of Hosts, by all adored! Thy name we praise with one ac-cord;

The earth and heavens are full of Thee, Thy light, Thy love, Thy ma-jes-ty.

87   *"Te Deum laudamus."*

LORD God of Hosts, by all adored!
Thy name we praise with one accord;
The earth and heavens are full of Thee,
Thy light, Thy love, Thy majesty.

2 Loud hallelujahs to Thy name
Angels and seraphim proclaim;
Eternal praise to Thee is given
By all the powers and thrones in heaven.

3 The apostles join the glorious throng;
The prophets aid to swell the song;
The noble and triumphant host
Of martyrs make of Thee their boast.

4 The holy church in every place
Throughout the world exalts Thy praise;
Both heaven and earth do worship Thee,
Thou Father of eternity!

5 From day to day, O Lord, do we
Highly exalt and honor Thee!
Thy name we worship and adore,
World without end, for evermore.

88   *"I will praise Thee, O Lord, among the people."*

BE Thou exalted, O my God!
Above the heavens where angels dwell;
Thy power on earth be known abroad,
And land to land Thy wonders tell.

2 My heart is fixed: my song shall raise
Immortal honors to Thy name;

Awake, my tongue, to sound His praise,
My tongue, the glory of my frame.

3 High o'er the earth Thy mercy reigns,
And reaches to the utmost sky;
Thy truth to endless years remains,
When lower worlds dissolve and die.

4 Be Thou exalted, O my God!
Above the heavens where angels dwell;
Thy power on earth be known abroad,
And land to land Thy wonders tell.
ISAAC WATTS.

89   *"Serve the Lord with gladness."*

ALL people that on earth do dwell,
Sing to the Lord with cheerful voice:
Him serve with fear, His praise forth tell,
Come ye before Him, and rejoice.

2 The Lord, ye know, is God indeed,
Without our aid He did us make:
We are His flock, He doth us feed,
And for His sheep He doth us take.

3 Oh, enter then His gates with praise,
Approach with joy His courts unto:
Praise, laud, and bless His name always,
For it is seemly so to do.

4 For why? the Lord our God is good,
His mercy is for ever sure;
His truth at all times firmly stood,
And shall from age to age endure.
WILLIAM KETHE.

MELITA. L. M. 6 lines.

The Lord my pasture shall prepare, And feed me with a shepherd's care; His presence shall my wants supply,

And guard me with a watchful eye; My noonday walks He shall at-tend, And all my midnight hours defend.

90 *"The Lord is my shepherd."*

THE Lord my pasture shall prepare,
And feed me with a shepherd's care ;
His presence shall my wants supply,
And guard me with a watchful eye ;
My noonday walks He shall attend,
And all my midnight hours defend.

2 When in the sultry globe I faint,
Or on the thirsty mountain pant,
To fertile vales, and dewy meads.
My weary. wandering feet He leads ;
Where peaceful rivers, soft and slow,
Amid the verdant landscape flow.

3 Though in the paths of death I tread,
With gloomy horrors overspread.
My steadfast heart shall fear no ill,
For Thou, O Lord. art with me still ;
Thy friendly rod shall give me aid,
And guide me through the dreadful shade.

4 Though in a bare and rugged way,
Through devious, lonely wilds I stray,
Thy presence shall my pains beguile ;
The barren wilderness shall smile.
With sudden greens and herbage crowned ;
And streams shall murmur all around.

JOSEPH ADDISON.

CATHEDRAL. L. M.

Before Jehovah's awful throne, Ye nations, bow with sacred joy; Know that the Lord is God a-lone ; He can create, and He destroy.

91 *"Jubilate Deo."*

BEFORE Jehovah's awful throne,
Ye nations, bow with sacred joy ;
Know that the Lord is God alone ;
He can create, and He destroy.

2 His sovereign power, without our aid,
Made us of clay, and formed us men ;
And when like wandering sheep we strayed,
He brought us to His fold again.

3 We'll crowd Thy gates with thankful
songs,
High as the heavens our voices raise ;
And earth, with her ten thousand tongues
Shall fill Thy courts with sounding praise.

4 Wide as the world is Thy command,
Vast as eternity Thy love ;
Firm as a rock Thy truth must stand,
When rolling years shall cease to move.

ISAAC WATTS.

MALVERN. L. M.

Thou, Lord, of all the pa - rent art, Of all things Thou a - lone the end:

On Thee still fix our wavering heart; To Thee let all our ac - tions tend.

92 *"Faithful is He that calleth you."*

Thou, Lord, of all the parent art,
 Of all things Thou alone the end :
On Thee still fix our wavering heart ;
 To Thee let all our actions tend.

2 Thou, Lord, art light ; Thy native ray
 No change nor shadow ever knows ;
To our dark souls Thy light display,
 The glory of Thy face disclose.

3 Thou, Lord, art love ; the fountain Thou
 Whence mercy unexhausted flows ;
On barren hearts, O shed it now,
 And make the desert bear the rose !

4 So shall our every power to Thee
 In love and holy service rise ;
And body, soul, and spirit be
 Thy ever-living sacrifice.

93 *"All things are naked and opened unto the eyes of Him with whom we have to do."*

Lord, Thou hast searched and seen me thro' ;
Thine eye commands with piercing view
My rising and my resting hours,
My heart and flesh with all their powers.

2 My thoughts, before they are my own,
Are to my God distinctly known ;
He knows the words I mean to speak,
Ere from my opening lips they break.

3 Within Thy circling power I stand ;
On every side I find Thy hand :

Awake, asleep, at home, abroad,
I am surrounded still with God.

4 Amazing knowledge, vast and great !
What large extent ! what lofty hight !
My soul with all the powers I boast
Is in the boundless prospect lost.

5 O may these thoughts possess my breast,
Where'er I rove, where'er I rest !
Nor let my weaker passions dare
Consent to sin, for God is there.
      ISAAC WATTS.

94 *"I will praise Thy name, O Lord, for it is good."*

O Thou whom neither time nor space
 Can circle in, unseen, unknown,
Nor faith in boldest flight can trace,
 Save through Thy Spirit and Thy Son !

2 And Thou that from Thy bright abode,
 To us in mortal weakness shown,
Didst graft the manhood into God,
 Eternal, Co-eternal Son !

3 And Thou, whose unction from on high
 By comfort, light, and love is known !
Who with the Parent Deity,
 Dread Spirit, art for ever one !

4 Great First and Last ! Thy blessing give ;
 And grant us faith, Thy gift alone,
To love and praise Thee while we live,
 And do whate'er Thou would'st have done !
      REGINALD HEBER.

CREATION. L. M. D.

The spacious firmament on high, With all the blue e - the - real sky, And spangled

heav'ns, a shining frame, Their great Original proclaim. Th' unwearied sun from day to day,

Does his Creator's power display, And publishes to ev'ry land The work of an Almighty hand.

95   *"The heavens declare the glory of God."*

THE spacious firmament on high,
With all the blue ethereal sky,
And spangled heavens, a shining frame,
Their great Original proclaim.
The unwearied sun from day to day,
Does his Creator's power display,
And publishes to every land
The work of an Almighty hand.

2 Soon as the evening shades prevail,
The moon takes up the wondrous tale,
And nightly to the listening earth
Repeats the story of her birth:
Whilst all the stars that round her burn,
And all the planets, in their turn,
Confirm the tidings, as they roll,
And spread the truth from pole to pole.

3 What though in solemn silence all
Move round the dark terrestrial ball?
What though nor real voice nor sound
Amid their radiant orbs be found?
In reason's ear they all rejoice,
And utter forth a glorious voice,
For ever singing, as they shine,
'The Hand that made us is divine.'

JOSEPH ADDISON.

96   *"Thou crownest the year with Thy goodness."*

ETERNAL source of every joy!
Well may Thy praise our lips employ,
While in Thy temple we appear,
Whose goodness crowns the circling year.
Wide as the wheels of nature roll,
Thy hand supports and guides the whole!
The sun is taught by Thee to rise,
And darkness when to veil the skies.

2 The flowery spring, at Thy command,
Perfumes the air and paints the land;
The summer rays with vigor shine
To raise the corn and cheer the vine,
Thy hand in autumn richly pours
Through all our coasts redundant stores:
And winters, softened by Thy care,
No more the face of horror wear.

3 Seasons and months, and weeks and days,
Demand successive songs of praise;
And be the grateful homage paid
With morning light and evening shade.
Here in Thy house let incense rise,
And circling Sabbaths bless our eyes,
Till to those lofty hights we soar,
Where days and years revolve no more.

PHILIP DODDRIDGE.

DUNDEE. C. M.

Great God! how infinite art Thou! What worthless worms are we! Let the whole race of creatures bow, And pay their praise to Thee.

97 *"Thou, O Lord, remainest forever."*

GREAT God! how infinite art Thou!
  What worthless worms are we!
Let the whole race of creatures bow,
  And pay their praise to Thee.

2 Thy throne eternal ages stood,
  Ere seas or stars were made :
Thou art the ever-living God,
  Were all the nations dead.

3 Eternity, with all its years,
  Stands present in Thy view ;
To Thee there's nothing old appears—
  Great God! there's nothing new.

4 Our lives thro' various scenes are drawn,
  And vexed with trifling cares ;
While Thine eternal thought moves on
  Thine undisturbed affairs.

5 Great God! how infinite art Thou!
  What worthless worms are we!
Let the whole race of creatures bow,
  And pay their praise to Thee.
        ISAAC WATTS.

98 *"Te Deum laudamus."*

O GOD! we praise Thee, and confess
  That Thou the only Lord
And everlasting Father art,
  By all the earth adored.

2 To Thee, all angels cry aloud ;
  To Thee the powers on high,
Both cherubim and seraphim,
  Continually do cry :—

3 O holy, holy, holy Lord,
  Whom heavenly hosts obey,
The world is with the glory filled
  Of Thy majestic sway !

4 The apostles' glorious company,
  And prophets crowned with light,
With all the martyrs' noble host,
  Thy constant praise recite.

5 The holy church throughout the world,
  O Lord, confesses Thee,
That Thou th' eternal Father art,
  Of boundless majesty.
        NAHUM TATE.

ST. ANN'S. C. M.

Keep silence, all cre - a-ted things! And wait your Maker's nod; My soul stands trembling,while she sings The honors of her God.

99 *"Let all the earth keep silence before Him."*

KEEP silence, all created things !
  And wait your Maker's nod ;
My soul stands trembling, while she sings
  The honors of her God.

2 Life, death, and hell, and worlds unknown,
  Hang on His firm decree ;
He sits on no precarious throne,
  Nor borrows leave to be.

3 His providence unfolds the book,
  And makes His counsels shine ;
Each opening leaf, and every stroke,
  Fulfills some deep design.

4 In Thy fair book of life and grace,
  Oh ! may I find my name
Recorded in some humble place,
  Beneath my Lord, the Lamb.
        ISAAC WATTS.

HELP. C. M.

Our God, our Help in a - ges past, Our Hope for years to come,

Our Shel - ter from the storm - y blast, And our E - ter - nal Home!

100 *"Even from everlasting to everlasting, Thou art God."*

Our God, our Help in ages past,
Our Hope for years to come,
Our Shelter from the stormy blast,
And our Eternal Home!

2 Under the shadow of Thy throne
Thy saints have dwelt secure;
Sufficient is Thine arm alone,
And our defence is sure.

3 Before the hills in order stood,
Or earth received her frame,

From everlasting Thou art God,
To endless years the same.

4 A thousand ages in Thy sight
Are like an evening gone;
Short as the watch that ends the night,
Before the rising sun.

5 Our God, our Help in ages past,
Our Hope for years to come,
Be Thou our Guard while troubles last,
And our Eternal Home!

ISAAC WATTS.

WATCH. C. M.

Ho-ly and rev'rend is the name Of our E-ter-nal King: Thrice holy Lord! the angels cry; Thrice ho-ly! let us sing.

101 *"Holiness, without which no man shall see the Lord."*

Holy and reverend is the name
Of our Eternal King:
Thrice holy Lord! the angels cry;
Thrice holy! let us sing.

2 The deepest reverence of the mind,
Pay, O my soul, to God;
Lift with thy hands a holy heart
To His sublime abode.

3 With sacred awe pronounce His name
Whom words nor thoughts can reach;
A contrite heart shall please Him more
Than noblest forms of speech.

4 Thou holy God! preserve our souls
From all pollution free;
The pure in heart are Thy delight,
And they Thy face shall see.

JOHN NEEDHAM.

NEWBURG. H. M.

O Zi-on, tune thy voice And raise thy hands on high; Tell all the earth thy joys, And boast salvation nigh: Cheer-

ful in God, A - rise and shine, While rays di - vine Stream all a-round.

102 *"His glory is above the earth and heaven."*

1 O ZION, tune thy voice
 And raise thy hands on high ;
 Tell all the earth thy joys,
  And boast salvation nigh :
Cheerful in God, | While rays divine
Arise and shine, | Stream all abroad.

2 He gilds thy mourning face
 With beams that cannot fade ;
 His all-resplendent grace
  He pours around thy head ;
The nations round | With lustre new
Thy form shall view | Divinely crowned.

3 In honor to his name
 Reflect that sacred light :
 And loud that grace proclaim,
  Which makes thy darkness bright ;
Pursue his praise, | In worlds above,
Till sovereign love, | The glory raise.

4 There on his holy hill
 A brighter sun shall rise
 And with his radiance fill
  Those fairer, purer skies ;
While round his throne | In nobler spheres,
Ten thousand stars, | His influence own.
     PHILIP DODDRIDGE.

103 *"My help cometh from the Lord."*

1 Upward I lift mine eyes ;
 From God is all my aid ;
 The God that built the skies,
  And earth and nature made :
God is the tower | His grace is nigh
To which I fly ; | In every hour.

2 My feet shall never slide,
 Nor fall in fatal snares,
 Since God, my Guard and Guide,
  Defends me from my fears :
Those wakeful eyes | Shall Israel keep
That never sleep, | When dangers rise.

3 No burning heats by day,
 Nor blasts of evening air,
 Shall take my health away,
  If God be with me there :
Thou art my Sun, | To guard my head
And Thou my Shade, | By night or noon.

4 Hast Thou not given Thy word
 To save my soul from death ?
 And I can trust my Lord
  To keep my mortal breath :
I'll go and come, | Till from on high
Nor fear to die, | Thou call me home.
     ISAAC WATTS.

MAIKAMMER. C. M.

Lift up to God the voice of praise, Whose breath our souls inspired; Loud and more loud the anthem raise, With grateful ardor fired.

104 *"With the voice of joy and praise."*

LIFT up to God the voice of praise,
  Whose breath our souls inspired ;
Loud and more loud the anthem raise,
  With grateful ardor fired.

2 Lift up to God the voice of praise,
  Whose goodness, passing thought,
Loads every minute, as it flies,
  With benefits unsought.

3 Lift up to God the voice of praise,
  From whom salvation flows,
Who sent His Son our souls to save
  From everlasting woes.

4 Lift up to God the voice of praise,
  For hope's transporting ray,
Which lights, thro' darkest shades of death,
  To realms of endless day.
                    RALPH WARDLAW.

105   *"Praise ye the Lord."*

WITH songs and honors sounding loud,
  Address the Lord on high :
Over the heavens He spreads His cloud,
  And waters vail the sky.

2 He sends His showers of blessings down,
  To cheer the plains below :
He makes the grass the mountains crown,
  And corn in valleys grow.

3 His steady counsels change the face
  Of the declining year ;
He bids the sun cut short his race,
  And wintry days appear.

4 His hoary frost, His fleecy snow,
  Descend and clothe the ground :
The liquid streams forbear to flow,
  In icy fetters bound.

5 He sends His word and melts the snow,
  The fields no longer mourn ;
He calls the warmer gales to blow,
  And bids the spring return.

6 The changing wind, the flying cloud,
  Obey His mighty word :
With songs and honors sounding loud,
  Praise ye the sovereign Lord.
                    ISAAC WATTS.

PHUVAH. C. M.

The Lord descended from above, and bowed the heavens most high; And underneath His feet He cast The darkness of the sky.

106 *"Bow Thy heavens, O Lord, and come down."*

THE Lord descended from above,
  And bowed the heavens most high ;
And underneath His feet He cast
  The darkness of the sky.

2 On cherubs and on cherubim
  Full royally He rode,
And on the wings of mighty winds
  Came flying all abroad.

3 The Lord doth sit upon the floods,
  Their fury to restrain ;

And He, as sovereign Lord and King,
  For evermore shall reign.

4 The Lord will give His people strength
  Whereby they shall increase :
And He will bless His chosen flock
  With everlasting peace.

5 Give glory to His holy name,
  And honor Him alone :
Give worship to His majesty
  Upon His holy throne.
                    THOMAS STERNHOLD.

Laus Dei

HOPKINS. 10s.

O Thou whose power o'er mov-ing worlds pre-sides Whose voice cre - a - ted and whose wisdom guides,

On darkling man in full effulgence shine And cheer the clouded mind with light divine.

107 *"In Him we live and move and have our being."*

O THOU whose power o'er moving worlds
 presides,
Whose voice created and whose wisdom
 guides,
On darkling man in full effulgence shine
And cheer the clouded mind with light
 divine.

2 'T is Thine alone to calm the pious
 breast
With silent confidence and holy rest;
From Thee, great God, we spring, to
 Thee we tend,
Path, motive, guide, original, and end.

DR. SAMUEL JOHNSON.

O. PESARO. L. M.

Thee we a - dore, E - ter - nal God! We praise Thy Name with one accord;

Thy saints, who here Thy goodness see, Through all the world do worship Thee.

108 *"Who can show forth all His praise?"*

THEE we adore, Eternal Lord!
We praise Thy Name with one accord;
Thy saints, who here Thy goodness see,
Through all the world do worship Thee.

2 To Thee aloud all angels cry,
And ceaseless raise their songs on high,
Both cherubin and seraphin,
The heavens and all the powers therein.

3 The apostles join the glorious throng;
The prophets swell the immortal song;
The martyrs' noble army raise
Eternal anthems to Thy praise.

4 Thee, Holy, holy, holy King!
Thee, O Lord God of hosts, they sing;
Thus earth below, and heaven above,
Resound Thy glory and Thy love.

THOMAS COTTERILL.

FORMOSA. H. M.

The Lord Je - ho - vah reigns,His throne is built on high; The garments He assumes,

Are light and majes- ty ; His glories shine with beams so bright, No mortal eye can bear the sight.

109 *"He is clothed with majesty."*

The Lord Jehovah reigns,
  His throne is built on high ;
The garments He assumes,
  Are light and majesty ;
His glories shine with beams so bright,
No mortal eye can bear the sight.

2 The thunders of His hand
  Keep the wide world in awe ;
His wrath and justice stand
  To guard His holy law ;
And where His love resolves to bless,
His truth confirms and seals the grace.

3 Through all His perfect work,
  Surprising wisdom shines ;
Confounds the powers of hell,
  And breaks their cursed designs :
Strong is the arm — and shall fulfil
His great decrees, His sovereign will.

4 And can this mighty King
  Of glory condescend —
And will He write His name,
  My Father and my Friend !
I love His name, I love His word ;
Join, all my powers, and praise the Lord !

ISAAC WATTS.

LÜTZEN. C. M.

The Lord our God is full of might; The winds o-bey His will; He speaks,and in his heavenly bight The rolling sun stands still.

110 *"The Lord hath His way in the whirlwind and in the storm."*

The Lord our God is full of might ;
  The winds obey His will ;
He speaks, and in His heavenly bight
  The rolling sun stands still.

2 Rebel, ye waves, and o'er the land
  With threatening aspect roar :
The Lord uplifts His awful hand,
  And chains you to the shore.

3 Howl,winds of night ; your force combine ;
  Without His high behest,

Ye shall not in the mountain pine
  Disturb the sparrow's nest.

4 His voice sublime is heard afar,
  In distant peals it dies ;
He yokes the whirlwind to His car,
  And sweeps the howling skies.

5 Ye nations, bend, in reverence bend ;
  Ye monarchs, wait His nod :
And bid the choral song ascend
  To celebrate our God.

HENRY KIRKE WHITE.

FRATERNITAS. S. P. M.

The Lord Jehovah reigns, And royal state maintains, His head with awful glories crowned:

Arrayed in robes of light, Begirt with sovereign might, And rays of majesty a - round.

111 *-"The Lord reigneth; let the earth rejoice."*

THE Lord Jehovah reigns,
And royal state maintains,
His head with awful glories crowned ;
Arrayed in robes of light,
Begirt with sovereign might,
And rays of majesty around.

2 Upheld by Thy commands,
The world securely stands,
And skies and stars obey Thy word ;

Thy throne was fixed on high
Ere stars adorned the sky :
Eternal is Thy kingdom, Lord.

3 Thy promises are true,
Thy grace is ever new ;
There fixed, Thy church shall ne'er remove ;
Thy saints with holy fear
Shall in Thy courts appear,
And sing Thine everlasting love.

ISAAC WATTS.

MEAR. C. M.

Come, ye that know and fear the Lord, And raise your tho'ts above: Let every heart and voice accord, To sing that "God is love."

112 *"The love which passeth knowledge."*

COME, ye that know and fear the Lord,
And raise your thoughts above :
Let every heart and voice accord,
To sing that 'God is love.'

2 This precious truth His word declares,
And all His mercies prove ;
Jesus, the gift of gifts, appears,
To show that 'God is love.'

3 Behold His patience, bearing long
With those who from Him rove ;
Till mighty grace their hearts subdues,
To teach them— 'God is love.'

4 Oh, may we all, while here below,
This best of blessings prove ;
Till warmer hearts, in brighter worlds,
Proclaim that 'God is love.'

GEORGE BURDER.

LANDSTUHL. C. M.

In all my vast concerns with Thee   In vain my soul would try   To

shun Thy presence, Lord, or flee, To shun Thy presence, Lord, or flee   The notice of Thine eye.

113   *"The eyes of the Lord are in every place."*

In all my vast concerns with Thee
In vain my soul would try
To shun Thy presence, Lord, or flee
The notice of Thine eye.

2 Thy all-surrounding sight surveys
My rising and my rest,
My public walks, my private ways,
And secrets of my breast.

3 My thoughts lie open to the Lord,
Before they're formed within ;

And ere my lips pronounce the word,
He knows the sense I mean.

4 O wondrous knowledge, deep and high !
Where can a creature hide?
Within Thy circling arms I lie,
Beset on every side.

5 So let Thy grace surround me still,
And like a bulwark prove,
To guard my soul from every ill,
Secured by sovereign love.

ISAAC WATTS.

BARNBY. 11s, 5s.

Lord of our life, and God of our salvation, Star of our night, and hope of every nation.

Hear and re-ceive Thy peo-ple's sup-pli-ca-tion, Lord God Al-migh-ty.

114   *"My high tower and my Deliverer."*

Lord of our life, and God of our salva-   2 Lord, Thou canst help when earthly
tion,   armor faileth,   [saileth.
Star of our night, and hope of every nation,   Lord, Thou canst save when deadly sin as-
Hear and receive Thy people's supplication,   Lord, o'er Thy rock nor death nor hell pre-
Lord God Almighty.   Grant us Thy peace, Lord.   [vaileth.

PHILIP PUSEY.

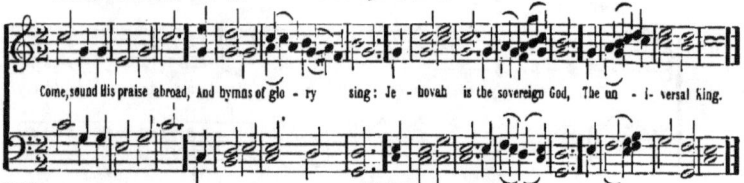

Come, sound His praise abroad, And hymns of glo - ry sing: Je - hovah is the sovereign God, The un - i - versal King.

115 *"Make a joyful noise unto Him."*

COME, sound His praise abroad,
 And hymns of glory sing:
Jehovah is the sovereign God,
 The universal King.

2 He formed the deeps unknown;
 He gave the seas their bound;
The watery worlds are all His own,
 And all the solid ground.

3 Come, worship at His throne,
 Come, bow before the Lord:
We are His work, and not our own,
 He formed us by His word.

4 To-day attend His voice,
 Nor dare provoke His rod;
Come, like the people of His choice,
 And own your gracious God.
 ISAAC WATTS.

116 *"The Lord is merciful and gracious."*

O BLESS the Lord, my soul!
 Let all within me join,
And aid my tongue to bless His name,
 Whose favors are divine.

2 O bless the Lord, my soul!
 Nor let His mercies lie
Forgotten in unthankfulness,
 And without praises die.

3 He fills the poor with good,
 He gives the sufferers rest:
The Lord hath judgments for the proud,
 And justice for the opprest.

4 His wondrous works and ways
 He made by Moses known;
But sent the world His truth and grace
 By His beloved Son.
 ISAAC WATTS.

DIX. 7s. 6 lines.

Holy, ho - ly, ho - ly Lord, God of hosts,e - ternal King, } Chanting ever - lastingly To the blessed Trini - ty.
By the heavens and earth adored; Angels and archangels sing,

117 *"Holy, holy, holy is the Lord God of Hosts."*

HOLY, holy, holy Lord,
 God of hosts, eternal King,
By the heavens and earth adored;
 Angels and archangels sing,
Chanting everlastingly
To the blessèd Trinity.
2 Thousands, tens of thousands stand,
 Spirits blest, before the throne,
Speeding thence at Thy command,
 And, when Thy commands are done,
Singing everlastingly
To the blessèd Trinity.
3 Cherubim and seraphim
 Vail their faces with their wings;
Eyes of angels are too dim

To behold the King of kings,
While they sing eternally
To the blessèd Trinity.
4 Thee apostles, prophets Thee,
 Thee the noble martyr band,
Praise with solemn jubilee,
 Thee, the church in every land;
Singing everlastingly
To the blessèd Trinity.
5 Hallelujah! Lord, to Thee,
 Father, Son, and Holy Ghost;
Godhead one, and Persons three;
 Join us with the heavenly host,
Singing everlastingly
To the blessèd Trinity. CHRISTOPHER WORDSWORTH

SWANWICK. C. M.

When all Thy mer - cies, O my God, My ris - ing soul surveys, Transported with the view, I'm lost In wonder, love, and praise, In wonder, love, and praise.

118 *"His mercy endureth forever."*

When all Thy mercies, O my God,
  My rising soul surveys,
Transported with the view, I'm lost
  In wonder, love, and praise.
2 Unnumbered comforts on my soul
  Thy tender care bestowed,
Before my infant heart conceived
  From whom those comforts flowed.
3 Ten thousand thousand precious gifts
  My daily thanks employ ;

Nor is the least a cheerful heart,
  That tastes those gifts with joy.
4 Through every period of my life,
  Thy goodness I'll pursue ;
And after death, in distant worlds,
  The glorious theme renew.
5 Through all eternity, to Thee
  A joyful song I'll raise :
For, O! eternity's too short
  To utter all Thy praise !

ISAAC WATTS.

LEIGHTON. S. M.

My Maker and my King! To Thee my all I owe; Thy sovereign boun - ty is the spring Whence all my blessings flow.

119 *"The Lord hath been mindful of us."*

My Maker and my King !
  To Thee my all I owe ;
Thy sovereign bounty is the spring
  Whence all my blessings flow.
2 The creature of Thy hand,
  On Thee alone I live ;
My God, Thy benefits demand
  More praise than life can give.

3 Lord, what can I impart,
  When all is Thine before ?
Thy love demands a thankful heart :
  The gift, alas, how poor !
4 Shall I withhold Thy due ?
  And shall my passions rove ?
Lord, form this wretched heart anew,
  And fill it with Thy love.

ANNE STEELE.

SEIR. S. M.

The Lord my shepherd is, I shall be well supplied; Since He is mine, and I am His, What can I want be-side?

120 *"He shall feed His flock like a shepherd."*

X THE Lord my shepherd is,
  I shall be well supplied ;
Since He is mine, and I am His,
  What can I want beside ?

2 He leads me to the place
  Where heavenly pasture grows,
Where living waters gently pass,
  And full salvation flows.

3 If e'er I go astray,
  He doth my soul reclaim,
And guides me in His own right way,
  For His most holy name.

4 While He affords His aid
  I cannot yield to fear ;   [shade,
Though I should walk through death's dark
  My Shepherd 's with me there.

5 In spite of all my foes,
  Thou dost my table spread ;
My cup with blessings overflows,
  And joy exalts my head.

6 The bounties of Thy love
  Shall crown my following days ;
Nor from Thy house will I remove,
  Nor cease to speak Thy praise.

ISAAC WATTS.

BATTELL. S. M. For Quartett.

The Lord my shepherd is, I shall be well supplied; Since He is mine, and I am His, What can I want beside ?

WILMOT. 8s, 7s.

Praise the Lord! ye heav'ns, adore Him ; Praise Him, angels in the hight; Sun and moon, rejoice before Him; Praise Him, all ye stars of light!

121 *"Praise Him in the firmament of His power."*

PRAISE the Lord ! ye heavens, adore Him ;
  Praise Him, angels in the hight ;
Sun and moon, rejoice before Him ;
  Praise Him, all ye stars of light !

2 Praise the Lord—for He hath spoken ;
  Worlds His mighty voice obeyed ;
Laws which never shall be broken,
  For their guidance He hath made.

3 Praise the Lord—for He is glorious ;
  Never shall His promise fail ;
God hath made His saints victorious,
  Sin and death shall not prevail.

4 Praise the God of our salvation,
  Hosts on high His power proclaim ;
Heaven and earth, and all creation,
  Laud and magnify His name !

LYONS. 10s, 11s.

Ye servants of God, your Master proclaim, And publish abroad His wonder-ful name;

The name all-victorious of Jesus ex-tol; His kingdom is glorious, He rules o-ver all.

122 *"An everlasting kingdom."*

YE servants of God, your Master proclaim,
And publish abroad His wonderful name;
The name all-victorious of Jesus extol;
His kingdom is glorious, He rules over all.

2 God ruleth on high, almighty to save;
And still He is nigh—His presence we
  have;
The great congregation His triumph shall
  sing,
Ascribing salvation to Jesus our king.

3 Salvation to God, who sits on the
  throne,
Let all cry aloud, and honor the Son:
The praises of Jesus the angels proclaim,
Fall down on their faces, and worship the
  Lamb.

4 Then let us adore, and give Him His
  right.—
All glory and power, and wisdom and
  might;
All honor and blessing, with angels above,
And thanks never ceasing, and infinite
  love.   CHARLES WESLEY.

123 *"O Lord my God, Thou art very great."*

O WORSHIP the King, all glorious above;
O gratefully sing His power and His love:
Our Shield and Defender, the Ancient of
  days,
Pavilioned in splendor, and girded with
  praise.

2 O tell of His might, O sing of His grace,
Whose robe is the light, whose canopy
  space;
His chariots of wrath deep thunder-clouds
  form,
And dark is His path on the wings of the
  storm.

3 Frail children of dust, and feeble as frail,
In Thee do we trust, nor find Thee to fail:
Thy mercies how tender! how firm to the
  end!
Our Maker, Defender, Redeemer, and
  Friend!

4 O measureless Might! ineffable Love!
While angels delight to hymn Thee above,
The humbler creation, though feeble their
  lays,
With true adoration shall lisp to Thy praise.
                    SIR ROBERT GRANT.

GERMANY. L. M.

Bless, O my soul, the liv-ing God, Call home thy tho'ts that rove a-broad,

Let all the pow'rs with-in me join In work and wor-ship so di-vine.

124 *"Bless the Lord. O my soul."*

BLESS, O my soul, the living God,
Call home thy thoughts that rove abroad,
Let all the powers within me join
In work and worship so divine.
2 Bless, O my soul, the God of grace;
His favors claim thy highest praise;
Why should the wonders He hath wrought
Be lost in silence and forgot?

3 'Tis He, my soul, that sent His Son
To die for crimes which thou hast done;
He owns the ransom; and forgives
The hourly follies of our lives.
4 Let the whole earth His power confess,
Let the whole earth adore His grace;
The Gentile with the Jew shall join
In work and worship so divine.

ISAAC WATTS.

DUKE STREET L. M.

O God, beneath Thy guid-ing hand, Our ex-iled fa-thers crossed the sea,

And when they trod the win-try strand, With pray'r and psalm they worshiped Thee.

125 *"So didst Thou lead Thy people."*

O GOD, beneath Thy guiding hand,
　Our exiled fathers crossed the sea,
And when they trod the wintry strand,
　With prayer and psalm they worshiped
　　Thee.
2 Thou heard'st, well pleased, the song, the
　　prayer,—
Thy blessing came; and still its power
Shall onward through all ages bear
The memory of that holy hour.

3 Laws, freedom, truth, and faith in God
　Came with those exiles o'er the waves;
And where their pilgrim feet have trod,
　The God they trusted guards their graves.

4 And here Thy name, O God of love,
　Their children's children shall adore,
Till these eternal hills remove,
　And spring adorns the earth no more.

LEONARD BACON.

PERRY. 7s. D.

Let us with a gladsome mind Praise the Lord, for He is kind. For His mercies aye endure, Ev - er faith-ful, ev - er sure.

Let us sound His name abroad, For of gods He is the God, For His mercies aye endure Ever faith - ful, ev - er sure.

126 *"His mercy endureth forever."*

LET us with a gladsome mind
Praise the Lord, for He is kind,
For His mercies aye endure,
Ever faithful, ever sure.
Let us sound His name abroad,
For of gods He is the God,
For His mercies aye endure,
Ever faithful, ever sure.

2 He by wisdom did create
Heaven's expanse and all its state,
By His all-commanding might,
Filled the new-made world with light:

Caused the golden-tressèd sun
All the day his course to run;
And the moon to shine by night,
'Mid her spangled sisters bright.

3 All His creatures God doth feed,
His full hand supplies their need;
Let us, therefore, warble forth
His high majesty and worth.
He His mansion hath on high,
'Bove the reach of mortal eye;
And His mercies aye endure,
Ever faithful, ever sure.

JOHN MILTON. (ALTERED.)

TRUST. 8s, 7s.

Blest be Thou, O God of Israel, Thou our Father and our Lord; Blest Thy Maj-es-ty for ev-er, Ev-er be Thy name adored.

127 *"Thine is the kingdom, and the power, and the glory."*

BLEST be Thou, O God of Israel,
Thou our Father and our Lord;
Blest Thy Majesty for ever,
Ever be Thy name adored.

2 Thine, O Lord, are power and greatness,
Glory, victory, are Thine own;
All is Thine in earth and heaven;
Over all Thy boundless throne.

3 Riches come of Thee, and honor,
Power and might to Thee belong;
Thine it is to make us prosper,
Only Thine to make us strong.

4 Lord our God, for these Thy bounties
Hymns of gratitude we raise;
To Thy name, for ever glorious,
Ever we address our praise.

DEUX ANGES. 7s. D.

Ho-ly, ho-ly, ho-ly Lord! Be Thy glorious name a - dored; Lord, Thy mercies nev-er fail: Hail, celestial goodness hail!

Tho' unworthy of Thine ear, Deign our humble songs to hear; Purer praise we hope to bring, When around Thy throne we sing.

128 *"Holy, holy, holy, is the Lord of hosts."*

HOLY, holy, holy Lord!
Be Thy glorious name adored;
Lord, Thy mercies never fail:
Hail, celestial goodness, hail!
Though unworthy of Thine ear,
Deign our humble songs to hear;
Purer praise we hope to bring,
When around Thy throne we sing.

2 While on earth ordained to stay,
Guide our footsteps in Thy way,
Till we come to dwell with Thee,
Till we all Thy glory see.
Lord, Thy mercies never fail;
Hail, celestial goodness, hail!
Holy, holy, holy Lord!
Be Thy glorious name adored.

BENJAMIN WILLIAMS.

IRENE. C. M.

Lord, when my raptur'd tho't surveys Creation's beauties o'er, All nature joins to teach Thy praise And bid my soul a - dore.

129 *"All Thy works shall praise Thee, O Lord."*

LORD, when my raptured thought surveys
Creation's beauties o'er,
All nature joins to teach Thy praise,
And bid my soul adore.

2 Where'er I turn my gazing eyes,
Thy radiant footsteps shine;
Ten thousand pleasing wonders rise,
And speak their source divine.

3 On me Thy providence has shone
With gentle smiling rays;
O let my lips and life make known
Thy goodness and Thy praise.

4 All-bounteous Lord, Thy grace impart;
O teach me to improve
Thy gifts with humble, grateful heart,
And crown them with Thy love.

ANNE STEELE.

PASTORALE. 11s.

The Lord is my Shep-herd, no want shall I know, I feed in green pas-tures, safe-fold-ed I rest;

He lead-eth my soul where the still waters flow, Re-stores me when wandering, re-deems when op-prest.

130 *"He leadeth me in the paths of righteousness."*

THE Lord is my Shepherd, no want shall
I know,
I feed in green pastures, safe-folded I
rest ;
He leadeth my soul where the still waters
flow,
Restores me when wandering, redeems
when opprest.

2 Through the valley and shadow of death
though I stray,
Since Thou art my Guardian, no evil
I fear ;
Thy rod shall defend me, Thy staff be my
stay ;
No harm can befall, with my Comforter
near.

3 In the midst of affliction my table is
spread ;
With blessings unmeasured my cup run-
neth o'er ;
With perfume and oil Thou anointest my
head ;
O! what shall I ask of Thy providence
more?

4 Let goodness and mercy, my bountiful
God !
Still follow my steps till I meet Thee
above ;
I seek — by the path which my fore-
fathers trod,
Through the land of their sojourn —
Thy kingdom of love.
JAMES MONTGOMERY.

131 *"They that endure to the end shall be saved."*

THOUGH faint, yet pursuing, we go on our
way ;
The Lord is our Leader, His word is our
stay ;
Though suffering and sorrow and trial be
near,
The Lord is our Refuge, and whom can
we fear?

2 He raiseth the fallen, He cheereth the
faint ;
The weak and opprest—He will hear their
complaint ;
The way may be weary, and thorny the
road,
But how can we falter?—our help is in
God !

3 And to His green pastures our footsteps
He leads ;
His flock in the desert. how kindly He
feeds !
The lambs in His bosom He tenderly
bears,
And brings back the wanderers all safe
from the snares.

4 Though clouds may surround us. our
God is our light ;
Though storms rage around us, our God
is our might ;
So faint, yet pursuing, still onward we
come ;
The Lord is our Leader, and Heaven is our
home !
JOHN NELSON DARBY.

ALLEIN GOTT. P. M.

Lord, Thou hast been Thy people's rest, Thro' all their gen - e - ra - tions,

Their re-fuge when by danger prest, Their hope in tri-bu - la - tions; Thou, ere the mountains

sprang to birth, Or ev-er Thou hadst form'd the earth, Art God from ev-er - last - ing!

132 *"O satisfy us early with Thy mercy."*

LORD, Thou hast been Thy people's rest,
  Through all their generations.
Their refuge when by danger prest,
  Their hope in tribulations ;
Thou, ere the mountains sprang to birth,
Or ever Thou hadst formed the earth,
  Art God from everlasting!
2 Lo! Thou hast set before Thine eyes
  All our misdeeds and errors :
Our secret sins from darkness rise,
  At Thine awakening terrors :

Who shall abide the trying hour?
Who knows the thunder of Thy power?
  We flee unto Thy mercy.
3 Lord, teach us so to mark our days
  That we may prize them duly ;
So guide our feet in wisdom's ways,
  That we may love Thee truly :
Return, O Lord! our griefs behold,
And with Thy goodness, as of old,
  O satisfy us early !

JAMES MONTGOMERY.

ITALIAN HYMN. 6s, 4s.

Come, Thou Al - migh - ty King, Help us Thy Name to sing, Help us to praise ;

Father all glo-ri-ous, O'er all vic - to - rious, Come and reign o - ver us, Ancient of days.

ABRAHAM. L. M.

O, for a strong, a last-ing faith To cred-it what th' Almight-y saith!

To embrace the message of His Son! And call the joys of heaven our own!

---

133 *"An anchor of the soul, both sure and steadfast."*

O, for a strong, a lasting faith
To credit what the Almighty saith!
To embrace the message of His Son!
And call the joys of heaven our own!

2 Then, should the earth's old pillars shake,
And all the wheels of nature break,
Our steady souls should fear no more
Than solid rocks when billows roar.

ISAAC WATTS.

---

134 *"Praise ye the Name of the Lord."*

COME, Thou Almighty King,
Help us Thy Name to sing,
   Help us to praise :
Father all glorious,
O'er all victorious,
Come and reign over us,
   Ancient of days.

2 Jesus, our Lord, arise ;
Scatter our enemies.
   And make them fall ;
Let Thine almighty aid
Our sure defence be made ;
Our souls on Thee be stayed ;
   Lord, hear our call.

3 Come, Thou Incarnate Word,
Gird on Thy mighty sword,
   Our prayer attend :

Come, and Thy people bless,
And give Thy word success :
Spirit of holiness,
   On us descend.

4 Come, Holy Comforter,
Thy sacred witness bear
   In this glad hour :
Thou who Almighty art,
Now rule in every heart,
And ne'er from us depart,
   Spirit of power.

5 To the great One and Three
Eternal praises be
   Hence, evermore :
His sovereign majesty
May we in glory see,
And to eternity
   Love and adore.

CHARLES WESLEY

64

Our Lord Jesus Christ.'

Stockel

ANTHEM. 8s, 7s, 4s.

Angels, from the realms of glo-ry, Wing your flight o'er all the earth; Ye who sang crea-tion's story, Now pro-claim Mes-

ti-ah's birth; Come and worship, Wor-ship Christ, Come and worship Christ, Wor-ship Christ, the new-born King.

135 *"We have seen His star in the east, and are come to worship Him."*

ANGELS, from the realms of glory,
  Wing your flight o'er all the earth;
Ye who sang creation's story,
  Now proclaim Messiah's birth;
    Come and worship,
Worship Christ, the new-born King.

2 Shepherds, in the field abiding,
  Watching o'er your flocks by night,
God with man is now residing,
  Yonder shines the infant light;
    Come and worship,
Worship Christ, the new-born King.

3 Sages, leave your contemplations,
  Brighter visions beam afar;
Seek the great Desire of nations,

Ye have seen His natal star;
    Come and worship,
Worship Christ, the new-born King.

4 Saints, before the altar bending,
  Watching long in hope and fear,
Suddenly the Lord, descending,
  In His temple shall appear;
    Come and worship,
Worship Christ, the new-born King.

5 Sinners, wrung with true repentance,
  Doomed for guilt to endless pains,
Justice now revokes the sentence,
  Mercy calls you,—break your chains!
    Come and worship,
Worship Christ, the new-born King.

JAMES MONTGOMERY.

HARMONY GROVE. L. M.

All praise to Thee, e-ter-nal Lord, Clothed in the garb of flesh and blood;

Choosing a man-ger for Thy throne, While worlds on worlds are Thine a-lone.

BETHLEHEM. 11s, 10s.

Brightest and best of the sons of the morning! Dawn on our darkness, and lend us Thine aid!

Star of the east, the ho - ri - zon a - dorning, Guide where our in - fant Redeemer is laid!

---

136 *"When they saw the star, they rejoiced with exceeding great joy."*

BRIGHTEST and best of the sons of the morning!
Dawn on our darkness, and lend us Thine aid!
Star of the east, the horizon adorning,
Guide where our infant Redeemer is laid!

2 Cold on His cradle the dew-drops are shining,
Low lies His head with the beasts of the stall,
Angels adore Him in slumber reclining —
Maker, and Monarch, and Saviour of all.

3 Say, shall we yield Him, in costly devotion,
Odors of Edom, and offerings divine?

Gems of the mountain, and pearls of the ocean,
Myrrh from the forest, or gold from the mine?

4 Vainly we offer each ample oblation;
Vainly with gifts would His favor secure;
Richer by far is the heart's adoration;
Dearer to God are the prayers of the poor.

5 Brightest and best of the sons of the morning!
Dawn on our darkness, and lend us Thine aid!
Star of the east, the horizon adorning,
Guide where our infant Redeemer is laid!

REGINALD HEBER.

---

137 *"Greater love hath no man than this."*

ALL praise to Thee, eternal Lord,
Clothed in the garb of flesh and blood;
Choosing a manger for Thy throne,
While worlds on worlds are Thine alone.

2 Once did the skies before Thee bow;
A Virgin's arms contain Thee now;
Angels who did in Thee rejoice
Now listen for Thine infant voice.

3 A little child Thou art our guest,
That weary ones in Thee may rest;

Forlorn and lowly is Thy birth,
That we may rise from heaven to earth.

4 Thou comest in the darksome night,
To make us children of the light,
To make us, in the realms divine,
Like Thine own angels round Thee shine.

5 All this for us Thy love hath done;
By this to Thee our love is won;
For this we tune our cheerful lays,
And shout our thanks in ceaseless praise.

MARTIN LUTHER.

JERUSALEM. C. M. D.

It came upon the midnight clear,—That glorious song of old, From angels bending near the earth To touch their harps of gold:

'Peace on the earth, good-will to men, From heaven's all-gracious King!' The world in solemn stillness lay To hear the an-gels sing.

138   "*We have peace with God through our Lord Jesus Christ.*"

It came upon the midnight clear,—
That glorious song of old,
From angels bending near the earth
To touch their harps of gold:
'Peace on the earth, good-will to men,
From heaven's all-gracious King!'
The world in solemn stillness lay
To hear the angels sing.

2 Still through the cloven skies they come,
With peaceful wings unfurled;
And still their heavenly music floats
O'er all the weary world:
Above its sad and lowly plains
They bend on hovering wing,
And ever o'er its Babel sounds
The blessed angels sing.

3 Yet with the woes of sin and strife
The world has suffered long;
Beneath the angel-strain have rolled
Two thousand years of wrong;
And men, at war with men, hear not
The love-song which they bring:
O hush the noise, ye men of strife,
And hear the angels sing!

4 And ye, beneath life's crushing load
Whose forms are bending low,
Who toil along the climbing way
With painful steps and slow;
Look now! for glad and golden hours
Come swiftly on the wing:
O rest beside the weary road,
And hear the angels sing!

5 For lo! the days are hastening on,
By prophet-bards foretold,
When with the ever-circling years
Comes round the age of gold;
When peace shall over all the earth
Its ancient splendors fling,
And the whole world send back the song
Which now the angels sing.

EDMUND HAMILTON SEARS.

139 "*The Word was made flesh and dwelt among us.*"

Calm on the listening ear of night,
Come heaven's melodious strains,
Where wild Judea stretches far
Her silver-mantled plains.
Celestial choirs, from courts above,
Shed sacred glories there,
And angels, with their sparkling lyres,
Make music on the air.

2 The answering hills of Palestine
Send back the glad reply,
And greet from all their holy hights
The Dayspring from on high:
O'er the blue depths of Galilee
There comes a holier calm;
And Sharon waves in solemn praise
Her silent groves of palm.

3 'Glory to God!' the lofty strain
The realm of ether fills;
How sweeps the song of solemn joy
O'er Judah's sacred hills!
'Glory to God!' the sounding skies
Loud with their anthems ring:
'Peace on the earth; good-will to men,
From heaven's eternal King.'

EDMUND HAMILTON SEARS.

HERALD ANGELS. 7s. D.

Hark, the herald an-gels sing, 'Glo - ry to the new-born King! Peace on earth, and mer-cy mild, God and

sinners re - con - cil'd! Joy-ful, all ye nations, rise, Join the triumph of the skies; Un - i - ver - sal nature

say, 'Christ the Lord is born to - day,' Un - i - ver - sal na - ture say, 'Christ the Lord is born to - day.'

140 *"Unto you is born this day . . a Saviour which is Christ the Lord."*

HARK, the herald angels sing,
'Glory to the new-born King!
Peace on earth, and mercy mild,
God and sinners reconciled!'
Joyful, all ye nations, rise,
Join the triumph of the skies;
Universal nature say,
'Christ the Lord is born to-day.'

2 Christ, by highest heaven adored,
Christ, the Everlasting Lord!
Late in time behold Him come,
Offspring of a Virgin's womb!
Veiled in flesh the Godhead see,
Hail, the incarnate Deity!
Pleased as man with men to dwell,
Jesus, our Immanuel.

3 Hail, the heavenly Prince of peace!
Hail, the Sun of righteousness!
Light and life to all He brings,
Risen with healing in His wings.
Mild He lays His glory by,
Born that man no more may die,
Born to raise the sons of earth,
Born to give them second birth.

4 Come, Desire of nations, come,
Fix in us Thy humble home;
Rise, the woman's conquering Seed,
Bruise in us the serpent's head.
Now display Thy saving power,
Ruined nature now restore;
Now in mystic union join
Thine to ours, and ours to Thine.
                                    CHARLES WESLEY.

141 C. M. D. *"God sent His only begotten Son."*

THE Saviour! O, what endless charms
Dwell in the blissful sound!
Its influence every fear disarms,
And spreads sweet comfort round.
The almighty Former of the skies
Stooped to our vile abode,
While angels viewed with wondering eyes
And hailed the incarnate God.

2 O, the rich depths of love divine!
Of bliss a boundless store!
Dear Saviour, let me call Thee mine;
I cannot wish for more.
On Thee alone my hope relies,
Beneath Thy cross I fall;
My Lord, my Life, my Sacrifice,
My Saviour and my All!
                                    ANNE STEELE.

DAVID. H. M.

Join all the glorious names Of wisdom, love, and pow'r, That ev - er mortal knew, That

an - gels ev - er bore ; All are too mean to speak His worth, Too mean to set my Saviour forth.

142 *"Christ is all, and in all."*

JOIN all the glorious names
  Of wisdom, love, and power,
That ever mortals knew,
  That angels ever bore ;
All are too mean to speak His worth,
Too mean to set my Saviour forth.

2 Great Prophet of my God,
  My tongue would bless Thy name ;
By Thee the joyful news
  Of our salvation came ;
The joyful news of sins forgiven,
Of hell subdued, and peace with heaven.

3 Jesus, my great High-Priest,
  Offered His blood and died ;
My guilty conscience seeks
  No sacrifice beside ;
His powerful blood did once atone,
And now it pleads before the throne.

4 My dear Almighty Lord,
  My Conqueror and my King,
Thy scepter and Thy sword,
  Thy reigning grace, I sing :
Thine is the power : behold I sit
In willing bonds beneath Thy feet !

ISAAC WATTS.

CHIMES. C. M.

In - fi - nite ex - cel - lence is Thine, Thou glori - ous Prince of grace,

Thine un - cre - a - ted beau - ties shine With nev - er fad - ing rays.

GLAD TIDINGS. C. M. D.

While shepherds watch'd their flocks by night, All seated on the ground; The an-gel of the
Lord came down, And glo - ry shone a - round. 'Fear not,' said he,—for mighty dread Had
seiz'd their troubled mind,— 'Glad ti-dings of great joy I bring, To you and all mankind.'

143 *"Unto you is born this day in the city of David, a Saviour, which is Christ the Lord."*

WHILE shepherds watched their flocks by [night,
All seated on the ground ;
The angel of the Lord came down,
And glory shone around.
'Fear not,' said he,—for mighty dread
Had seized their troubled mind,—
'Glad tidings of great joy I bring,
To you and all mankind.'

2 'To you in David's town this day,
Is born of David's line,
The Saviour, who is Christ, the Lord,
And this shall be the sign ;—

The heavenly babe you there shall find
To human view displayed,
All meanly wrapped in swathing bands,
And in a manger laid.'

3 Thus spake the seraph—and forthwith
Appeared a shining throng
Of angels, praising God, who thus
Addressed their joyful song :—
'All glory be to God on high,
And to the earth be peace ;
Good-will henceforth from heaven to men
Begin, and never cease !'

NAHUM TATE.

144 *"A light to lighten the Gentiles."*

INFINITE excellence is Thine,
Thou glorious Prince of grace !
Thine uncreated beauties shine
With never-fading rays.

2 Sinners. from earth's remotest end,
Come bending at Thy feet ;
To Thee their prayers and songs ascend,
In Thee their wishes meet.

3 Millions of happy spirits live
On Thine exhaustless store ;
From Thee they all their bliss receive,
And still Thou givest more.

4 Thou art their triumph and their joy ;
They find their all in Thee ;
Thy glories will their tongues employ
Through all eternity.

JOHN FAWCETT.

LANCASHIRE. 7s, 6s.

O word of God in-car-nate, O Wis-dom from on high, O Truth unchang'd, unchanging, O Light of our dark sky!

We praise Thee for the radiance That from the hallow'd page, A lantern to our footsteps, Shines on from age to age.

145 *"Thy word is a lamp unto my feet."*
O WORD of God incarnate,
  O Wisdom from on high,
O Truth unchanged, unchanging,
  O Light of our dark sky!
We praise Thee for the radiance
  That from the hallowed page,
A lantern to our footsteps,
  Shines on from age to age.

2 The Church from her dear Master
  Received the gift divine,
And still that light she lifteth
  O'er all the earth to shine.
It is the golden casket
  Where gems of truth are stored,
It is the heaven-drawn picture
  Of Christ the living Word.

3 Oh, make Thy Church, dear Saviour,
  A lamp of burnished gold,
To bear before the nations
  Thy true light as of old;
Oh, teach Thy wandering pilgrims
  By this their path to trace,
Till, clouds and darkness ended,
  They see Thee face to face.
          WILLIAM WALSHAM HOW.

146 *"Hosanna to the Son of David."*
ALL glory, laud, and honor,
  To Thee, Redeemer King!
To whom the lips of children
  Made sweet Hosannas ring!
Thou art the King of Israel;
  Thou David's Royal Son;
Who in the Lord's name comest,
  The King and Blessed One.

2 The company of angels
  Are praising Thee on high:
And mortal men and all things
  Created make reply.
The people of the Hebrews
  With palms before Thee went;
Our praise, and prayer, and anthems
  Before Thee we present.

3 To Thee before Thy Passion,
  They raised their hymns of praise:
To Thee amid Thy glory,
  Our melody we raise.
Thou didst accept their praises;
  Accept the prayers we bring,
Who in all good delightest,
  Thou good and gracious King!
          JOHN MASON NEALE.

147 *"Seek those things which are above."*
FROM every earthly pleasure,
  From every transient joy;
From every mortal treasure,
  That soon will fade and die,
No longer these desiring,
  Our wishes upward tend,
To nobler bliss aspiring
  And joys that never end.

2 Our hope is in the Saviour,
  So graciously revealed;
Our strength, His grace and favor,
  His mighty arm our shield.
Rejoice we then before Him,
  Our Prophet, Priest, and King,
With grateful hearts adore Him,
  And loud hosannas sing.
          DAVIS.

FRANCONIA. C. M.

The race that long in darkness walked Have seen a glorious light; The people dwell in day, who dwelt In death's surrounding night.

148 *"Mine eyes have seen Thy salvation."*

THE race that long in darkness walked
  Have seen a glorious light ;
The people dwell in day, who dwelt
  In death's surrounding night.

2 To hail Thy rise, Thou better Sun,
  The gathering nations come ;
They joy as when the reapers bear
  The harvest-treasures home.

3 For unto us a Child is born,
  To us a Son is given ;

And on His shoulder ever rests
  All power in earth and heaven.

4 His name shall be the Prince of peace,
  The God by all adored,
The Wonderful, the Counsellor,
  The Everlasting Lord.

5 His power increasing still shall spread,
  His reign no end shall know,
Justice and judgment guard His throne,
  And peace abound below.
                              JOHN MORRISON.

CORONATION. C. M.

All hail the power of Je-sus' name! Let an-gels prostrate fall; Bring forth the roy-al di-a-dem.

To crown Him Lord of all! Bring forth the roy-al di-a-dem, To crown Him Lord of all!

149 *"King of Kings, and Lord of Lords."*

ALL hail the power of Jesus' name !
  Let angels prostrate fall ;
Bring forth the royal diadem,
  To crown Him Lord of all !

2 Crown Him, ye morning stars of light,
  Who fixed this floating ball ;
Now hail the Strength of Israel's might,
  And crown Him Lord of all !

3 Ye chosen seed of Israel's race,
  Ye ransomed of the fall,

Hail Him who saves you by His grace,
  And crown Him Lord of all !

4 Sinners, whose love can ne'er forget
  The wormwood and the gall,
Go, spread your trophies at His feet,
  And crown Him Lord of all !

5 Let every tribe and every tongue
  That hear the Saviour's call,
Now shout in universal song,
  And crown Him Lord of all !
                              EDWARD PERRONET.

ANTIOCH. C. M.

Joy to the world! the Lord is come; Let earth re-ceive her King; Let ev'-ry heart pre-

pare Him room, And heav'n and nature sing, And heav'n and nature sing, And heav'n and heav'n and nature sing.

And heav'n and nature sing, And heav'n and nature sing.

150 *"Behold, I bring you good tidings of great joy."*

Joy to the world! the Lord is come ;
Let earth receive her King ;
Let every heart prepare Him room,
And heaven and nature sing.

2 Joy to the earth! the Saviour reigns ;
Let men their songs employ ; [plains
While fields and floods, rocks, hills, and
Repeat the sounding joy.

3 No more let sin and sorrows grow,
Nor thorns infest the ground ;
He comes to make His blessings flow
Far as the curse is found.

4 He rules the world with truth and grace,
And makes the nations prove
The glories of His righteousness,
And wonders of His love.

ISAAC WATTS.

OSWALD. 8s, 7s.

Hark! what mean those holy voices, Sweetly sounding thro' the skies! Lo! the angelic host rejoices; Loudest hal-le - lu - jahs rise.

151 *"A multitude of the heavenly host, praising God."*

HARK! what mean those holy voices,
Sweetly sounding through the skies?
Lo! the angelic host rejoices ;
Loudest hallelujahs rise.

2 Listen to the wondrous story,
Which they chant in hymns of joy :—
'Glory in the highest, glory!
Glory be to God most high!

3 'Peace on earth, good-will from heaven,
Reaching far as man is found ;

Souls redeemed, and sins forgiven ;—
Loud our golden harps shall sound.

4 'Christ is born, the great Anointed ;
Heaven and earth His praises sing!
Glad receive whom God appointed,
For your Prophet, Priest and King!

5 'Hasten, mortals, to adore Him ;
Learn His name, and taste His joy ;
Till in heaven ye sing before Him,—
Glory be to God most high!'

JOHN CAWOOD.

MALVERN. L. M.

Come, let us sing the song of songs,—The saints in heaven be-gan the strain,—

The homage which to Christ be-longs: 'Worthy the Lamb, for He was slain!'

152 *"Worthy is the Lamb that was slain."*

COME, let us sing the song of songs,—
  The saints in heaven began the strain,—
The homage which to Christ belongs:
  'Worthy the Lamb, for He was slain!'

2 Slain to redeem us by His blood,
  To cleanse from every sinful stain,
And make us kings and priests to God:
  'Worthy the Lamb, for He was slain!'

3 To Him who suffered on the tree,
  Our souls at His soul's price to gain,

Blessing, and praise, and glory be:
  'Worthy the Lamb, for He was slain!'

4 To Him enthroned by filial right,
  All power in heaven and earth pertain,
Honor, and majesty, and might:
  'Worthy the Lamb, for He was slain!'

5 Come, Holy Spirit, from on high,
  Our faith, our hope, our love sustain,
Living to sing, and dying cry,
  'Worthy the Lamb, for He was slain!'
                        JAMES MONTGOMERY.

RATHBUN. 8s, 7s.

In the cross of Christ I glory, Towering o'er the wrecks of time; All the light of sacred story Gathers round its head sublime.

153 *"God forbid that I should glory, save in the cross of our Lord Jesus Christ."*

IN the cross of Christ I glory,
  Towering o'er the wrecks of time;
All the light of sacred story
  Gathers round its head sublime.

2 When the woes of life o'ertake me,
  Hopes deceive, and fears annoy,
Never shall the cross forsake me;
  Lo, it glows with peace and joy.

3 When the sun of bliss is beaming
  Light and love upon my way,

From the cross the radiance streaming
  Adds more luster to the day.

3 Bane and blessing, pain and pleasure,
  By the cross are sanctified;
Peace is there, that knows no measure,
  Joys that through all time abide.

5 In the cross of Christ I glory,
  Towering o'er the wrecks of time;
All the light of sacred story
  Gathers round its head sublime.
                        JOHN BOWRING.

CAMBRIDGE. C. M.

Hark, the glad sound, the Saviour comes, The Saviour promis'd long! Let every heart prepare a throne, And every voice a song, And every voice a song, And every voice a song.

154 *"The oil of joy for mourning, the garment of praise*
for the spirit of heaviness."

HARK, the glad sound, the Saviour comes,
The Saviour promised long !
Let every heart prepare a throne,
And every voice a song.

2 On Him, the Spirit, largely poured,
Exerts its sacred fire ;
Wisdom and might, and zeal and love,
His holy breast inspire.

3 He comes the prisoners to release,
In Satan's bondage held ;
The gates of brass before Him burst,
The iron fetters yield.

4 He comes, from thickest films of vice
To clear the mental ray ;
And, on the eyes opprest with night,
To pour celestial day.

5 He comes. the broken heart to bind,
The bleeding soul to cure ;
And, with the treasures of His grace,
To enrich the humble poor.

6 Our glad hosannas, Prince of peace,
Thy welcome shall proclaim ;
And heaven's eternal arches ring
With Thy beloved name.

PHILIP DODDRIDGE.

HOLY TRINITY. C. M.

How condescending and how kind Was God's e-ternal Son ! Our misery reach'd His heavenly mind, And pity brought Him down.

155   *"Even the death of the cross."*

How condescending and how kind
Was God's eternal Son !
Our misery reached His heavenly mind,
And pity brought Him down.

2 He sunk beneath our heavy woes,
To raise us to His throne ;
There's ne'er a gift His hand bestows,
But cost His heart a groan.

3 This was compassion, like a God,
That when the Saviour knew
The price of pardon was His blood,
His pity ne'er withdrew.

4 Now, though He reigns exalted high,
His love is still as great ;
Well He remembers Calvary,
Nor let His saints forget.

ISAAC WATTS.

AVISON. 11s, 10s.
Chorus.

Shout the glad tidings, ex-ulting-ly sing; . . . Je-ru - sa-lem triumphs, Mes- si - ah is King. Zi - 'on,the mar-vel-ous

sto - ry be tell-ing, The Son of the Highest, how low - ly His birth; The brightest arch-an- gel in glo-ry ex - cell-ing,

CLOSE WITH 1 CHORUS. CHORUS AFTER LAST VERSE.

He stoops to re - deem thee, He reigns up - on earth. Shout the glad ti - dings, ex -

ultingly sing, . . Je - ru - sa-lem triumphs,Mes - si - ah is King, Mes - si - ah is King, Mes - si - ah is King.

156 *"Good tidings of great joy."*

Cho.—SHOUT the glad tidings, exultingly
  sing ;
  Jerusalem triumphs, Messiah is
  King.

ZION, the marvelous story be telling,
  The Son of the Highest, how lowly His
  birth ;
Thebrightest archangel in glory excelling,
  He stoops to redeem thee, He reigns
  upon earth.
  Cho.—Shout the glad tidings, etc.

  Cho.—Shout the glad tidings, etc.
2 Tell how He cometh ; from nation to
  nation,
  The heart-cheering news let the earth
  echo round ;

How free to the faithful He offers salvation !
How His people with joy everlasting are
  crowned !
  Cho.—Shout the glad tidings, etc.

  Cho.—Shout the glad tidings, etc.

3 Mortals, your homage be gratefully
  bringing,
  And sweet let the gladsome hosanna
  arise ;
Ye angels, the full hallelujah be singing ;
  One chorus resound through the earth
  and the skies.
  Cho.—Shout the glad tidings, etc.
  WILLIAM AUGUSTUS MUHLENBERG.

ARIEL. C. P. M.

O could I speak the match-less worth, O could I sound the glo-ries forth, Which in my Saviour shine! I'd

soar, and touch the heav'nly strings, And vie with Gabriel while he sings In notes almost di-vine, In notes al-most di-vine.

157 *"Make His praise glorious."*

O COULD I speak the matchless worth,
O could I sound the glories forth,
 Which in my Saviour shine !
I'd soar, and touch the heavenly strings,
And vie with Gabriel while he sings
 In notes almost divine.

2 I'd sing the precious blood He spilt,
My ransom from the dreadful guilt
 Of sin and wrath divine :
I'd sing His glorious righteousness,
In which all-perfect, heavenly dress
 My soul shall ever shine.

3 I'd sing the characters he bears,
And all the forms of love He wears,
 Exalted on His throne :
In loftiest songs of sweetest praise,
I would to everlasting days
 Make all His glories known.

4 Well, the delightful day will come,
When my dear Lord will bring me home,
 And I shall see His face :
Then, with my Saviour, Brother, Friend,
A blest eternity I'll spend,
 Triumphant in His grace.

SAMUEL MEDLEY.

DOLCE. 7s.

Sweet-er sounds than mu-sic knows, Charm me in Im-man-uel's name;

All her hopes my spi-rit owes, To His birth, and cross, and shame.

FEDERAL STREET. L. M.

My dear Redeem - er and my Lord, I read my du - ty in Thy word;

But in Thy life the law ap - pears, Drawn out in liv - ing char - ac - ters.

158 *"Behold My Servant, whom I have chosen."*

My dear Redeemer and my Lord,
I read my duty in Thy word ;
But in Thy life the law appears
Drawn out in living characters.

2 Such was Thy truth, and such Thy zeal,
Such deference to Thy Father's will,
Such love, and meekness so divine,
I would transcribe and make them mine.

3 Cold mountains, and the midnight air,
Witnessed the fervor of Thy prayer ;
The desert Thy temptations knew,
Thy conflict, and Thy victory too.

4 Be Thou my pattern ; make me bear
More of Thy gracious image here !
Then God, the Judge, shall own my name,
Among the followers of the Lamb.
ISAAC WATTS.

159 *"Never man spake like this Man."*

How sweetly flowed the gospel's sound
From lips of gentleness and grace,
When listening thousands gathered round,
And joy and reverence filled the place !

2 From heaven He came, of heaven He
spoke,
To heaven He led His followers' way ;
Dark clouds of gloomy night He broke,
Unveiling an immortal day.

3 'Come, wanderers, to My Father's home ;
Come, all ye weary ones, and rest :'
Yes, sacred Teacher, we will come,
Obey Thee, love Thee, and be blest.

4 Decay, then, tenements of dust ;
Pillars of earthly pride, decay :
A nobler mansion waits the just,
And Jesus has prepared the way.
JOHN BOWRING.

160 *"Bless the Lord, O my soul."*

SWEETER sounds than music knows
Charm me in Immannuel's name ;
All her hopes my spirit owes
To His birth, and cross, and shame.

2 When He came, the angels sung,
'Glory be to God on high :'
Lord, unloose my stammering tongue ;
Who should louder sing than I ?

3 Did the Lord a man become,
That He might the law fulfill,

Bleed and suffer in my room,—
And canst thou, my tongue, be still ?

4 No ; I must my praises bring,
Though they worthless are, and weak ;
For should I refuse to sing,
Sure the very stones would speak.

5 O my Saviour ! Shield and Sun,
Shepherd, Brother, Lord, and Friend —
Every precious name in one !
I will love Thee without end.
JOHN NEWTON.

CRAMER. L. M.

Je-sus! and shall it ev - er be, A mor-tal man a - shamed of Thee?

Asham'd of Thee whom an - gels praise, Whose glories shine thro' end - less days?

161   *"If we deny Him, He also will deny us."*

JESUS! and shall it ever be,
A mortal man ashamed of Thee?
Ashamed of Thee whom angels praise,
Whose glories shine thro' endless days?

2 Ashamed of Jesus! sooner far
Let evening blush to own a star;
He sheds the beams of light divine
O'er this benighted soul of mine.

3 Ashamed of Jesus! that dear Friend
On whom my hopes of heaven depend!

No; when I blush—be this my shame,
That I no more revere His name.

4 Ashamed of Jesus! yes, I may,
When I've no guilt to wash away;
No tear to wipe, no good to crave,
No fear to quell, no soul to save.

5 Till then, nor is my boasting vain,
Till then I boast a Saviour slain!
And O may this my glory be,
That Christ is not ashamed of me!

JOSEPH GRIGG.

CRUSADERS' HYMN. P. M.

Fair-est Lord Je - sus! Ruler of all na - ture, O Thou of God and man the Son!

Thee will I cher - ish, Thee will I hon - or, Thou! my soul's glory, joy, and crown.

LUX MUNDI. 7s, 6s. D.

O Je - sus, our sal - va - tion, Low at Thy cross we lie; Lord, in Thy great com-
pas - sion, Hear our be - wail-ing cry. We come to Thee with mourning, We
come to Thee in woe; With contrite hearts re - turning, And tears that o-ver - flow.

162   *"Hear my cry, O God."*

O JESUS, our salvation,
  Low at Thy cross we lie ;
Lord, in Thy great compassion,
  Hear our bewailing cry.
We come to Thee with mourning,
  We come to Thee in woe :
With contrite hearts returning,
  And tears that overflow.

2 O gracious Intercessor,
  O Priest within the veil,
Plead, for each lost transgressor,
  The blood that cannot fail.

We spread our sins before Thee,
  We tell them one by one ;
O, for Thy name's great glory,
  Forgive all we have done.

3 O, by Thy cross and passion,
  Thy tears and agony,
And crown of cruel fashion,
  And death on Calvary ;
By all that untold suffering,
  Endured by Thee alone ;
O Priest, O spotless offering,
  Plead for us, and atone.

HAMILTON.

163   *"How great is His goodness."*

FAIREST Lord Jesus ! Ruler of all nature !
  O Thou of God and man the Son !
Thee will I cherish, Thee will I honor,
  Thou ! my soul's glory, joy, and crown.

2 Fair are the meadows, fairer still the woodlands,
  Robed in the blooming garb of spring :

Jesus is fairer ! Jesus is purer !
  Who makes the woeful heart to sing.

3 Fair is the sunshine, fairer still the moonlight,
  And the twinkling starry host :
Jesus shines brighter ! Jesus shines purer !
  Than all the angels heaven can boast.

RICHARD STORRS WILLIS.

DYKES. L. M.

O Love, how deep! how broad! how high! It fills the heart with ec-sta-cy,

That God, the Son of God, should take Our mor-tal form for mor-tals' sake.

164   *"The unsearchable riches of Christ."*

O Love, how deep! how broad! how
   high!
It fills the heart with ecstacy,
That God, the Son of God, should take
Our mortal form for mortals' sake.

2 He sent no angel to our race,
Of higher or of lower place,
But clothed Himself in human frame
And to redeem this lost world came.

3 For us He prayed, for us He taught,
For us His daily works He wrought,
By words, and signs, and actions, thus
Still seeking not Himself, but us.

4 For us to wicked men betrayed,
Scourged, mocked, in purple robe arrayed,
He bore the shameful cross and death,
For us at length gave up His breath.

5 For us He rose from death again,
For us He went on high to reign,
For us He sent His Spirit here
To guide, to strengthen, and to cheer.

6 To Him whose boundless love has won
Salvation for us through the Son,
To God the Father, glory be,
Both now and through eternity.

JOHN MASON NEALE.

CALVARY. 7s. 6 lines.

{ From the cross up-lift-ed high, Where the Sav-iour deigns to die, }
{ What me-lo-dious sounds I hear, Burst-ing on my rav-ish'd ear! }

'Love's re-deem-ing work is done, Come and wel-come, sin-ner, come.'

PHRYGIA. 7s, 6s.

O Sa-cred Head! once wound-ed, With grief and shame weighed down, Once scorn-ful-ly sur-round-ed With thorns, Thy on-ly crown; O Sa-cred Head! what glo-ry,

What bliss, till now was Thine; Yet, though despis'd and go-ry, joy to call Thee mine.

---

165 *"Who loved me, and gave Himself for me."*

O SACRED Head! once wounded,
  With grief and shame weighed down,
Once scornfully surrounded
  With thorns, Thy only crown;
O Sacred Head! what glory,
  What bliss, till now was Thine;
Yet, though despised and gory,
  I joy to call Thee mine.

2 What Thou, my Lord, hast suffered,
  Was all for sinners' gain:
Mine, mine, was the transgression,
  But Thine the deadly pain.
Lo! here I fall, my Saviour;
  'Tis I deserve Thy place;
Look on me with Thy favor,
  Vouchsafe to me Thy grace.

3 What language shall I borrow
  To thank Thee, dearest Friend,
For this, Thy dying sorrow,
  Thy pity without end!

O make me Thine for ever;
  And should I fainting be,
Lord, let me never, never,
  Outlive my love to Thee.

4 And when I am departing,
  O part not Thou from me!
When mortal pangs are darting,
  Come, Lord, and set me free!
And when my heart must languish
  Amid the final throe,
Release me from mine anguish
  By Thine own pain and woe!

5 Be near me when I'm dying,
  O show Thy cross to me;
And, for my succor flying,
  Come, Lord, and set me free!
These eyes new faith receiving
  From Jesus shall not move;
For he who dies believing,
  Dies safely through Thy love.
                              PAUL GERHARDT.

---

166 *"And I, if I be lifted up from the earth, will draw all men unto Me."*

FROM the cross uplifted high
Where the Saviour deigns to die,
What melodious sounds I hear,
Bursting on my ravished ear!
'Love's redeeming work is done,
Come and welcome, sinner, come!

2 'Sprinkled now with blood the throne,
Why beneath thy burdens groan?
On My pierced body laid,
Justice owns the ransom paid:
Bow the knee, and kiss the Son,
Come and welcome, sinner, come!

3 'Spread for thee, the festal board
See with richest dainties stored:
To thy Father's bosom prest
Yet again a child confest,
Never from His house to roam;
Come and welcome, sinner, come!

4 'Soon the days of life shall end:
Lo I come, your Saviour, Friend!
Safe your spirit to convey
To the realms of endless day,
Up to My eternal home:
Come and welcome, sinner, come!'
                              THOMAS HAWEIS.

ROCK OF AGES. 7s. 6 lines.

FINE.   D.C.

Son of God! to Thee I cry: By the ho - ly mys-ter - y   Of Thy dwell-ing here on earth, By Thy pure and ho-ly birth,
Lord, Thy presence let me see, Man - i - fest Thyself to me.

167   *"And I will love him, and will manifest myself to him."*

Son of God! to Thee I cry:
By the holy mystery
Of Thy dwelling here on earth,
By Thy pure and holy birth,
Lord, Thy presence let me see,
Manifest Thyself to me.

2 Lamb of God! to Thee I cry:
By Thy bitter agony,
By Thy pangs to us unknown,
By Thy spirit's parting groan,
Lord, Thy presence let me see,
Manifest Thyself to me.

3 Prince of Life! to Thee I cry:
By Thy glorious majesty,
By Thy triumph o'er the grave,
Meek to suffer, strong to save,
Lord, Thy presence let me see,
Manifest Thyself to me.

4 Lord of glory, God most high,
Man exalted to the sky;
With Thy love my bosom fill,
Prompt me to perform Thy will;
Then Thy glory I shall see,
Thou wilt bring me home to Thee.

RICHARD MANT.

AVON. C. M.

A - las! and did my Sav - iour bleed? And did my Sovereign die?

Would He de - vote that sa - cred head For such a worm as I?

168   *"Christ also suffered for us."*

Alas! and did my Saviour bleed?
And did my Sovereign die?
Would He devote that sacred head
For such a worm as I?

2 Was it for crimes that I had done
He groaned upon the tree?
Amazing pity! grace unknown!
And love beyond degree!

3 Well might the sun in darkness hide,
And shut his glories in,

When Christ, the Lord of glory, died
For man the creature's sin.

4 Thus might I hide my blushing face
While His dear cross appears,
Dissolve my heart in thankfulness,
And melt mine eyes to tears.

5 But drops of grief can ne'er repay
The debt of love I owe:
Here, Lord, I give myself away;
'Tis all that I can do.

ISAAC WATTS.

ALLELUIA. S. M. D.

'The Lord is risen in-deed;' The grave hath lost its prey; With Him shall rise the ransomed seed To reign in endless day.'The Lord is ris'n in-deed;' He lives,to die no more; He lives the sin-ner's cause to plead, Whose curse and shame He bore.

169 *"Death is swallowed up in victory."*

'The Lord is risen indeed;'
   The grave hath lost its prey :
With Him shall rise the ransomed seed
   To reign in endless day.
'The Lord is risen indeed;'
   He lives, to die no more ;
He lives the sinner's cause to plead,
   Whose curse and shame He bore.

2 'The Lord is risen indeed ;'
   Attending angels, hear ;
Up to the courts of heaven, with speed,
   The joyful tidings bear.
Then take your golden lyres,
   And strike each cheerful chord ;
Join all the bright celestial choirs,
   To sing our risen Lord.
                                    THOMAS KELLY.

170 *"And on His head were many crowns."*

Crown Him with crowns of gold,
   All nations great and small,
Crown Him, ye martyred saints of old,
   The Lamb once slain for all ;
The Lamb once slain for them
   Who bring their praises now,
As jewels for the diadem
   That girds His sacred brow.

2 Crown Him the Son of God
   Before the worlds began,
And ye who tread where He hath trod,
   Crown Him the Son of Man ;
Who every grief hath known
   That wrings the human breast,
And takes and bears them for His own
   That all in Him may rest.

3 Crown Him the Lord of light,
   Who o'er a darkened world
In robes of glory infinite
   His fiery flag unfurled,
And bore it raised on high,
   In heaven,—in earth,—beneath,
To all the sign of victory
   O'er Satan, sin, and death.

4 Crown Him the Lord of life,
   Who triumphed o'er the grave,
And rose victorious in the strife
   For those He came to save ;
His glories now we sing
   Who died, and rose on high,
Who died, eternal life to bring,
   And lives, that death may die.
                                    GODFREY THRING.

               Our Lord Jesus Christ.

TRIUMPH. H. M.

Yes, the Re-deem - er rose; The Sav - iour left the dead; And o'er our hell - ish foes

High rais'd His con - quering head. In wild dis - may, The guards around Fell to the ground, And sunk a - way.

171   *"O grace, where is thy victory?"*

YES, the Redeemer rose ;
  The Saviour left the dead ;
And o'er our hellish foes
  High raised His conquering head.
In wild dismay, | Fell to the ground,
The guards around | And sunk away.

2 Lo! the angelic bands
  In full assembly meet,
To wait His high commands,
  And worship at His feet:
Joyful they come, | From realms of day
And wing their way | To such a tomb.

3 Then back to heaven they fly,
  The joyful news to bear :
Hark! as they soar on high,

What music fills the air !
Their anthems say, | Hath left the dead ;
'Jesus, who bled, | He rose to-day.'

4 Ye mortals, catch the sound,
  Redeemed by Him from hell ;
And send the echo round
  The globe on which you dwell ;
Transported cry, | Hath left the dead,
'Jesus, who bled, | No more to die.'

5 All hail, triumphant Lord,
  Who sav'st us with Thy blood !
Wide be Thy name adored,
  Thou rising, reigning God !
With Thee we rise, | And empires gain
With Thee we reign. | Beyond the skies.

                               PHILIP DODDRIDGE.

OLIVET. 6s, 4s.

Glo -ry to God on high! Let praises fill the sky! Praise ye His name! An-gels His

name a-dore, Who all our sor-rows bore, Saints cry for ev - er-more, Worthy the Lamb!

GREENPORT. C. M. D.

There is a green hill far away, Without a ci-ty wall, Where the dear Lord was

cru-ci-fied, Who died to save us all. We may not know, we can-not tell

What pains He had to bear; But we believe it was for us He hung and suffered there.

172 *" While we were yet sinners, Christ died for us."*

THERE is a green hill far away,
  Without a city wall,
Where the dear Lord was crucified,
  Who died to save us all.
We may not know, we cannot tell
  What pains He had to bear;
But we believe it was for us
  He hung and suffered there.

2 He died that we might be forgiven,
  He died to make us good,
That we might go at last to heaven,
  Saved by His precious blood.

There was no other good enough
  To pay the price of sin;
He only could unlock the gate
  Of heaven and let us in.

3 Oh, dearly, dearly, has He loved,
  And we must love Him too,
And trust in His redeeming blood,
  And try His works to do.
For there's a green hill far away,
  Without a city wall,
Where the dear Lord was crucified,
  Who died to save us all.
CECIL FRANCES ALEXANDER.

173 *" Worthy is the Lamb that was slain."*

GLORY to God on high!
  Let praises fill the sky!
    Praise ye His name!
Angels His name adore,
Who all our sorrows bore;
Saints cry for evermore,
    Worthy the Lamb!

2 All they around the throne
Cheerfully join in one,
    Praising His name:

We, who have felt His blood
Sealing our peace with God,
Spread His dear name abroad,
    Worthy the Lamb!

3 Though we must change our place,
Our souls shall never cease
    Praising His name;
To Him we'll tribute bring,
Hail Him our gracious King,
And without ceasing sing,
    Worthy the Lamb!
JAMES ALLEN.

FILII ET FILIAE. P. M.

Al - le - lu - ia, Al-le - lu - ia, Al - le - lu - ia; Ye sons and daughters of the Lord!

The King of Glo-ry, King ador'd, This day Himself from death restor'd. Alle-lu - ia.

174 *"He is not here; He is risen."*

Ye sons and daughters of the Lord!
The King of Glory, King adored,
This day Himself from death restored.

2 On Sunday morn, at break of day,
The faithful women went their way,
To see the tomb where Jesus lay.

3 Then straightway one in white they see,
Who saith, 'Ye seek the Lord; but He
Is risen, and gone to Galilee.'

4 That night the apostles met in fear,
But Christ did in their midst appear,—
'My peace,' He said, 'be on all here!'

5 When Thomas first these tidings heard,
He doubted if it were the Lord,
Until He came and spake this word:—

6 'Behold my side, O Thomas! see,
My hands, my feet, I show to thee;
Nor faithless, but believing be.'

7 When Thomas saw that wounded side,
The truth no longer he denied;
'Thou art my Lord and God?' he cried.

8 How blest are they who have not seen,
And yet whose faith hath constant been!
For they eternal life shall win.

JOHN MASON NEALE.

LATOUR. C. M.

Thou art the Way—to Thee a - lone From sin and death 'we flee; And he who

would the Father seek, Must seek him, Lord, by Thee, Must seek him, Lord, by Thee.

HUMMEL. C. M.

Come, let us join our songs of praise To our as-cend-ed Priest;

He en-tered heaven with all our names En-grav-en on His breast.

175 *" We have not an High Priest, which cannot be touched with the feeling of our infirmities."*

Come, let us join our songs of praise
To our ascended Priest;
He entered heaven with all our names
Engraven on His breast.

2 Below He washed our guilt away,
By His atoning blood;
Now He appears before the throne,
And pleads our cause with God.

3 Clothed with our nature still, He knows
The weakness of our frame,
And how to shield us from the foes
Whom He Himself o'ercame.

4 Nor time, nor distance, e'er shall quench
The fervor of His love;
For us He died in kindness here,
For us He lives above.

5 O may we ne'er forget His grace,
Nor blush to bear His name;
Still may our hearts hold fast His faith,
Our lips His praise proclaim.
ALEXANDER PIRIE.

176 *" He that glorieth, let him glory in the Lord."*

O Christ! our Hope, our heart's Desire,
Redemption's only Spring,
Creator of the world art Thou,
Its Saviour and its King!

2 How vast the mercy and the love
Which laid our sins on Thee,
And led Thee to a cruel death,
To set Thy people free!

3 But now the bonds of death are burst,
The ransom hath been paid;
And Thou art on Thy Father's throne,
In glorious might arrayed.

4 O may Thy wondrous love prevail
Our sinful souls to spare!
O may we come before Thy throne,
And find acceptance there!

5 O Christ, be Thou our present Joy,
Our future great Reward;
Our only glory may it be
To glory in the Lord.
JOHN CHANDLER.

177 *" No man cometh unto the Father, but by Me."*

Thou art the Way—to Thee alone
From sin and death we flee;
And He who would the Father seek,
Must seek him. Lord, by Thee.

2 Thou art the Truth—Thy word alone
True wisdom can impart;
Thou only canst inform the mind,
And purify the heart.

3 Thou art the Life—the rending tomb
Proclaims Thy conquering arm,
And those who put their trust in Thee
Nor death, nor hell shall harm.

4 Thou art the Way—the Truth—the Life;
Grant us that Way to know,
That Truth to keep, that Life to win,
Whose joys eternal flow.
GEORGE WASHINGTON DOANE.

ECCE DEUS. P. M.

Behold the Lamb of God! O Thou for sin - ners slain, Let it not be in vain That Thou hast died:

Thee for my Sav - iour let me take, My on-ly re - fuge let me make Thy pierc - ed Side.

178 *"Behold the Lamb of God which taketh away the sins of the world."*

BEHOLD the Lamb of God!
O Thou for sinners slain,
Let it not be in vain
That Thou hast died:
Thee for my Saviour let me take,
My only refuge let me make
Thy piercèd Side.

2 Behold the Lamb of God!
Into the sacred flood,
Of Thy most precious Blood
My soul I cast.
Wash me and keep me clean within,
And keep me pure from every sin,
Till life is past.

3 Behold the Lamb of God!
All hail, Incarnate Word,
Thou everlasting Lord,
Saviour most blest.
Fill us with love that never faints,
Grant us with all Thy blessèd saints
Eternal rest.

4 Behold the Lamb of God!
Worthy is He alone
That sitteth on the throne
Of God above;
One with the Ancient of all days,
One with the Comforter in praise,
All Light and Love.

MATTHEW BRIDGES.

WATCH. C. M.

The Head that once was crown'd with thorns Is crown'd with glo -ry now;

A roy - al di - a - dem a -dorns The migh - ty Vic - tor's brow.

SCHUMANN. L. M.

How beauteous were the marks di - vine, That in Thy meekness used to shine,

That lit Thy lone - ly path-way, trod In wondrous love, O Son of God!

---

179 *"He humbled Himself and became obedient unto death, even the death of the cross."*

How beauteous were the marks divine,
That in Thy meekness used to shine,
That lit Thy lonely pathway, trod
In wondrous love, O Son of God!

2 O, who like Thee, so calm, so bright,
So pure, so made to live in light?
O, who like Thee did ever go
So patient though a world of woe!

3 O, who like Thee so humbly bore
The scorn, the scoffs of men, before?

So meek, forgiving, godlike, high,
So glorious in humility?

4 Ev'n death, which sets the prisoner free,
Was pang, and scoff, and scorn to Thee:
Yet love through all Thy torture glowed,
And mercy with Thy life-blood flowed.

5 O, in Thy light be mine to go,
Illuming all my way of woe!
And give me ever on the road
To trace Thy footsteps, Son of God.

ARTHUR CLEVELAND COXE.

---

180 *"Perfect through sufferings."*

THE Head that once was crowned with
Is crowned with glory now ; [thorns
A royal diadem adorns
The mighty Victor's brow.

2 The highest place that heaven affords,
Is His, is His by right.
The King of kings, and Lord of lords,
And heaven's eternal Light.

3 The Joy of all who dwell above,
The Joy of all below
To whom He manifests His love,
And grants His name to know.

4 To them the cross, with all its shame,
With all its grace, is given :
Their name, an everlasting name,
Their joy, the joy of heaven.

5 They suffer with their Lord below,
They reign with Him above ;
Their profit and their joy to know
The mystery of His love.

6 The cross He bore is life and health,
Though shame and death to Him :
His people's hope, His people's wealth,
Their everlasting theme.

THOMAS KELLY.

HASTINGS. L. M. 6 lines.

How calm and beau - ti - ful the morn That gilds the sa - cred tomb, Where Christ the cru - ci - fied was borne

And veiled in midnight gloom! O weep no more the Sav - iour slain! The Lord is ris'n, He lives a - gain!

181   *"If we be dead with Him, we shall also live with Him."*

How calm and beautiful the morn
  That gilds the sacred tomb,
Where Christ the crucified was borne
  And veiled in midnight gloom!
O weep no more the Saviour slain!
The Lord is risen, He lives again!'

2 Ye mourning saints, dry every tear
  For your departed Lord;
Behold the place. He is not here,
  The tomb is all unbarred:
The gates of death were closed in vain,
The Lord is risen, He lives again.

3 How tranquil now the rising day!
  'Tis Jesus still appears,
A risen Lord, to chase away
  Your unbelieving fears:
O weep no more your comforts slain!
The Lord is risen, He lives again!

4 And when the shades of evening fall,
  When life's last hour draws nigh,
If Jesus shines upon the soul,
  How blissful then to die!
Since He has risen that once was slain,
Ye die in Christ to live again.

                      THOMAS HASTINGS.

ROTHWELL L. M.

O Lord most high, E - ter - nal King, By Thee redeem'd Thy praise we sing:

The bonds of death are burst by Thee, And grace has won the vic - to - ry.

MOZART. 7s.

Christ the Lord is ris'n a-gain, Christ hath brok-en ev'-ry chain; Hark! an-gel - ic

voi-ces cry, Singing ev - er-more on high, Hal-le - lu - jah! Praise the Lord.

182 *"Death is swallowed up in victory."*

Christ the Lord is risen again,
Christ hath broken every chain;
Hark! angelic voices cry,
Singing evermore on high,
  Hallelujah! Praise the Lord!

2 He who bore all pain and loss,
Comfortless, upon the cross,
Lives in glory now on high,
Pleads for us and hears our cry:
  Hallelujah! Praise the Lord!

3 He who slumbered in the grave
Is exalted now to save;
Now through Christendom it rings
That the Lamb is King of kings:
  Hallelujah! Praise the Lord!

4 Now He bids us tell abroad
How the lost may be restored,
How the penitent forgiven,
How we, too, may enter heaven:
  Hallelujah! Praise the Lord!
CAROLINE WINKWORTH.

183 *"Now is Christ risen from the dead."*

Jesus Christ is risen to-day,
Our triumphant holy day,
Who did once upon the cross
Suffer to redeem our loss.

2 Hymns of praise then let us sing
Unto Christ our Heavenly King,
Who endured the cross and grave,
Sinners to redeem and save.

3 But the pain which He endured,
Our salvation has procured;
Now above the sky He's King,
Where the angels ever sing.

4 Sing we to our God above
Praise eternal as His love;
Praise Him, all ye heavenly host,
Father, Son, and Holy Ghost.

184 *"All power is given unto Me, in heaven and in earth."*

O Lord most high, Eternal King,
By Thee redeemed Thy praise we sing:
The bonds of death are burst by Thee,
And grace has won the victory.

2 Ascending to the Father's throne,
Thou claim'st the kingdom as Thine own;
Thy days of mortal weakness o'er,
All power is Thine for evermore.

3 To Thee the whole creation now
Shall, in its threefold order, bow,
Of things on earth, and things on high,
And things that underneath us lie.

4 Be Thou our Joy, O mighty Lord,
As Thou wilt be our great Reward;
Let all our glory be in Thee
Both now and through eternity.
JOHN MASON NEALE.

DUKE STREET. L. M.

He lives, the great Re - deem - er lives,—What joy the blest as - sur - ance gives:

And now, be - fore His Fa - ther, God, Pleads the full mer - it of His blood.

185 *"He ever liveth to make intercession for us."*

He lives, the great Redeemer lives.—
What joy the blest assurance gives:
And now, before His Father, God,
Pleads the full merit of His blood.

2 Hence then, ye black, despairing thoughts:
Above our fears, above our faults,
His powerful intercessions rise.
And guilt recedes, and terror dies.

3 In every dark, distressful hour,
When sin and Satan join their power,
Let this dear hope repel the dart,
That Jesus bears us on His heart.

4 Great Advocate, Almighty Friend!
On Him our humble hopes depend;
Our cause can never, never fail,
For Jesus pleads, and must prevail.

ANNE STEELE.

WOODSTOCK. C. M.

Behold the glories of the Lamb, A - mid His Fath-er's throne; Pre-pare new honors for His name, And songs be-fore unknown.

186 *"And I heard the voice of many angels round about the Throne."*

Behold the glories of the Lamb,
Amid His Father's throne;
Prepare new honors for His name,
And songs before unknown.

2 Let elders worship at His feet;
The church adore around:
With vials full of odors sweet,
And harps of sweeter sound.

3 Those are the prayers of all the saints,
And these the hymns they raise:
Jesus is kind to our complaints;
He loves to hear our praise.

4 Now to the Lamb, that once was slain,
Be endless blessings paid;
Salvation, glory, joy, remain
For ever on Thy head.

5 Thou hast redeemed our souls with blood,
Hast set the prisoners free,
Hast made us kings and priests to God,
And we shall reign with Thee!

6 The worlds of nature and of grace
Are put beneath Thy power;
Then shorten these delaying days,
And bring the promised hour.

ISAAC WATTS.

OLD MELODY. 6s, 5s.

Glo-ry be to Je-sus, Who in bit-ter pains, Pour'd for me the life-blood From His sa-cred veins!

187 *"Cleanseth us from all sin."*

GLORY be to Jesus,
Who in bitter pains,
Poured for me the life-blood
From His sacred veins!

2 Grace and life eternal
In that blood I find;
Blest be His compassion
Infinitely kind.

3 Blest through endless ages
Be the precious stream
Which from endless torments
Did the world redeem.

4 Oft as earth exulting,
Wafts its praise on high,
Angel-hosts rejoicing,
Make their glad reply.

EDWARD CASWALL.

EMMELAR. 6s, 5s.

Nearer, ev-er near-er, Christ, we draw to Thee, Deep in a-do-ra-tion, Bend-ing low the knee.

a-do-ration, bending low the knee.

188 *"O Lord, my strength and refuge."*

NEARER, ever nearer,
Christ, we draw to Thee,
Deep in adoration,
Bending low the knee.

2 Thou for our redemption
Camest on earth to die;
Thou, that we might follow,
Hast gone up on high.

3 Onward, ever onward,
Journeying o'er the road
Worn by saints before us
Journeying on to God.

4 All we have to offer,
All we hope to be,
Body, Soul, and Spirit,
All we yield to Thee.

GODFREY THRING.

189 *"Come unto Me, for I am meek, and lowly of heart."*

JESUS, meek and gentle,
Son of God most high,
Pitying, loving Saviour,
Hear Thy children's cry.

2 Pardon our offences,
Loose our captive chains,
Break down every idol
Which our soul detains.

3 Give us holy freedom,
Fill our hearts with love;
Draw us, holy Jesus,
To the realms above.

4 Lead us on our journey,
Be Thyself the way
Through terrestrial darkness
To celestial day.

GEORGE RUNDELL PRYNNE.

SMART. 8s, 7s. D.

Jesus, hail, enthron'd in glory, There for ev-er to a - bide; All the heavenly hosts adore Thee, Seated at Thy Father's side.

There for sinners Thou art pleading; There Thou dost our place prepare; Ev-er for us in - ter-ced-ing Till in glory we ap-pear.

190   *"God hath highly exalted Him."*

Jesus, hail, enthroned in glory,
  There for ever to abide ;
All the heavenly hosts adore Thee,
  Seated at Thy Father's side.
There for sinners Thou art pleading ;
  There Thou dost our place prepare ;
Ever for us interceding
  Till in glory we appear.

2 Worship, honor, power and blessing
  Thou art worthy to receive ;
Loudest praises, without ceasing,
  Meet it is for us to give.
Help, ye bright angelic spirits,
  Bring your sweetest, noblest lays ;
Help to sing our Saviour's merits,
  Help to chant Immanuel's praise.

JOHN BAKEWELL.

WALES. 11s & 10s.

1. 'We would see Je-sus !'—for the shadows lengthen Across this little landscape of our life ;

'We would see Jesus !' our weak faith to strengthen For the last weariness, the fi - nal strife.

SECOND HALF OF VERSES 2, 3, AND 4.

2. Nor life nor death, with all their a-gi-ta-tion, Can thence re-move us, if we see His face.
3. We would see Thee, Thyself our hearts reminding What Thou hast suffer'd, our great debt to pay.
4. 'We would see Jesus !' dying, risen, pleading ; Then, welcome day, and farewell mortal night !

Praise to the Holiest in the hight, And in the depth be praise : In all His words most wonder-ful, Most sure in all His ways! O lov-ing wisdom of our God! When all was sin and shame, A sec-ond A-dam to the fight And to the res-cue came.

191   *"Truly this man was the Son of God."*

PRAISE to the Holiest in the hight,
  And in the depth be praise :
In all His words most wonderful,
  Most sure in all His ways!
O loving wisdom of our God!
  When all was sin and shame,
A second Adam to the fight
  And to the rescue came.
2 O wisest love! that flesh and blood,
  Which did in Adam fail,
Should strive afresh against the foe,
  Should strive and should prevail ;

And that a higher gift than grace
  Should flesh and blood refine,
God's presence and His very Self,
  And Essence all-divine.
3 O generous love! that He who smote
  In man for man the foe,
The double agony in man
  For man should undergo ;
And in the garden secretly,
  And on the cross on high,
Should teach His brethren and inspire
  To suffer and to die !

JOHN HENRY NEWMAN.

192   *"We shall be like Him, for we shall see Him as He is."*

'WE would see Jesus!'—for the shadows
  lengthen
Across this little landscape of our
  life ;
'We would see Jesus!' our weak faith to
  strengthen
For the last weariness, the final strife.
2 'We would see Jesus!' the great Rock-
  foundation,
Whereon our feet were set by sovereign
  grace ;
Nor life nor death, with all their agita-
  tion,
Can thence remove us, if we see His
  face.

3 'We would see Jesus!' sense is all too
  blinding,
And heaven appears too dim, too far away ;
We would see Thee, Thyself our hearts
  reminding
What Thou hast suffered, our great debt
  to pay.
4 'We would see Jesus!' this is all we're
  needing ;
Strength, joy, and willingness come with
  the sight ;
'We would see Jesus!' dying, risen,
  pleading ;
Then, welcome day, and farewell mortal night !

The Holy Spirit.

ALLELUIA. S. M. D.

Come, Spi - rit, source of light, Thy grace is un - con-fin'd; Dis - pel the gloomy shades of night, The darkness of the mind. Now to our eyes dis-play The truth Thy words re-veal; . . Cause us to run the heavenly way, De - light - ing in Thy will.

193 *"In Thy light shall we see light."*

COME, Spirit, source of light,
  Thy grace is unconfined ;
Dispel the gloomy shades of night,
  The darkness of the mind.
Now to our eyes display
  The truth Thy words reveal ;
Cause us to run the heavenly way,
  Delighting in Thy will.

2 Thy teachings make us know
  The mysteries of Thy love,
The vanity of things below,
  The joy of things above.
While through this maze we stray,
  O, spread Thy beams abroad ;
Disclose the dangers of the way,
  And guide our steps to God.

BENJAMIN BEDDOME.

194 *"The Comforter, which is the Holy Ghost."*

COME, Holy Spirit, come,
  Let Thy bright beams arise,
Dispel the darkness from our minds,
  And open all our eyes.
Revive our drooping faith,
  Our doubts and fears remove,
And kindle in our breasts the flame
  Of never-dying love.

2 Convince us of our sin,
  Then lead to Jesus' blood,
And to our wondering view reveal
  The secret love of God.
'T is Thine to cleanse the heart,
  To sanctify the soul,
To pour fresh life in every part,
  And new-create the whole.

JOSEPH HART.

195 *"He dwelleth with you and shall be in you."*

LORD, bid Thy light arise
  On all Thy people here,
And when we raise our longing eyes,
  O, may we find Thee near.
Thy Holy Spirit send,
  To quicken every soul ;
And hearts the most rebellious bend
  To Thy divine control.

2 Let all that own Thy name
  Thy sacred image bear,
And light in every heart the flame
  Of watchfulness and prayer.
Since in Thy love we see
  Our only sure relief,
O, raise our earthly minds to Thee,
  And help our unbelief.

WILLIAM HILEY BATHURST.

ST. JOHN. H. M.

O Thou that hear-est prayer, At-tend our hum-ble cry; And let Thy ser-vants share

Thy bless-ing from on high: We plead the prom-ise of Thy word; Grant us Thy Ho-ly Spir-it, Lord!

196 *"Ask, and it shall be given you."*

O Thou that hearest prayer,
  Attend our humble cry;
And let Thy servants share
  Thy blessing from on high:
We plead the promise of Thy word;
Grant us Thy Holy Spirit, Lord!

2 If earthly parents hear
  Their children when they cry;
If they, with love sincere,
  Their children's wants supply:
Much more wilt Thou Thy love display,
And answer when Thy children pray.

3 Our Heavenly Father Thou;
  We, children of Thy grace;
O let Thy Spirit now
  Descend, and fill the place:
That all may feel the heavenly flame,
And all unite to praise Thy name.

4 O send Thy Spirit down
  On all the nations, Lord,
With great success to crown
  The preaching of Thy word;
Till heathen lands may own Thy sway,
And cast their idol-gods away.

JOHN BURTON.

SPIRITUS SANCTUS. 7s, 5s.

Ho-ly Ghost, the In-fi-nite! Shine upon our nature's night With Thy blessed inward light, Comfort-er Di-vine!

197 *"The Comforter, which is the Holy Ghost."*

Holy Ghost, the Infinite!
Shine upon our nature's night
With Thy blessed inward light,
  Comforter Divine!

2 We are sinful: cleanse us, Lord;
We are faint: Thy strength afford;
Lost,—until by Thee restored.

3 Like the dew, Thy peace distill;
Guide, subdue our wayward will,
Things of Christ unfolding still.

4 In us, for us, intercede,
And with voiceless groanings, plead
Our unutterable need.

5 In us 'Abba, Father,' cry,—
Earnest of our bliss on high,
Seal of immortality.

6 Search for us the depths of God;
Bear us up the starry road,
To the height of Thine abode.

GEORGE RAWSON.

GLUCK. C. M.

Spir - it Di - vine, at - tend our prayers, And make this house Thy home;

De - scend with all Thy gra - cious powers, O come, Great Spir - it, come!

---

198   *"The love of God is shed abroad in our hearts by the Holy Ghost."*

SPIRIT Divine, attend our prayers,
  And make this house Thy home;
Descend with all Thy gracious powers,
  O come, Great Spirit, come!

2 Come as the light: to us reveal
  Our emptiness and woe,
And lead us in those paths of life
  Where all the righteous go.

3 Come as the fire, and purge our hearts
  Like sacrificial flame;
Let our whole soul an offering be
  To our Redeemer's name.

4 Come as the dove, and spread Thy wings,
  The wings of peaceful love;
And let Thy church on earth become
  Blest as the church above.
ANDREW REED.

199   *"The Spirit giveth life."*

COME, Holy Spirit, Heavenly Dove,
  With all Thy quickening powers;
Kindle a flame of sacred love
  In these cold hearts of ours.

2 Look how we grovel here below,
  Fond of these trifling toys:
Our souls can neither fly, nor go,
  To reach eternal joys.

3 In vain we tune our formal songs,
  In vain we strive to rise;
Hosannas languish on our tongues,
  And our devotion dies.

4 Come, Holy Spirit, Heavenly Dove,
  With all Thy quickening powers;
Come, shed abroad a Saviour's love,
  And that shall kindle ours.
ISAAC WATTS.

SEYMOUR. 7s.

Ho-ly Spirit, in my breast Grant that lively faith may rest, And subdue each rebel thought To believe what Thou hast taught.

---

200   *"The fruit of the Spirit."*

HOLY Spirit, in my breast
Grant that lively faith may rest,
And subdue each rebel thought
To believe what Thou hast taught.

2 Faith, and hope, and charity,
Comforter, descend from Thee;

Thou the anointing Spirit art,
These Thy gifts to us impart;—

3 Till our faith be lost in sight,
Hope be swallowed in delight,
Love return to dwell with Thee,
In the threefold Deity!
RICHARD MANT.

GERMANY. L. M.

Come, O Cre - a - tor Spir - it blest, And in our souls take up Thy rest;

Come, with Thy grace and heavenly aid, And fill the hearts which Thou hast made.

201 *"As many as are led by the Spirit of God, they are the sons of God."*

Come, O Creator Spirit blest,
And in our souls take up Thy rest ;
Come, with Thy grace and heavenly aid,
And fill the hearts which Thou hast made.

2 Great Paraclete, to Thee we cry :
O highest gift of God most high,
O Fount of life, O Fire of love,
And sweet Anointing from above !

3 Thou in Thy sevenfold gifts art known ;
Thee, Finger of God's hand, we own :
The promise of the Father Thou,
Who dost the tongue with power endow.

4 Our senses kindle from above,
And make our hearts o'erflow with love :
With Thine unfailing strength refresh
The weakness of our mortal flesh.

5 Drive far from us the foe we dread,
And grant us Thy true peace instead :
With Thee for Guardian, Thee for Guide,
No evil can our steps betide.

6 O let Thy grace on us bestow
The Father and the Son to know,
And Thee, through endless time confest,
Of Both the Eternal Spirit blest.
EDWARD CASWALL.

202 *"He will guide you into all truth."*

Come, Holy Spirit, Heavenly Dove,
My sinful maladies remove ;
Be Thou my Light, be Thou my Guide,
O'er every thought and step preside.

2 The light of truth to me display,
That I may know and choose my way ;

Plant holy fear within mine heart,
That I from God may ne'er depart.

3 Conduct me safe, conduct me far
From every sin and hurtful snare ;
Lead me to God, my final rest,
In His enjoyment to be blest.

4 Lead me to Christ, the Living Way,
Nor let me from His pastures stray :
Lead me to heaven, the seat of bliss,
Where pleasure in perfection is.

5 Lead me to holiness, the road
That I must take to dwell with God ;
Lead to Thy word, that rules must give,
And sure directions how to live.

6 Lead me to means of grace, where I
May own my wants, and seek supply :
Lead to Thyself, the Spring from whence
To fetch all quickening influence.
SIMON BROWNE.

203 *"The Spirit also helpeth our infirmities."*

Come, Holy Ghost, who ever One
Art with the Father and the Son :
Come, Holy Ghost, our souls possess
With Thy full flood of holiness.

2 Let flesh, and heart, and lips, and mind,
Sound forth our witness to mankind ;
And love light up our mortal frame,
Till others catch the living flame.

3 Thou ever-blessed Three in One,
O Father and Coequal Son,
O Holy Ghost the Comforter,
Thy grace on Thy redeemed confer.
JOHN HENRY NEWMAN.

LAST HOPE. 7s.

In the midst do Thou ap - pear,—Lord re - veal . . Thy pres-ence here;

Sanc - ti - fy us now, and bless; Breathe Thy spi - rit, give Thy peace.

204   *"That they also may be one."*

In the midst do Thou appear,—
Lord, reveal Thy presence here ;
Sanctify us now, and bless ;
Breathe Thy Spirit, give Thy peace.

2 While we walk with God in light
God our hearts doth still unite ;
Sweetly each with each combined,
In the bonds of duty joined.

3 Father, still our faith increase ;
Cleanse from all unrighteousness :
Thee the unholy cannot see ;
Make, O make us meet for Thee.

CHARLES WESLEY.

205 *"The fruit of the Spirit is love, joy, peace."*

Gracious Spirit, Dove Divine !
Let Thy light within me shine ;

All my guilty fears remove,
Fill me with Thy heavenly love.

2 Speak Thy pardoning grace to me,
Set the burdened sinner free ;
Lead me to the Lamb of God,
Wash me in His precious blood.

3 Life and peace to me impart ;
Seal salvation on my heart ;
Breathe Thyself into my breast,
Earnest of immortal rest.

4 Let me never from Thee stray ;
Keep me in the narrow way ;
Fill my soul with joy divine,
Keep me, Lord, for ever Thine.

JOHN STOCKER.

UXBRIDGE. L. M.

Spirit of God, that mov'd of old Upon the water's darken'd face, Come, when our faithless hearts are cold, And stir them with an inward grace.

PESARO. L M.

Come, bless-ed Spir - it! Source of light, Whose power and grace are un - con-fin'd,

Dis - pel the gloom - y shades of night, The thick - er dark - ness of the mind.

206 *"He shall teach you all things."*

COME, blessed Spirit! Source of light,
Whose power and grace are unconfined,
Dispel the gloomy shades of night,
The thicker darkness of the mind.

2 To mine illumined eyes display
The glorious truths Thy word reveals;
Cause me to run the heavenly way;
The book unfold, and loose the seals.

3 Thine inward teachings make me know
The mysteries of redeeming love,
The emptiness of things below,
And excellence of things above.

4 While through this dubious maze I stray,
Spread, like the sun, Thy beams abroad,
To show the dangers of the way,
And guide my feeble steps to God.

BENJAMIN BEDDOME.

207 *"Walk in the Spirit, and ye shall not fulfill the lust of the flesh."*

ETERNAL Spirit! we confess
And sing the wonders of Thy grace;
Thy power conveys our blessings down
From God the Father and the Son.

2 Enlightened by Thy heavenly ray,
Our shades and darkness turn to day;
Thine inward teachings make us know
Our danger, and our refuge too.

3 Thy power and glory work within,
And break the chains of reigning sin;
Do our imperious lusts subdue,
And form our wretched hearts anew.

4 The troubled conscience knows Thy voice;
Thy cheering words awake our joys;
Thy words allay the stormy wind,
And calm the surges of the mind.

ISAAC WATTS.

208 *"Ye are the temple of the living God."*

SPIRIT of God, that moved of old
Upon the water's darkened face,
Come, when our faithless hearts are cold,
And stir them with an inward grace.

2 Thou that art power and peace combined,
All highest strength, all purest love,
The rushing of the mighty wind,
The brooding of the gentle dove:

3 Come, give us still Thy powerful aid,
And urge us on, and make us Thine;
Nor leave the hearts that once were made
Fit temples for Thy grace divine.

CECIL FRANCES ALEXANDER.

Redemption.

STAR OF BETHLEHEM. L. M. D.

When marshaled on the nightly plain, The glittering host be-stud the sky,
One star a-lone, of all the train, Can fix the sin-ner's wandering eye.

Hark! hark! to God the chorus breaks, From every host, from ev-ery gem; But

one alone the Saviour speaks, It is the Star of Bethlehem, It is the Star of Beth-le - hem.

209 *"We have seen His star in the east."*

WHEN marshaled on the nightly plain,
  The glittering host bestud the sky,
One star alone, of all the train,
  Can fix the sinner's wandering eye.

2 Hark! hark! to God the chorus breaks,
  From every host, from every gem;
But one alone the Saviour speaks,
  It is the Star of Bethlehem.

3 Once on the raging seas I rode,
  The storm was loud, the night was dark.
The ocean yawned, and rudely blowed
  The wind that tost my foundering bark.

4 Deep horror then my vitals froze;
  Death-struck, I ceased the tide to stem;
When suddenly a star arose,—
  It was the Star of Bethlehem.

5 It was my guide, my light, my all:
  It bade my dark forebodings cease;
And, through the storm and danger's thrall,
  It led me to the port of peace.

6 Now safely moored, my perils o'er,
  I'll sing, first in night's diadem,
For ever and for evermore,
  The Star—the Star of Bethlehem.

HENRY KIRKE WHITE.

ASHFORD. L. M.

How shall a con-trite spir-it pray, A bro-ken heart its griefs make known,

A wea-ry wanderer find the way To peace and rest?—Thro' Christ a-lone.

210 *"He is the propitiation for our sins."*

How shall a contrite spirit pray,
A broken heart its griefs make known,
A weary wanderer find the way
To peace and rest?—Thro' Christ alone.

2 He died that we might die to sin ;
He rose that we to God might rise ;
By His own blood He entered in
The holy place beyond the skies.

3 Father, in Him we claim our part ;
For Thy Son's sake accept us now ;
In Him well pleased Thou always art,
Well pleased with us thro' Him be Thou.

4 O look on Thine anointed One ;
Thy gift in Him is all our plea ;
Our righteousness, what He hath done ;
Our prayer, His prayer for us to Thee.

5 So, while He intercedes above,
In His dear name may we believe,
And all the fullness of Thy love
Into our inmost souls receive.
JAMES MONTGOMERY.

211 *"With His stripes we are healed."*

We sing the praise of Him who died,
Of Him who died upon the cross ;
The sinner's hope let men deride,
For this we count the world but loss.

2 Inscribed upon the cross we see,
In shining letters, 'God is love ;'
He bears our sins upon the tree,
He brings us mercy from above.

3 The cross ! it takes our guilt away ;
It holds the fainting spirit up :
It cheers with hope the gloomy day,
And sweetens every bitter cup ;

4 It makes the coward spirit brave,
And nerves the feeble arm for fight ;
It takes its terror from the grave,
And gilds the bed of death with light.

5 The balm of life, the cure of woe,
The measure and the pledge of love,
The sinner's refuge here below,
The angels' theme in heaven above.
THOMAS KELLY.

212 *"God forbid that I should glory, save in the cross of our Lord Jesus Christ."*

When I survey the wondrous cross
On which the Prince of glory died,
My richest gain I count but loss,
And pour contempt on all my pride.

2 Forbid it, Lord, that I should boast,
Save in the death of Christ, my God ;
All the vain things that charm me most,
I sacrifice them to His blood.

3 See from His head, His hands, His feet,
Sorrow and love flow mingled down !
Did e'er such love and sorrow meet,
Or thorns compose so rich a crown ?

4 Were the whole realm of nature mine,
That were a present far too small ;
Love so amazing, so divine,
Demands my soul, my life, my all.
ISAAC WATTS.

COME, YE DISCONSOLATE.   11s, 10s.

Duo.

Come, ye dis-con - so-late, wher - e'er ye languish: Come to the mer-cy - seat, fer - vent-ly kneel;

Here bring your wounded hearts, here tell your anguish; Earth has no sorrow that heaven can-not heal.

CHORUS.

Here bring your wounded hearts, here tell your an - guish; Earth has no sor - row that heaven cannot heal.

213   *"Come unto Me, all ye that labor and are heavy laden, and I will give you rest."*

COME, ye disconsolate, where'er ye languish :
Come to the mercy-seat, fervently kneel ;
Here bring your wounded hearts, here tell
    your anguish ;   [heal.
Earth has no sorrow that heaven cannot

2 Joy of the desolate, Light of the straying,
Hope of the penitent, fadeless and pure,
Here speaks the Comforter, tenderly saying,

Earth has no sorrow that heaven cannot
    cure.
3 Here see the bread of life ; see waters flowing
    Forth from the throne of God, pure from
      above ;
Come to the feast of love ; come, ever knowing
    Earth has no sorrow but heaven can
      remove.

THOMAS MOORE.

COWPER. C. M.

There is a fountain fill'd with blood Drawn from Immanuel's veins,

And sinners, plung'd beneath that flood, Lose all their guilty stains, Lose all their guilty stains.

BACON. 7s.

Wake the song of ju - bi - lee, Let it ech - o o'er the sea!

Now is come the pro - mised hour; Je - sus reigns with glorious power!

---

214 *"Of His kingdom there shall be no end."*

WAKE the song of jubilee,
Let it echo o'er the sea!
Now is come the promised hour;
Jesus reigns with glorious power!

2 All ye nations, join and sing,
Praise your Saviour, praise your King;
Let it sound from shore to shore,—
'Jesus reigns for evermore!'

3 Hark! the desert lands rejoice;
And the islands join their voice;
Joy! the whole creation sings,—
'Jesus is the King of kings!'
LEONARD BACON.

215 *"In His days shall the righteous flourish."*

HASTEN, Lord, the glorious time,
When, beneath Messiah's sway,

---

216 *"Him that lov'd us, and washed us from our sins in His own blood."*

THERE is a fountain filled with blood
Drawn from Immanuel's veins;
And sinners, plunged beneath that flood,
Lose all their guilty stains.

2 The dying thief rejoiced to see
That fountain in his day;
And there have I, as vile as he,
Washed all my sins away.

3 Dear dying Lamb! Thy precious blood
Shall never lose its power,
Till all the ransomed church of God
Be saved, to sin no more.

4 E'er since, by faith, I saw the stream
Thy flowing wounds supply,

Every nation, every clime,
Shall the gospel call obey.

2 Mightiest kings His power shall own,
Heathen tribes His name adore;
Satan and his host, o'erthrown,
Bound in chains, shall hurt no more.

3 Then shall wars and tumults cease,
Then be banished grief and pain;
Righteousness, and joy, and peace,
Undisturbed shall ever reign.

4 Bless we, then, our gracious Lord,
Ever praise His glorious name;
All His mighty acts record,
All His wondrous love proclaim.
HARRIET AUBER.

Redeeming love has been my theme,
And shall be till I die.

5 Then in a nobler, sweeter song
I'll sing Thy power to save,
When this poor lisping, stammering tongue
Lies silent in the grave.

6 Lord, I believe Thou hast prepared,
Unworthy though I be,
For me a blood-bought free reward,
A golden harp for me.

7 'Tis strung, and tuned for endless years,
And formed by power divine,
To sound in God the Father's ears
No other name but Thine.
WILLIAM COWPER.

HELP. C. M.   Redemption.

Plung'd in a gulf of dark de-spair We wretch-ed sin-ners lay,

With-out one cheer-ful beam of hope, Or spark of glimmering day.

217   *"The light of the glorious gospel of Christ."*

PLUNGED in a gulf of dark despair
  We wretched sinners lay,
Without one cheerful beam of hope,
  Or spark of glimmering day.

2 With pitying eyes the Prince of grace
  Beheld our helpless grief:
He saw, and O! amazing love!
  He ran to our relief.

3 Down from the shining seats above
  With joyful haste He fled;
Entered the grave in mortal flesh,
  And dwelt among the dead.

4 O! for this love, let rocks and hills
  Their lasting silence break,
And all harmonious human tongues
  The Saviour's praises speak!

            ISAAC WATTS.

218   *"Christ Jesus came into the world to save sinners, of whom I am chief."*

AMAZING grace,—how sweet the sound,—
  That saved a wretch like me!
I once was lost, but now am found;
  Was blind, but now I see.

2 'Twas grace that taught my heart to fear,
  And grace my fears relieved;
How precious did that grace appear,
  The hour I first believed!

3 Through many dangers, toils, and snares,
  Have I already come;
But grace has brought me safe thus far,
  And grace will lead me home.

4 Yes, when this flesh and heart shall fail,
  And mortal life shall cease,
I shall possess, within the veil,
  A life of joy and peace.

            JOHN NEWTON.

WINCHESTER. L. M.

Now to the Lord a no-ble song! A-wake, my soul, a-wake, my tongue;

Ho-san-na to th'e-ter-nal name, And all His bound-less love proclaim.

LANE. S. M.

Grace! 'tis a charming sound! Harmonious to my ear! Heaven with the ech - o

shall resound, And all the earth shall hear, And all the earth shall hear.

and all

219 *"By grace ye are saved."*

GRACE! 't is a charming sound!
Harmonious to my ear!
Heaven with the echo shall resound,
And all the earth shall hear.

2 Grace first contrived a way
To save rebellious man;
And all the steps that grace display,
Which drew the wondrous plan.

3 Grace taught my wandering feet
To tread the heavenly road;
And new supplies each hour I meet,
While pressing on to God.

4 Grace all the work shall crown,
Through everlasting days;
It lays in heaven the topmost stone,
And well deserves the praise.
                  PHILIP DODDRIDGE.

220 *"Justified freely by His grace."*

AH, how shall fallen man
Be just before his God!

If He contend in righteousness,
We sink beneath His rod.

2 If He our ways should mark
With strict inquiring eyes,
Could we for one of thousand faults
A just excuse devise?

3 All-seeing, powerful God!
Who can with Thee contend?
Or who that tries the unequal strife,
Shall prosper in the end?

4 The mountains, in Thy wrath,
Their ancient seats forsake!
The trembling earth deserts her place,
Her rooted pillars shake!

5 Ah, how shall guilty man
Contend with such a God!
None, none can meet Him, and escape,
But through the Saviour's blood.

221 *"The exceeding riches of His grace."*

NOW to the Lord a noble song!
Awake, my soul; awake, my tongue;
Hosanna to the eternal name,
And all His boundless love proclaim.

* 2 See where it shines in Jesus' face,
The brightest image of His grace;
God, in the person of His Son,
Has all His mightiest works outdone.

3 Grace! 'tis a sweet, a charming theme;
My thoughts rejoice at Jesus' name!
Ye angels, dwell upon the sound!
Ye heavens, reflect it to the ground!

4 O may I live to reach the place
Where He unveils His lovely face!
Where all His beauties you behold,
And sing His name to harps of gold!
                   ISAAC WATTS.

BENEVENTO. 7s. D.

Hark! the song of Ju-bi-lee; Loud as mighty thunders roar, Or the fullness of the sea, When it breaks upon the shore:

Hal-le-lu-jah! for the Lord God Omni-po-tent shall reign; Hal-le-lu-jah! let the word Ech-o round the earth and main.

222 *"Alleluia, for the Lord God Omnipotent reigneth."*

HARK! the song of Jubilee;
  Loud as mighty thunders roar,
Or the fullness of the sea,
  When it breaks upon the shore:
Hallelujah! for the Lord
  God Omnipotent shall reign;
Hallelujah! let the word
  Echo round the earth and main.

2 Hallelujah! hark! the sound,
  From the center to the skies,
Wakes above, beneath, around,
  All creation's harmonies;

See Jehovah's banner furled,
  Sheathed His sword; He speaks—'tis done,
And the kingdoms of this world
  Are the kingdoms of His Son.

3 He shall reign from pole to pole
  With illimitable sway;
He shall reign, when like a scroll
  Yonder heavens have past away:
Then the end;—beneath His rod,
  Man's last enemy shall fall;
Hallelujah! Christ in God,
  God in Christ, is all in all.
                    JAMES MONTGOMERY.

WESLEY. 11s, 10s.

Hail to the brightness of Zion's glad morning, Joy to the lands that in darkness have lain!

Hush'd be the accents of sorrow and mourning, Zi-on in triumph begins her mild reign.

MISSIONARY CHANT. L. M.

Je - sus shall reign where'er the sun Does his suc-ces - sive jour - neys run;

His king-dom stretch from shore to shore, Till moons shall wax and wane no more.

223 *"His name shall endure for ever."*

Jesus shall reign where'er the sun
Does his successive journeys run ;
His kingdom stretch from shore to shore,
Till moons shall wax and wane no more.

2 For Him shall endless prayer be made,
And praises throng to crown His head ;
His name, like sweet perfume, shall rise
With every morning sacrifice.

3 People and realms of every tongue
Dwell on His love with sweetest song ;
And infant voices shall proclaim
Their early blessings on His name.

4 Blessings abound where'er He reigns ;
The prisoner leaps to loose his chains ;
The weary find eternal rest,
And all the sons of want are blest.

5 Let every creature rise and bring
Peculiar honors to our King ;

Angels descend with songs again,
And earth repeat the loud Amen !

ISAAC WATTS.

224 *"Christ, the Power of God and the Wisdom of God."*

NATURE with open volume stands,
To spread her Maker's praise abroad,
And every labor of His hands
Shows something worthy of a God.

2 But in the grace that rescued man,
His brightest form of glory shines ;
Here on the cross, 't is fairest drawn
In precious blood, and crimson lines.

3 Oh ! the sweet wonders of that cross,
Where God the Saviour loved, and died !
Her noblest life my spirit draws
From His dear wounds and bleeding side.

4 I would for ever speak His name,
In sounds to mortal ears unknown ;
With angels join to praise the Lamb,
And worship at His Father's throne.

ISAAC WATTS.

225 *"Thy saving health among all nations."*

HAIL to the brightness of Zion's glad morning !
Joy to the lands that in darkness have lain !
Hushed be the accents of sorrow and mourning ;
Zion in triumph begins her mild reign.

2 Hail to the brightness of Zion's glad morning,
Long by the prophets of Israel foretold ;
Hail to the millions from bondage return-ing ;
Gentiles and Jews the blest vision behold.

3 Lo, in the desert rich flowers are springing
Streams ever copious are gliding along ;
Loud from the mountain-tops echoes are ringing ;
Wastes rise in verdure, and mingle in song.

4 See, from all lands, from the isles of the ocean,
Praise to Jehovah ascending on high ;
Fallen are the engines of war and commo-tion ;
Shouts of salvation are rending the sky.

THOMAS HASTINGS.

ZERAH. C. M.   Redemption.

Sal - vation! O, the joyful sound! 'T is pleasure to our ears; A sov'reign balm for ev'ry wound,

A cordial for our fears, A sov'reign balm for ev'ry wound, A cordial for our fears.

226 *"Blessed is he whose transgression is forgiven."*

SALVATION! O, the joyful sound!
'T is pleasure to our ears;
A sovereign balm for every wound,
A cordial for our fears.

2 Buried in sorrow and in sin,
At hell's dark door we lay;
But we arise by grace divine,
To see a heavenly day.

3 Salvation! let the echo fly
The spacious earth around;
While all the armies of the sky,
Conspire to raise the sound.

4 Salvation! O Thou bleeding Lamb!
To Thee the praise belongs;
Salvation shall inspire our hearts,
And dwell upon our tongues.

ISAAC WATTS.

FEDERAL STREET. L. M.

'Come hither, all ye wea - ry souls, Ye heavy la - den sin - ners, come;

I'll give you rest from all your toils, And raise you to my heavenly home.'

227 *"His commandments are not grievous."*

'COME hither, all ye weary souls,
Ye heavy laden sinners, come;
I'll give you rest from all your toils,
And raise you to My heavenly home.

2 'They shall find rest that learn of Me;
I 'm of a meek and lowly mind;
But passion rages like the sea,
And pride is restless as the wind.

3 'Blest is the man whose shoulders take
My yoke, and bear it with delight!
My yoke is easy to his neck,
My grace shall make the burden light.'

4 Jesus, we come at Thy command;
With faith, and hope, and humble zeal,
Resign our spirits to Thy hand,
To mold and guide us at Thy will.

ISAAC WATTS.

LANCASHIRE. 7s 6s.

'Come unto Me, ye wea-ry, And I will give you rest.' O blessed voice of Jesus, Which comes to hearts opprest!

It tells of bene - dic - tion, Of pardon, grace, and peace; Of joy that hath no ending, Of love which cannot cease.

228 *"Him that cometh unto Me, I will in no wise cast out."*

'COME unto Me, ye weary,
And I will give you rest.'
O blessed voice of Jesus,
Which comes to hearts opprest!
It tells of benediction,
Of pardon, grace, and peace;
Of joy that hath no ending,
Of love which cannot cease.

2 'Come unto me, ye wanderers,
And I will give you light.'
O loving voice of Jesus,
Which comes to cheer the night!
Our hearts were filled with sadness,
And we had lost our way,
But morning brings us gladness,
And songs the break of day.

3 'Come unto me, ye fainting,
And I will give you life.'
O cheering voice of Jesus,
Which comes to aid our strife!
The foe is stern and eager,
The fight is fierce and long;
But Thou hast made us mighty,
And stronger than the strong.

4 'And whosoever cometh,
I will not cast him out.'
O welcome voice of Jesus,
Which drives away our doubt!
Which calls us, very sinners,
Unworthy though we be
Of love so free and boundless,
To come, dear Lord, to Thee!

WILLIAM CHATTERTON DIX.

GORTON. S. M.

O cease, my wandering soul, On restless wing to roam; All the wide world, to either pole, Has not for thee a home.

229 *"We which have believed do enter into rest."*

O CEASE, my wandering soul,
On restless wing to roam;
All the wide world, to either pole,
Has not for thee a home.

2 Behold the ark of God;
Behold the open door;

Hasten to gain that dear abode,
And rove, my soul, no more.

3 There safe thou shalt abide,
There sweet shall be thy rest,
And every longing satisfied,
With full salvation blest.

WILLIAM AUGUSTUS MUHLENBERG.

LENOX. H. M.

A - rise, my soul, a - rise! Shake off thy guilt - y fears; The bleeding Sac - ri - fice In

my behalf ap - pears; Before the throne my Surety stands: My name is written on His hands, My name is written on His hands.

230 *"The blood of Christ cleanseth from all sin."*

ARISE, my soul, arise !
  Shake off thy guilty fears ;
  The bleeding Sacrifice
  In my behalf appears ;
Before the throne my Surety stands :
My name is written on His hands.

2 He ever lives above,
  For me to intercede,
  His all-redeeming love,

His precious blood to plead ;
  His blood atoned for all our race,
And sprinkles now the throne of grace.

3 My God is reconciled :
  His pardoning voice I hear ;
  He owns me for His child ;
  I can no longer fear ;
With confidence I now draw nigh,
And 'Father, Abba, Father,' cry.
               CHARLES WESLEY.

EISENACH. S. M.

How heavy is the night That hangs up - on our eyes, Till Christ with His re - viving light O - ver our souls a - rise!

231 *"The wages of sin is death ; but the gift of God is eternal life through Jesus Christ our Lord."*

HOW heavy is the night
  That hangs upon our eyes,
Till Christ with His reviving light
  Over our souls arise !

2 Our guilty spirits dread
  To meet the wrath of heaven !
But, in His righteousness arrayed,
  We see our sins forgiven.

3 Unholy and impure
  Are all our thoughts and ways :

His hands infected nature cure
  With sanctifying grace.

4 The powers of hell agree
  To hold our souls in vain ;
He sets the sons of bondage free,
  And breaks the cursèd chain.

5 Lord, we adore Thy ways
  To bring us near to God,
Thy sovereign power, Thy healing grace,
  And Thine atoning blood.
               ISAAC WATTS.

VOLKSLIED. L. M.

O Saviour! is Thy promise fled! Nor longer might Thy grace endure To heal the sick, and

raise the dead, And preach Thy gospel to the poor? And preach Thy gospel to the poor!

232 *"Where is the word of the Lord? Let it come now."*

O Saviour! is Thy promise fled?
Nor longer might Thy grace endure
To heal the sick, and raise the dead,
And preach Thy gospel to the poor?

2 Come, Jesus, come! return again;
With brighter beam Thy servants bless,
Who long to feel Thy perfect reign,
And share Thy kingdom's happiness!

3 Come, Jesus, come! and as of yore
The prophet went to clear Thy way,
A harbinger Thy feet before,
A dawning to Thy brighter day;

4 So now may grace, with heavenly shower,
Our stony hearts for truth prepare;
Sow in our souls the seed of power,
Then come, and reap Thy harvest there!
REGINALD HEBER.

233 *"I will pour out of My Spirit upon all flesh."*

O Spirit of the living God!
In all Thy plenitude of grace,
Where'er the foot of man hath trod,
Descend on our apostate race.

2 Give tongues of fire and hearts of love,
To preach the reconciling word;
Give power and unction from above,
Whene'er the joyful sound is heard.

3 Be darkness, at Thy coming, light;
Confusion, order in Thy path;
Souls without strength inspire with might,
Bid mercy triumph over wrath.

4 O Spirit of the Lord! prepare
All the round world her God to meet;
Breathe Thou abroad like morning air,
Till hearts of stone begin to beat.

5 Baptize the nations; far and nigh
The triumphs of the cross record;
The name of Jesus glorify,
Till every kindred call Him Lord.
JAMES MONTGOMERY.

234 *"He left not Himself without witness."*

The heavens declare Thy glory, Lord,
In every star Thy wisdom shines;
But when our eyes behold Thy word,
We read Thy name in fairer lines.

2 The rolling sun, the changing light,
And nights and days Thy power confess;
But the blest volume Thou hast writ
Reveals Thy justice and Thy grace.

3 Sun, moon, and stars convey Thy praise
Round the whole earth, and never stand;
So, when Thy truth began its race,
It touched and glanced on every land.

4 Great Sun of righteousness, arise;
Bless the dark world with heavenly light;
Thy gospel makes the simple wise;
Thy laws are pure, Thy judgments right.

5 Thy noblest wonders here we view,
In souls renewed and sins forgiven;
Lord, cleanse my sins, my soul renew,
And make Thy word my guide to heaven.
ISAAC WATTS.

DETROIT. S. M.

The Spirit, in our hearts, Is whispering, 'Sinner, come;' The Bride, the Church of Christ, proclaims To all His children, 'Come!'

235 *"The Spirit and the Bride say Come."*
THE Spirit, in our hearts,
Is whispering, 'Sinner, come;
The Bride, the Church of Christ, proclaims
To all His children, ' Come!'

2 Let him that heareth say
To all about him, ' Come!'
Let him that thirsts for righteousness,
To Christ, the Fountain, come!

3 Yes, whosoever will,
O let him freely come,
And freely drink the stream of life;
'T is Jesus bids him come.

4 Lo! Jesus, who invites,
Declares, 'I quickly come:'
Lord, even so! I wait Thine hour;
Jesus, my Saviour, come!

HENRY USTICK ONDERDONK.

236 *"Let God arise, let His enemies be scattered."*
O LORD our God, arise,
The cause of truth maintain,
And wide o'er all the peopled world
Extend her blessèd reign.

2 Thou Prince of life, arise,
Nor let Thy glory cease;
Far spread the conquests of Thy grace,
And bless the earth with peace.

3 Thou Holy Ghost, arise,
Expand Thy quickening wing,
And o'er a dark and ruined world
Let light and order spring.

4 O all ye nations, rise,
To God the Saviour sing;
From shore to shore, from earth to heaven,
Let echoing anthems ring.

RALPH WARDLAW.

HAVEN. L. M.

Why will ye waste on tri-fling cares That life which God's compassion spares,

While, in the va-rious range of thought, The one thing needful is for-got.

AURORA. 7s. D.

Watchman! tell us of the night, What its signs of promise are: Traveler! o'er yon mountain hight, See that glory-beaming star! Watchman! does its beauteous ray Aught of hope or joy foretell! Traveler! yes; it brings the day, Promised day of Is - ra - el.

237   *"The morning cometh."*

WATCHMAN! tell us of the night,
  What its signs of promise are:
Traveler! o'er yon mountain hight.
  See that glory-beaming star!
Watchman! does its beauteous ray
  Aught of hope or joy foretell?
Traveler! yes; it brings the day.
  Promised day of Israel.

2 Watchman! tell us of the night;
  Higher yet that star ascends;
Traveler! blessedness and light.
  Peace and truth its course portends!

Watchman! will its beams alone
  Gild the spot that gave them birth?
Traveler! ages are its own,
  See, it bursts o'er all the earth!

3 Watchman! tell us of the night,
  For the morning seems to dawn:
Traveler! darkness takes its flight,
  Doubt and terror are withdrawn.—
Watchman! let thy wanderings cease;
  Hie thee to thy quiet home:
Traveler! lo! the Prince of peace,
  Lo! the Son of God is come!
                  JOHN BOWRING.

238   *"Be ye doers of the word, and not hearers only."*

WHY will ye waste on trifling cares
That life which God's compassion spares,
While, in the various range of thought,
The one thing needful is forgot.

2 Shall God invite you from above?
Shall Jesus urge His dying love?
Shall troubled conscience give you pain?
And all these pleas unite in vain?

3 Not so your eyes will always view
Those objects which you now pursue;
Not so will heaven and hell appear,
When death's decisive hour is near.

4 Almighty God! Thy grace impart;
Fix deep conviction on each heart;
Nor let us waste on trifling cares
That life which Thy compassion spares.
                  PHILIP DODDRIDGE.

WEBB. 7s, 6s. D.

The morning light is breaking; The darkness disap - pears; The sons of earth are waking To peni - tential tears;

Each breeze that sweeps the ocean Brings tidings from a - far, Of nations in commotion, Prepar'd for Zion's war.

239   *"Arise, shine, for thy light is come."*

THE morning light is breaking;
The darkness disappears;
The sons of earth are waking
To penitential tears;
Each breeze that sweeps the ocean
Brings tidings from afar,
Of nations in commotion,
Prepared for Zion's war.

2 See heathen nations bending
Before the God we love,
And thousand hearts ascending
In gratitude above;
While sinners, now confessing,
The gospel call obey,
And seek the Saviour's blessing,—
A nation in a day.

3 Blest river of salvation!
Pursue thine onward way;
Flow thou to every nation,
Nor in thy richness stay:
Stay not till all the lowly
Triumphant reach their home:
Stay not till all the holy
Proclaim— 'The Lord is come!'
       SAMUEL F. SMITH.

240   *"All nations shall serve Him."*

HAIL to the Lord's Anointed!
Great David's greater Son!
Hail, in the time appointed,
His reign on earth begun!
He comes to break oppression,
To set the captive free;
To take away transgression,
And rule in equity.

2 He comes, with succor speedy
To those who suffer wrong;
To help the poor and needy,
And bid the weak be strong;
To give them songs for sighing,
Their darkness turn to light,
Whose souls, condemned and dying,
Were precious in His sight.

3 He shall come down like showers
Upon the fruitful earth,
And love and joy, like flowers,
Spring in His path to birth:
Before Him, on the mountains,
Shall peace the herald go,
And righteousness in fountains
From hill to valley flow.

4 Kings shall fall down before Him,
And gold and incense bring:
All nations shall adore Him,
His praise all people sing.
For Him shall prayer unceasing
And daily vows ascend;
His kingdom still increasing,
A kingdom without end.

5 O'er every foe victorious,
He on His throne shall rest,
From age to age more glorious,
All-blessing and all-blest:
The tide of time shall never
His covenant remove;
His name shall stand for ever;
That name to us is—love.
       JAMES MONTGOMERY.

MISSIONARY HYMN. 7s, 6s. D.

From Greenland's i-cy mountains, From India's coral strand, Where Afric's sunny foun-tains Roll down their golden sand,

From many an ancient riv - er, From many a palm-y plain, They call us to de - liv - er Their land from error's chain.

241   " Come over and help us."

From Greenland's icy mountains,
From India's coral strand,
Where Afric's sunny fountains
Roll down their golden sand,
From many an ancient river,
From many a palmy plain,
They call us to deliver
Their land from error's chain.

2 What though the spicy breezes
Blow soft o'er Ceylon's isle ;
Though every prospect pleases,
And only man is vile ;
In vain with lavish kindness
The gifts of God are strown ;
The heathen in his blindness
Bows down to wood and stone.

3 Can we, whose souls are lighted
With wisdom from on high,
Can we to men benighted
The lamp of life deny?
Salvation ! O salvation !
The joyful sound proclaim,
Till each remotest nation
Has learnt Messiah's Name.

4 Waft, waft, ye winds, His story,
And you, ye waters, roll,
Till like a sea of glory
It spreads from pole to pole ;
Till o'er our ransomed nature
The Lamb for sinners slain,
Redeemer, King, Creator,
In bliss returns to reign.
REGINALD HEBER.

ASCENSION. L. M.

Ascend Thy throne, almighty King, And spread Thy glories all a'road; Let Thine own arm salvation bring, And be Thou known the gracious God.

242   " The Lord God will come with strong hand."

Ascend Thy throne, almighty King,
And spread Thy glories all abroad ;
Let Thine own arm salvation bring,
And be Thou known the gracious God.

2 Let millions bow before Thy seat,
Let humble mourners seek Thy face,

Bring daring rebels to Thy feet,
Subdued by Thy victorious grace.

3 Oh, let the kingdoms of the world
Become the kingdoms of the Lord !
Let saints and angels praise Thy name,
Be Thou thro' heaven and earth adored.
BENJAMIN BEDDOME.

Redemption.

ZURICH. 7s.

'Come,' said Je - sus' sacred voice, 'Come and make my paths your choice; I will guide you

to your home: Weary pilgrim, hither come, Wea-ry pilgrim, hither come.'

243 *"Ye shall find rest unto your souls."*

'COME!' said Jesus' sacred voice,
'Come and make my paths your choice;
I will guide you to your home:
Weary pilgrim, hither come.

2 'Thou, who homeless, and forlorn,
Long hast borne the proud world's scorn,
Long hast roamed the barren waste,
Weary pilgrim, hither haste.

3 'Ye, who tost on beds of pain
Seek for ease, but seek in vain;
Ye, by fiercer anguish torn,
In remorse for guilt who mourn :- .

4 'Hither come, for here is found
Balm that flows for every wound!
Peace that ever shall endure,
Rest eternal, sacred, sure.'

ANNA LÆTITIA BARBAULD.

244 *"Lord, Thou knowest that I love Thee."*

HARK! my soul! it is the Lord;
'T is the Saviour—hear His word;
Jesus speaks. and speaks to thee:
'Say, poor sinner, lov'st thou me?

2 'I delivered thee when bound,
And when bleeding, healed thy wound :
Sought thee wandering, set thee right,
Turned thy darkness into light.

3 'Mine is an unchanging love,
Higher than the hights above,
Deeper than the depths beneath,
Free and faithful, strong as death.'

4 Lord, it is my chief complaint,
That my love is cold and faint,
Yet I love Thee and adore,
O for grace to love Thee more.

WILLIAM COWPER.

ANVERN. L. M.

Triumph-ant Zi-on, lift your head From dust, and dark-ness, and the dead. Though humbled

long, a-wake at length, And gird thee with thy Sav-iour's strength, And gird thee with thy Sav-iour's strength.

rit.

RIGHINI. 6s, 4s.

Thou, whose Almighty word Cha - os and darkness heard, And took their flight; Hear us, we

humbly pray; And, where the gospel's day Sheds not its glorious ray, Let there be light!

245 *"Let there be light."*

Thou, whose Almighty word
Chaos and darkness heard,
　And took their flight;
Hear us, we humbly pray;
And, where the gospel's day
Sheds not its glorious ray,
　Let there be light!

2 Thou who didst come to bring
On Thy redeeming wing
　Healing and sight,
Health to the sick in mind,
Sight to the inly blind,
O now to all mankind
　Let there be light!

3 Spirit of truth and love,
Life-giving, holy Dove,
　Speed forth Thy flight!
Move on the waters' face,
Bearing the lamp of grace,
And in earth's darkest place
　Let there be light!

4 Holy and blessèd Three,
Glorious Trinity,
　Wisdom, Love, Might!
Boundless as ocean's tide
Rolling in fullest pride,
Through the earth, far and wide,
　Let there be light!

JOHN MARRIOTT.

246 *"Awake, awake: put on thy strength, O Zion."*

Triumphant Zion, lift thy head
From dust, and darkness, and the dead;
Though humbled long, awake at length,
And gird thee with thy Saviour's strength.

2 Put all thy beauteous garments on,
And let thy various charms be known:
The world thy glories shall confess,
Decked in the robes of righteousness.

3 No more shall foes unclean invade,
And fill thy hallowed walls with dread;
No more shall hell's insulting host
Their victory and thy sorrows boast.

4 God, from on high, thy groans will hear,
His hands thy ruins shall repair;
Nor will thy watchful monarch cease
To guard thee in eternal peace.

PHILIP DODDRIDGE.

247 *"He shall have dominion from sea to sea."*

Great God, whose universal sway
The known and unknown worlds obey,
Now give the kingdom to Thy Son,
Extend His power, exalt His throne.

2 As rain on meadows newly mown,
So shall He send His influence down;
His grace on fainting souls distils
Like heavenly dew on thirsty hills.

3 The heathen lands, that lie beneath
The shades of overspreading death,
Revive at His first dawning light,
And deserts blossom at the sight.

4 The saints shall flourish in His days,
Drest in the robes of joy and praise;
Peace, like a river, from His throne
Shall flow to nations yet unknown.

ISAAC WATTS.

BERESINA. 10s.

Rise, crown'd with light, imperial Salem, rise! Ex - alt thy towering head, and lift thine eyes;

See heav'n its sparkling portals wide display, And break up - on thee in a flood of day.

248   *"Arise, shine: for thy light is come, and the glory of the Lord is risen upon thee."*

RISE, crowned with light, imperial Salem, rise !

Exalt thy towering head, and lift thine eyes ;
See heaven its sparkling portals wide display,
And break upon thee in a flood of day.

2 See a long race thy spacious courts adorn :
See future sons and daughters yet unborn
In crowding ranks on every side arise,
Demanding life, impatient for the skies.

3 See barbarous nations at thy gates attend,
Walk in thy light, and in thy temple bend :
See thy bright altars thronged with pros-
    trate kings,
While every land its joyful tribute brings.

4 The seas shall waste, the skies to smoke
    decay,
Rocks fall to dust, and mountains melt away ;
But fixed His word, His saving power re-
    mains :   [reigns.
Thy realms shall last, thy own Messiah

ALEXANDER POPE.

ROBBINS. C. M.

Blest are the souls that hear and know The gos - pel's joy - ful sound;

Peace shall at - tend the path they go, And light their steps surround.

249   *"Blessed is the people that know the joyful sound."*

BLEST are the souls that hear and know
    The gospel's joyful sound ;
Peace shall attend the path they go,
    And light their steps surround.

2 Their joy shall bear their spirits up
    Through their Redeemer's name ;

His righteousness exalts their hope,
    Nor Satan dares condemn.

3 The Lord, our glory and defence,
    Strength and salvation gives ;
Israel, thy King for ever reigns,
    Thy God for ever lives.

ISAAC WATTS.

AUSTRIA 8s, 7s. D.

Hail, Thou once despised Jesus! Hail, Thou Ga'i - le - an King! Thou didst suffer to release us, Thou didst free salvation bring:

Hail, Thou agonizing Saviour, bear - er of our sin and shame; by Thy merits we find favor; Life is giv - en through Thy name!

250 *"Ye are Christ's, and Christ is God's."*

Hail, Thou once despised Jesus!
Hail, Thou Galilean King!
Thou didst suffer to release us,
Thou didst free salvation bring:
Hail, Thou agonizing Saviour,
Bearer of our sin and shame;
By Thy merits we find favor;
Life is given through Thy name!

2 Jesus, hail! enthroned in glory,
There for ever to abide:
All the heavenly host adore Thee,
Seated at Thy Father's side:
There for sinners Thou art pleading;
There Thou dost our place prepare;
Ever for us interceding
Till in glory we appear.

3 Worship, honor, power, and blessing,
Thou art worthy to receive;
Loudest praises, without ceasing,
Meet it is for us to give!
Help, ye bright angelic spirits,
Bring your sweetest, noblest lays;
Help to sing our Saviour's merits,
Help to chant Immanuel's praise!
JOHN BAKEWELL.

251 *"I will never leave thee, nor forsake thee."*

One there is above all others,
Well deserves the name of Friend;
His is love beyond a brother's,
Costly, free, and knows no end.
Which of all our friends, to save us,
Could or would have shed his blood?
But our Jesus died to have us
Reconciled in Him to God.

2 When He lived on earth abased,
Friend of sinners was His name;
Now above all glory raised,
He rejoices in the same.
O for grace our hearts to soften;
Teach us, Lord, at length to love;
We, alas, forget too often
What a Friend we have above.
JOHN NEWTON.

252 *"Justified freely by His grace."*

When I view my Saviour bleeding,
For my sins, upon the tree;
Oh, how wondrous!—how exceeding
Great His love appears to me!
Floods of deep distress and anguish,
To impede His labors, came;
Yet they all could not extinguish
Love's eternal, burning flame.

2 Now redemption is completed,
Full salvation is procured;
Death and Satan are defeated,
By the sufferings He endured.
Now the gracious Mediator
Risen to the courts of bliss,
Claims for me, a sinful creature,
Pardon, righteousness, and peace!

3 Sure such infinite affection
Lays the highest claims to mine;
All my powers, without exception,
Should in fervent praises join.
Jesus, fit me for Thy service;
Form me for Thyself alone;
I am Thy most costly purchase,—
Take possession of Thine own.
RICHARD LEE.

The Church.

HAYDN. S. M. D.

I love Thy kingdom, Lord, The house of Thine a-bode, The church our blest Re-deem-er sav'd

With His own precious blood. I love Thy church, O God! Her walls before Thee stand,

Dear as the ap-ple of Thine eye, And gra-ven on Thy hand, And gra-ven on Thy hand.

253 *"Pray for the peace of Jerusalem ; they shall prosper that love thee."*

I LOVE Thy kingdom, Lord,
  The house of Thine abode,
The church our blest Redeemer saved
  With His own precious blood.
I love Thy church, O God!
  Her walls before Thee stand,
Dear as the apple of Thine eye,
  And graven on Thy hand.

2 If e'er to bless Thy sons
  My voice or hands deny,
These hands let useful skill forsake,
  This voice in silence die.
If e'er my heart forget
  Her welfare or her wo,
Let every joy this heart forsake,
  And every grief o'erflow.

3 For her my tears shall fall,
  For her my prayers ascend ;
To her my cares and toils be given,
  Till toils and cares shall end.
Beyond my highest joy
  I prize her heavenly ways,
Her sweet communion, solemn vows,
  Her hymns of love and praise.

4 Jesus, Thou Friend Divine,
  Our Saviour and our King,
Thy hand from every snare and foe
  Shall great deliverance bring.
Sure as Thy truth shall last,
  To Zion shall be given
The brightest glories earth can yield,
  And brighter bliss of heaven.
             TIMOTHY DWIGHT.

254 *"The kingdom of God is come nigh unto you."*

COME, kingdom of our God,
  Sweet reign of light and love,
Shed peace and hope and joy abroad,
  And wisdom from above.
Over our spirits first
  Extend Thy healing reign ;
Then raise and quench that sacred thirst
  That never pains again.

2 Come, kingdom of our God,
  And make the broad earth Thine ;
Stretch o'er her lands and isles the rod
  That flowers with grace divine.
Come, kingdom of our God,
  And raise the glorious throne
In worlds by the undying trod
  When God shall bless His own.
             HENRY D. JOHNS.

GLAD TIDINGS. C. M. D.

Let saints below in con-cert sing With those to glory gone: For all the servants

of our King In earth and heav'n are one. One fa-mi-ly we dwell in Him, One

church, above, beneath, Tho' now di-vid-ed by the stream,The narrow stream of death.

255 *"That they all may be one."*

LET saints below in concert sing
  With those to glory gone:
For all the servants of our King
  In earth and heaven are one.
One family we dwell in Him,
  One church, above, beneath,
Though now divided by the stream,
  The narrow stream of death.

2 One army of the living God,
  To His command we bow;
Part of the host have crossed the flood,
  And part are crossing now.
Some to their everlasting home
  This solemn moment fly;
And we are to the margin come,
  And soon expect to die.

3 Ev'n now, by faith, we join our hands
  With those that went before,
And greet the ransomed blessèd bands
  Upon the eternal shore.
Lord Jesus, be our constant Guide:
  And, when the word is given,
Bid death's cold flood its waves divide,
  And land us safe in heaven.

CHARLES WESLEY.

256 *"Fellowcitizens with the saints, and of the household of God."*

NOT to the terrors of the Lord,
  The tempest, fire, and smoke;
Not to the thunder of that word
  Which God on Sinai spoke:—
But we are come to Zion's hill,
  The city of our God;
Where milder words declare His will
  And spread His love abroad.

2 Behold the innumerable host
  Of angels clothed in light!
Behold the spirits of the just,
  Whose faith is turned to sight!
Behold the blest assembly there,
  Whose names are writ in heaven!
And God, the judge of all, declare
  Their vilest sins forgiven!

3 The saints on earth, and all the dead,
  But one communion make;
All join in Christ, their living Head,
  And of His grace partake.
In such society as this
  My weary soul would rest;
The man that dwells where Jesus is,
  Must be for ever blest.

ISAAC WATTS.

WARD. L. M.

God is the re-fuge of His saints, When storms of sharp distress in-vade:

Ere we can of-fer our com-plaints, Behold Him pres - ent with His aid.

257   "God is our Refuge and Strength."

God is the refuge of His saints,
  When storms of sharp distress invade:
Ere we can offer our complaints,
  Behold Him present with His aid.

2 Let mountains from their seats be hurled
  Down to the deep, and buried there;
Convulsions shake the solid world;—
  Our faith shall never yield to fear.

3 Loud may the troubled ocean roar;—
  In sacred peace our souls abide,
While every nation, every shore,
  Trembles, and dreads the swelling tide.

4 There is a stream whose gentle flow
  Supplies the city of our God;
Life, love, and joy, still gliding through,
  And watering our divine abode.

5 That sacred stream, Thine holy word,
  Our grief allays, our fear controls:
Sweet peace Thy promises afford,
  And give new strength to fainting souls.

6 Zion enjoys her Monarch's love,
  Secure against a threatening hour;
Nor can her firm foundations move,
  Built on His truth, and armed with power.

ISAAC WATTS.

BOYLSTON. S. M.

Blest be the . tie that binds Our hearts in Chris - tian love,

The fel - low-ship of kindred minds, Is like to that a - bove.

ST. MATTHEW. C. M. D.

O where are kings and empires now, Of old that went and came. But, Lord, Thy church is

praying yet, A thousand years the same! We mark her ho - ly bat-tlements, And her found-

a-tions strong; And hear with-in her ceaseless voice, And her un-end-ing song.

258 *"Beautiful for situation, the joy of the whole earth, is Mount Zion."*

O WHERE are kings and empires now,
  Of old that went and came!
But, Lord, Thy church is praying yet,
  A thousand years the same!
We mark her holy battlements,
  And her foundations strong;
And hear within her ceaseless voice,
  And her unending song.

2 For not like kingdoms of the world,
  The holy church of God!   [her,
Though earthquake shocks be threatening
  And tempest is abroad;

Unshaken as eternal hills,
  Unmovable she stands,
A mountain that shall fill the earth,
  A house unbuilt by hands.

3 O ye that in these latter days
  The citadel defend,
Perchance for you the Saviour said,
  'I'm with you to the end':
Stand therefore girt about, and hold
  Your burning lamps in hand,
And standing listen for your Lord,
  And till He cometh—stand!

ARTHUR CLEVELAND COXE.

259 *"Every one members one of another."*

BLEST be the tie that binds
  Our hearts in Christian love;
The fellowship of kindred minds
  Is like to that above.

2 Before our Father's throne,
  We pour our ardent prayers;
Our fears, our hopes, our aims, are one,
  Our comforts and our cares.

3 We share our mutual woes,
  Our mutual burdens bear;
And often for each other flows
  The sympathizing tear.

4 When we asunder part,
  It gives us inward pain;
But we shall still be joined in heart,
  And hope to meet again.

5 This glorious hope revives
  Our courage by the way;
While each in expectation lives,
  And longs to see the day.

6 From sorrow, toil, and pain,
  And sin, we shall be free:
And perfect love and friendship reign
  Through all eternity.

JOHN FAWCETT.

126   The Church.

CASSEL. C. M. D.

Lord Jesus, are we one with Thee? O hight, O depth of love! Thou one with us on

Cal - va - ry, We one with Thee a - bove. Such was Thy love that for our sake Thou

didst from heav'n come down, Our mortal flesh and blood partake, In all our misery one.

260 *"Our fellowship is with the Father and with His Son Jesus Christ."*

Lord Jesus, are we one with Thee?
  O hight, O depth of love!
Thou one with us on Calvary,
  We one with Thee above.
Such was Thy love that for our sake
  Thou didst from heaven come down,
Our mortal flesh and blood partake,
  In all our misery one.

2 Our sins, our guilt, in love divine,
  Confessed and borne by Thee ;
The sting, the curse. the wrath, were Thine
  To set Thy members free.
Ascended now, in glory bright,
  Still one with us Thou art ;
Nor life, nor death, nor depth, nor hight,
  Thy saints and Thee can part.

3 Such was Thy love, that for our sake
  Thou didst from heaven come down ;
Our mortal blood and flesh partake,
  In all our misery one.
Ere long shall come that glorious day,
  When, seated on Thy throne,
Thou shalt to wondering worlds display
  That we in Thee are one.

                    JAMES GEORGE DECK.

261 *"And they sung as it were a new song before the throne."*

Sing we the song of those who stand
  Around the eternal throne,
Of every kindred, clime, and land,
  A multitude unknown.
Life's poor distinctions vanish here ;
  To-day the young, the old,
Our Saviour and His flock, appear
  One Shepherd and one fold.

2 Toil, trial, suffering, still await
  On earth the pilgrim-throng,
Yet learn we in our low estate
  The church-triumphant's song.
'Worthy the Lamb for sinners slain,'
  Cry the redeemed above,
'Blessing and honor to obtain,
  And everlasting love.'

3 'Worthy the Lamb !' on earth we sing,
  'Who died our souls to save ;
Henceforth, O Death ! where is thy sting?
  Thy victory, O Grave?'
Then hallelujah, power and praise
  To God in Christ be given ;
May all who now this anthem raise
  Renew the strain in heaven !

                    JAMES MONTGOMERY.

PARK STREET. L. M.

O Lord, in perfect bliss above Thou couldst not need cre - a - ted love; And yet Thou

didst Thy pow'r display, And earth's foundation firmly lay, And earth's foundation firmly lay.

262   *"Behold I create new heavens and a new earth."*

O LORD, in perfect bliss above
Thou couldst not need created love ;
And yet Thou didst Thy power display,
And earth's foundation firmly lay.

2 But even while the world came forth
In all the beauty of its birth,
In Thy deep thought Thou didst behold
Another world of nobler mold.

3 For Thou didst will that Christ should
A new creation by His name ;   [frame

Its seed, the living word of grace
He scatters wide in every place ;

4 Its home, when time shall be no more,
In heaven with Thee for evermore ;
Accepted in Thy boundless love
To share His throne and joy above.

5 O Father, bless, for they are Thine,
O Son, direct in love divine,
O Holy Ghost, with grace endue
The old creation and the new !

          ISAAC WILLIAMS.

LEIGHTON. S. M.

Awake, and sing the song Of Moses and the Lamb, Wake ev-'ry heart and ev-'ry tongue To praise the Saviour's name.

263   *"He hath put a new song in my mouth."*

AWAKE, and sing the song
Of Moses and the Lamb.
Wake every heart and every tongue
To praise the Saviour's name.

2 Sing of His dying love ;
Sing of His rising power ;
Sing how He intercedes above
For those whose sins He bore.

3 Sing, till we feel our hearts
Ascending with our tongues ;

Sing, till the love of sin departs,
And grace inspires our songs.

4 Sing on your heavenly way,
Ye ransomed sinners, sing ;
Sing on, rejoicing every day
In Christ, the Eternal King.

5 Soon shall ye hear Him say,
Ye blessèd children, come ;
Soon will He call you hence away,
And take His wanderers home.

          WILLIAM HAMMOND.

VOX DILECTI. C. M. D.

I heard the voice of Jesus say, 'Come unto Me and rest; Lay down, thou weary one, lay down Thy head upon My breast!' I came to Je-sus as I was, Wea-ry and worn and sad; I found in Him a resting-place, And He has made me glad.

264 *He that hath ears to hear, let him hear."*

I HEARD the voice of Jesus say,
 'Come unto me and rest;
Lay down, thou weary one, lay down
 Thy head upon My breast!'
I came to Jesus as I was,
 Weary and worn and sad;
I found in Him a resting-place,
 And He has made me glad.

2 I heard the voice of Jesus say,
 'Behold! I freely give
The living water; thirsty one,
 Stoop down, and drink, and live!'
I came to Jesus, and I drank
 Of that life-giving stream;
My thirst was quenched, my soul revived,
 And now I live in Him.

3 I heard the voice of Jesus say,
 'I am this dark world's Light;
Look unto Me, thy morn shall rise,
 And all thy day be bright.'

I looked to Jesus, and I found
 In Him my Star, my Sun;
And in that light of life I'll walk
 Till traveling days are done.
 HORATIUS BONAR.

265 *"Blessed are they that have not seen, and yet have believed."*

'REMEMBER Me,' the Saviour said,
 On that forsaken night,
When from His side the nearest fled,
 And death was close in sight.
Through all the following ages' track
 The world remembers yet;
With love and worship gazes back,
 And never can forget.

2 O, blest are they, who have not seen,
 And yet believe Him still!
They know Him, when His praise they mean,
 And when they do His will.
We hear His word along our way;
 We see His light above;—
Remember, when we strive and pray,
 Remember, when we love.
 NATHANIEL LANGDON FROTHINGHAM.

OLMUTZ. S. M.

Je-sus invites His saints To meet around His board; Here pardon'd rebels sit, and hold Communion with their Lord.

266 *"Blessed are they that are called to the marriage supper."*

Jesus invites His saints
  To meet around His board ;
Here pardoned rebels sit, and hold
  Communion with their Lord.

2 This holy bread and wine
  Maintains our fainting breath,
By union with our living Lord,
  And interest in His death.

3 Our heavenly Father calls
  Christ and His members one :
We, the young children of His love,
  And He, the first-born Son.

4 Let all our powers be joined,
  His glorious name to raise ;
Pleasure and love fill every mind,
  And every voice be praise.

5 To God, the Father, Son,
  And Spirit, glory be,
As was, and is, and shall remain
  Through all eternity !
                              ISAAC WATTS.

267 *"Christ our Passover is sacrificed for us."*

Not all the blood of beasts
  On Jewish altars slain
Could give the guilty conscience peace,
  Or wash away the stain.

2 But Christ, the Heavenly Lamb,
  Takes all our sins away.;
A sacrifice of nobler name
  And richer blood than they.

3 My faith would lay her hand
  On that dear head of Thine,
While like a penitent I stand,
  And there confess my sin.

4 My soul looks back to see
  The burdens Thou didst bear,
When hanging on the cursèd tree,
  And hopes her guilt was there.

5 Believing, we rejoice
  To see the curse remove ;
We bless the Lamb with cheerful voice,
  And sing His bleeding love.
                              ISAAC WATTS.

HANFORD. P. M.

By Christ redeem'd, in Christ restor'd, We keep the memo - ry ador'd, And show the death of our dear Lord, Un - til He come.

268 *"Ye do show the Lord's death till He come."*

By Christ redeemed, in Christ restored,
We keep the memory adored,
And show the death of our dear Lord,
    Until He come.

2 His body, broken in our stead,
Is here in this memorial bread ;
And so our feeble love is fed,
    Until He come.

3 His fearful drops of agony,
His life-blood shed for us we see :

The wine shall tell the mystery,
    Until He come.

4 Until the trump of God be heard,
Until the ancient graves be stirred,
And with the great, commanding word,
    The Lord shall come.

5 O blessed hope ! with this elate,
Let not our hearts be desolate,
But strong in faith, in patience wait,
    Until He come !
                              GEORGE RAWSON.

AURELIA. 7s, 6s. D.

O bread to pilgrims giv-en, O food that angels eat, O manna sent from heaven, For heaven-born natures meet:

Give us, for Thee, long pining, To eat till richly filled; Till, earth's delights resigning, Our ev-'ry wish is still'd!

269   *"Except ye eat the flesh of the Son of man, and drink His blood, ye have no life in you."*

O BREAD to pilgrims given,
  O food that angels eat,
O manna sent from heaven,
  For heaven-born natures meet:
Give us, for Thee, long pining,
  To eat till richly filled;
Till, earth's delights resigning,
  Our every wish is stilled!
2 O water, life-bestowing,
  From out the Saviour's heart,
A fountain purely flowing,
  A fount of love Thou art!

O let us, freely tasting,
  Our burning thirst assuage!
Thy sweetness, never wasting,
  Avails from age to age.
3 Jesus, this feast receiving,
  We Thee unseen adore;
Thy faithful word believing
  We take, and doubt no more:
Give us, Thou true and loving,
  On earth to live in Thee;
Then, death the veil removing,
  Thy glorious face to see.

RAY PALMER.

HEATHLAND. 7s, 6 lines.

Ma-ny cen-tu-ries have fled Since our Sa-viour broke the bread, And this sa-cred feast ordain'd,

Ev-er by His church retain'd: Those His bo-dy who dis-cern, Thus shall meet till His re-turn.

270   *"If ye love Me, keep My commandments."*

MANY centuries have fled
Since our Saviour broke the bread,
And this sacred feast ordained,
Ever by His church retained:
Those His body who discern,
Thus shall meet till His return.

2 Come, the blessed emblems share,
Which the Saviour's death declare;
Come, on truth immortal feed;
For His flesh is meat indeed:
Saviour—witness with the sign,
That our ransomed souls are Thine.

JOSIAH CONDER.

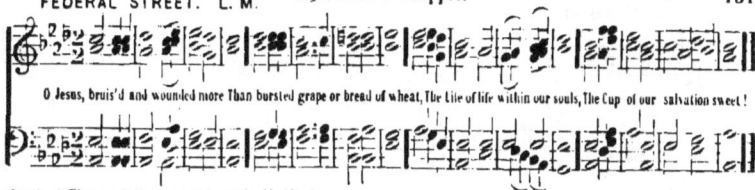

O Jesus, bruis'd and wounded more Than bursted grape or bread of wheat, The Life of life within our souls, The Cup of our salvation sweet!

271 *"This cup is the new testament in My blood, which is shed for you."*

O JESUS, bruised and wounded more
Than bursted grape, or bread of wheat,
The Life of life within our souls,
The Cup of our salvation sweet!

2 We come to show Thy dying hour,
Thy streaming vein, Thy broken flesh;
And still the blood is warm to save,
And still the fragrant wounds are fresh.

3 O Heart, that, with a double tide
Of blood and water, maketh pure;
O Flesh, once offered on the cross,
The gift that makes our pardon sure:

4 Let never more our sinful souls
The anguish of Thy cross renew;
Nor forge again the cruel nails
That pierced Thy victim body through.

CECIL FRANCES ALEXANDER.

272 *"He that cometh to Me shall never hunger."*

JESUS, thou Joy of loving hearts!
Thou Fount of Life! Thou Light of men!

From the best bliss that earth imparts,
We turn unfilled to Thee again.

2 Thy truth unchanged hath ever stood;
Thou savest those that on Thee call;
To them that seek Thee, Thou art good,
To them that find Thee, All in all!

3 We taste Thee, O Thou living Bread,
And long to feast upon Thee still!
We drink of Thee, the Fountain Head,
And thirst our souls from Thee to fill!

4 Our restless spirits yearn for Thee,
Where'er our changeful lot is cast;
Glad, when Thy gracious smile we see,
Blest, when our faith can hold Thee fast.

5 O Jesus, ever with us stay!
Make all our moments calm and bright!
Chase the dark night of sin away,
Shed o'er the world Thy holy light!

RAY PALMER.

CLOISTERS. 11s, 5s.

Father, Thy name be praised, Thy kingdom given; Thy will be done on earth as 'tis in heaven; Keep us in life; forgive our sins; de-li-ver Us now and ev - er.

273 *"Thy kingdom come."*

FATHER, Thy name be praised, Thy kingdom given;
Thy will be done on earth as 'tis in heaven;
Keep us in life; forgive our sins; deliver
Us now and ever.

2 Praise be to Thee through Jesus our salvation,
God, three in one, the Ruler of creation,
High throned, o'er all Thine eye of mercy casting,
Lord everlasting! CATHARINE WINKWORTH.

132

BEATITUDO C. M.

According to Thy gracious word, In meek hu-mi-li-ty, This will I do, my dying Lord! I will remember Thee!

274 *"This do in remembrance of Me."*

ACCORDING to Thy gracious word,
In meek humility,
This will I do, my dying Lord!
I will remember Thee!

2 Thy body, broken for my sake,
My bread from heaven shall be;
Thy testamental cup I take,
And thus remember Thee!

3 Gethsemane can I forget?
Or there Thy conflict see,
Thine agony and bloody sweat,
And not remember Thee?

4 When to the cross I turn mine eye,
And rest on Calvary,
O Lamb of God, my Sacrifice!
I must remember Thee:—

5 Remember Thee and all Thy pains
And all Thy love to me;
Yea, while a breath, a pulse remains,
Will I remember Thee.

6 And when these failing lips grow dumb,
And mind and memory flee,
When Thou shalt in Thy kingdom come,
Then, Lord, remember me!

JAMES MONTGOMERY.

275 *"Abide in Me, and I in you."*

IF human kindness meets return
And owns the grateful tie;
If tender thoughts within us burn,
To feel a friend is nigh;—

2 O, shall not warmer accents tell
The gratitude we owe
To Him, who died, our fears to quell—
Who bore our guilt and wo!

3 While yet in anguish He surveyed
Those pangs He would not flee,
What love His latest words displayed,
'Meet and remember Me!'

4 Remember Thee, Thy death, Thy shame,
Our sinful hearts to share!
O memory! leave no other name
But His recorded there.

GERALD THOMAS NOEL.

NORFOLK. 10s.

Lord, I am come! Thy promise is my plea, Without Thy word I dare not venture nigh!

But Thou hast call'd the burden'd soul to Thee; A weary, burden'd soul, O Lord, am I!

276 *"A broken and a contrite heart, O God, Thou will not despise."*

LORD, I am come! Thy promise is my plea,
Without Thy word I dare not venture nigh!
But Thou hast called the burdened soul to
 Thee;
A weary, burdened soul, O Lord, am I!

2 Bowed down beneath a heavy load of sin,

By Satan's fierce temptations sorely prest,
Beset without, and full of fears within,
Trembling and faint I come to Thee for rest.

3 Be Thou my refuge, Lord, my hiding-place;
I know no force can tear me from Thy side;
Unmoved I then may all accusers face
And answer every charge with—'Jesus died!'

JOHN NEWTON.

Repentance.

ETON. L. M.

God call - ing yet! shall I .not hear? Earth's pleasures shall I still hold dear?

Shall life's swift passing years all fly And still my soul in slum - ber lie!

277 *"Rise: He calleth thee."*

God calling yet! shall I not hear?
Earth's pleasures shall I still hold dear?
Shall life's swift passing years all fly
And still my soul in slumber lie?

2 God calling yet! shall I not rise?
Can I His loving voice despise
And basely His kind care repay?
He calls me still: can I delay?

3 God calling yet! and shall He knock,
And I my heart the closer lock?
He still is waiting to receive,
And shall I dare His Spirit grieve?

4 God calling yet! and shall I give
No heed, but still in bondage live?
I wait, but He does not forsake;
He calls me still: my heart, awake!

5 God calling yet! I cannot stay;
My heart I yield without delay:
Vain world, farewell, from thee I part,
The voice of God hath reached my heart.
GERHARD TERSTEEGEN.

278 *"Shall Thy loving kindness be declared in the grave?"*

While life prolongs its precious light,
Mercy is found, and peace is given;
But soon, ah! soon, approaching night
Shall blot out every hope of heaven.

2 While God invites, how blest the day!
How sweet the gospel's charming sound!
Come, sinners, haste, O, haste away,
While yet a pardoning God is found.

3 Soon, borne on time's most rapid wing,
Shall death command you to the grave,
Before His bar your spirits bring,
And none be found to hear or save.

4 In that lone land of deep despair
No Sabbath's heavenly light shall rise;
No God regard your bitter prayer,
Nor Saviour call you to the skies.

5 Now God invites—how blest the day!
How sweet the gospel's charming sound!
Come, sinners, haste, O, haste away,
While yet a pardoning God is found.
TIMOTHY DWIGHT.

279 *" Whatsoever thy hand findeth to do, do it with thy might."*

Life is the time to serve the Lord,
The time to insure the great reward;
And while the lamp holds out to burn
The vilest sinner may return.

2 Life is the hour that God hath given,
To escape from hell, and fly to heaven;
The day of grace, and mortals may
Secure the blessings of the day.

3 Then what my thoughts design to do,
My hands, with all your might pursue,
Since no device, nor work, is found,
Nor faith, nor hope, beneath the ground.

4 There are no acts of pardon past
In the cold grave to which we haste;
But darkness, death, and long despair
Reign in eternal silence there.
ISAAC WATTS.

WALDSTEIN. 7s, D.

Does the gospel word proclaim Rest for those that weary be? Then, my soul, as - sert thy

claim; Sure, that promise speaks to thee. Marks of grace I can - not show, All pol -

luted is my best; Yet I weary am, I know, And the weary long for rest.

280 *"Rest in the Lord, and wait patiently for Him."*

DOES the gospel word proclaim
  Rest for those that weary be?
Then, my soul, assert thy claim;
  Sure, that promise speaks to thee.
Marks of grace I cannot show,
  All polluted is my best;
Yet I weary am, I know,
  And the weary long for rest.

2 Burdened with a load of sin,
  Harassed with tormenting doubt,
Hourly conflicts from within,
  Hourly crosses from without:

All my little strength is gone,
  Sink I must without supply;
Sure, upon the earth is none
  Can more weary be than I.

3 In the ark the weary dove
  Found a welcome resting-place;
Thus my spirit longs to prove
  Rest in Christ, the Ark of grace;
Tempest-tost I long have been,
  And the flood increases fast;
Open, Lord, and draw me in,
  Till the storm be overpast!

JOHN NEWTON.

GOLGOTHA. C. M.

A - las! what hourly dangers rise! What snares beset my way! To heav'n, O let me lift mine eyes, And hourly watch and pray.

PENITENCE. 10s.

Weary of earth, and laden with my sin, I look at heav'n and long to enter in;

But there no e-vil thing may find a home; And yet I hear a voice that bids me come.

281 *"Redemption through His blood, the forgiveness of sins."*

WEARY of earth, and laden with my sin,
I look at heaven and long to enter in;
But there no evil thing may find a home,
And yet I hear a voice that bids me come.

2 It is the voice of Jesus that I hear;
His are the hands stretched out to draw me
near;

And His the Blood that can for all atone,
And set me faultless there before the throne.

3 Yea, Thou wilt answer for me, righteous
Lord;
Thine all the merits, mine the great reward;
Thine the sharp thorns, and mine the golden
crown;
Mine the life won, and Thine the life laid
down.

SAMUEL J. STONE.

282 *"In Him will I trust."*

ALAS, what hourly dangers rise!
What snares beset my way!
To heaven, O let me lift mine eyes,
And hourly watch and pray.

2 O gracious God, in whom I live,
My feeble efforts aid;
Help me to watch, and pray, and strive,
Though trembling and afraid.

3 Increase my faith, increase my hope,
When foes and fears prevail;
And bear my fainting spirit up,
Or soon my strength will fail.

4 Where'er temptations fright my heart,
Or lure my feet aside,
My God, Thy powerful aid impart,
My Guardian and my Guide.

5 O keep me in Thy heavenly way,
And bid the tempter flee,
And let me never, never stray
From happiness and Thee.

ANNE STEELE.

283 *"God shall bring every work into judgment."*

ALMIGHTY God, Thy piercing eye
Strikes through the shades of night;
And our most secret actions lie
All open to Thy sight.

2 There's not a sin that we commit,
Nor wicked word we say,
But in Thy dreadful book 't is writ
Against the judgment-day.

3 And must the crimes that I have done
Be read and published there,
Be all exposed before the sun,
While men and angels hear?

4 Lord! at Thy foot ashamed I lie,
Upward I dare not look;
Pardon my sins before I die,
And blot them from Thy book.

5 Remember all the dying pains
That my Redeemer felt,
And let His blood wash out my stains,
And answer for my guilt.

ISAAC WATTS.

GORTON. S. M.

And wilt Thou pardon, Lord, A sinner such as I,   Although Thy book his crimes record Of such a crimson dye?

284   *"If the righteous scarcely be saved, where shall the ungodly and the sinner appear?"*

AND wilt Thou pardon, Lord,
  A sinner such as I.
Although Thy book his crimes record
  Of such a crimson dye?

2 So deep are they engraved,
  So terrible their fear,—
The righteous scarcely shall be saved,
  And where shall I appear?

3 My soul, make all things known
  To Him who all things sees;
That so the Lamb shall yet atone
  For thine iniquities.

4 O Thou Physician blest,
  Make clean my guilty soul!
And me, by many a sin opprest
  Restore, and keep me whole!

5 I know not how to praise
  Thy mercy and Thy love:
But deign Thy servant to upraise,
  And I shall learn above!
          JOHN MASON NEALE.

285   *"To-day, if ye will hear His voice, harden not your hearts."*

O WHERE shall rest be found,
  Rest for the weary soul?
'T were vain the ocean depths to sound,
  Or pierce to either pole.

2 The world can never give
  The bliss for which we sigh:
'T is not the whole of life to live,
  Nor all of death to die.

2 Beyond this vale of tears,
  There is a life above,
Unmeasured by the flight of years;
  And all that life is love.

4 There is a death whose pang
  Outlasts the fleeting breath:
O what eternal horrors hang
  Around the second death!

5 Lord God of truth and grace,
  Teach us that death to shun,
Lest we be banished from Thy face,
  And evermore undone.
          JAMES MONTGOMERY.

DETROIT. S. M.

Did Christ o'er sinners weep, And shall our cheeks be dry! Let floods of pen-i-ten-tial grief Burst forth from ev'ry eye.

286   *"While we were yet sinners, Christ died for us."*

DID Christ o'er sinners weep.
  And shall our cheeks be dry?
Let floods of penitential grief
  Burst forth from every eye.

2 The Son of God in tears
  Angels with wonder see!

Be thou astonished. O my soul,
  He shed those tears for thee.

3 He wept that we might weep:
  Each sin demands a tear;
In heaven alone no sin is found,
  And there's no weeping there.
          BENJAMIN BEDDOME.

CHERITH. C. M.

O Thou, whose ten - der mer - cy hears Con - tri - tion's hum - ble sigh,

Whose hand in - dul - gent wipes the tears From sor - row's weep - ing eye;

287 *"Return unto Me, and I will return unto you, saith the Lord of hosts."*

O THOU, whose tender mercy hears
Contrition's humble sigh,
Whose hand indulgent wipes the tears
From sorrow's weeping eye ;

2 See, low before Thy throne of grace,
A wretched wanderer mourn ;
Hast Thou not bid me seek Thy face?
Hast Thou not said, Return?

3 Absent from Thee, my Guide, my Light,
Without one cheering ray,
Through dangers, fears, and gloomy night,
How desolate my way !

4 O shine on this benighted heart,
With beams of mercy shine !
And let Thy healing voice impart
A taste of joys divine !

ANNE STEELE.

288 *"Seek ye the Lord while He may be found."*

COME, trembling sinner, in whose breast
A thousand thoughts revolve,
Come, with your guilt and fear opprest,
And make this last resolve :—

2 'I'll go to Jesus, though my sin
Like mountains round me close ;
I know His courts, I'll enter in,
Whatever may oppose.

3 'Prostrate I'll lie before His throne,
And there my guilt confess ;
I'll tell Him I'm a wretch undone,
Without His sovereign grace.

4 'I'll to the gracious King approach,
Whose scepter pardon gives ;

Perhaps He may command my touch,
And then the suppliant lives.

5 'Perhaps He will admit my plea,
Perhaps will hear my prayer ;
But, if I perish, I will pray,
And perish only there.

6 'I can but perish, if I go—
I am resolved to try ;
For, if I stay away, I know
I must for ever die.'

EDMUND JONES.

289 *"With His stripes we are healed."*

I saw One hanging on a tree,
In agony and blood,
Who fixed His languid eyes on me,
As near His cross I stood.

2 Sure, never till my latest breath
Can I forget that look ;
It seemed to charge me with His death,
Though not a word He spoke.

3 Alas, I knew not what I did,
But all my tears were vain :
Where could my trembling soul be hid,
For I the Lord had slain.

4 A second look He gave, that said,
'I freely all forgive ;
This blood is for thy ransom paid ;
I die, that thou may'st live.'

5 Thus while His death my sin displays
In all its blackest hue,
Such is the mystery of grace,
It seals my pardon too !

JOHN NEWTON.

BURNHAM. H. M.

Blot out our sins of old, When erst we went a - stray, When, Father, from Thy fold

We wander'd far away; O King of heav'n, To Thee we cry, Ere yet we die, To be forgiv'n.

290   *"Hide Thy face from my sins, and blot out all mine iniquities."*

Blot out our sins of old,
    When erst we went astray,
    When, Father, from Thy fold
      We wandered far away;
O King of heaven, | Ere yet we die,
To Thee we cry, | To be forgiven.

2 In this our hour of need,
    In hope we fly to Thee:

Sow in our hearts the seed
      Of bright eternity;
O Lord, we pray, | Our strength renew
As morning dew, | From day to day.

3 Blot out our sins gone by,
    Blot out our sins to-day,
      And others ere we die;
      And give us, while we pray,
Undying faith | The victory
In Christ, to see | O'er sin and death.
            GODFREY THRING.

HEAVENLY LOVE. C. P. M.

Lord, Thou hast won, at length I yield, My heart by might - y grace compell'd, Sur - ren - ders all to Thee;

A - gainst Thy ter - rors long I strove, But who can stand a-gainst Thy love! Love con-quers e - ven me.

Mercy

LAST HOPE. 7s.

Repentance.

149

Hast thou sin - ned? sin no more; Par - don ask and par - don win;

Mer - cy sits at mer - cy's door, Bold - ly knock and en - ter in.

291 *"Let us therefore come boldly unto the throne of grace, that we may obtain mercy."*

HAST thou sinned? Sin no more ;
Pardon ask, and pardon win ;
Mercy sits at mercy's door,
Boldly knock and enter in.

2 Boldly to the throne of grace,
Weeping for the bitter past,
Go, though shame would hide its face,
Go, and find a rest at last.

3 Christ, who died the lost to save,
Never turned His face from pain ;
They who meekly pardon crave,
Never cry to Him in vain.

4 Christ Himself is calling, 'Come,'
Christ, who lived and died for thee,
'Hasten, helpless sinner, home ;
Lay your weary load on Me.'

5 Stand not still to count the cost,
Hasten while 't is yet to-day ;
Time, too precious to be lost,
Brooks not doubt ;—away, away !

6 Yes, in this thy sorest need,
Knock in faith at mercy's door ;
Go, and there for pardon plead,
Go, for grace to sin no more.
GODFREY THRING.

292 *"God is love."*

DEPTH of mercy ! can there be
Mercy still reserved for me ?
Can my God His wrath forbear,—
Me, the chief of sinners, spare ?

2 I have long withstood His grace ;
Long provoked Him to His face ;
Would not hearken to His calls,
Grieved Him by a thousand falls.

3 Lord, incline me to repent ;
Let me now my fall lament ;
Deeply my revolt deplore ;
Weep, believe, and sin no more.

4 There for me the Saviour stands,
Shows His wounds, and spreads His hands :
God is love ! I know, I feel ;
Jesus weeps, but loves me still.
CHARLES WESLEY.

293 *"Lord, what wilt Thou have me to do?"*

LORD, Thou hast won—at length I yield,
My heart, by mighty grace compelled,
Surrenders all to Thee ;
Against Thy terrors long I strove,
But who can stand against Thy love ?—
Love conquers even me.

2 If Thou hadst bid Thy thunders roll,
And lightnings flash to blast my soul,
I still had stubborn been :

But mercy has my heart subdued,
A bleeding Saviour I have viewed,
And now, I hate my sin.

3 Now, Lord, I would be Thine alone ;
Come, take possession of Thine own,
For Thou hast set me free :
Released from Satan's hard command,
See all my powers in waiting stand,
To be employed by Thee.
JOHN NEWTON.

OSGOOD. 8s, 7s, 4s. **Repentance.**

Come, ye sinners, poor and wretched, Weak and wounded, sick and sore ; }
Je - sus ready stands to save you, Full of pi - ty join'd with pow'r : } He is able,

He is a - ble, He is will-ing; doubt no more. He is willing; doubt no more.

294 *"Ho, every one that thirsteth."*

COME, ye sinners, poor and wretched,
Weak and wounded, sick and sore ;
Jesus ready stands to save you,
Full of pity, joined with power :
He is able,
He is willing ; doubt no more.

2 Ho, ye needy, come and welcome ;
God's free bounty glorify ;
True belief, and true repentance,
Every grace that brings us nigh,
Without money,
Come to Jesus Christ and buy.

3 Let not conscience make you linger,
Nor of fitness fondly dream ;
All the fitness He requireth
Is to feel your need of Him :
This He gives you ;
'T is the Spirit's rising beam.

4 Come, ye weary, heavy laden,
Lost and ruined by the fall !
If you tarry till you're better,
You will never come at all :
Not the righteous,
Sinners, Jesus came to call.
JOSEPH HART.

MANOAH. C. M.

Lord, as to Thy dear cross we flee And plead to be for - given, So let Thy life our pattern be, And form our souls for heav'n.

295 *"This is the love of God, that we keep His commandments."*

LORD, as to Thy dear cross we flee
And plead to be forgiven,
So let Thy life our pattern be,
And form our souls for heaven.

2 Help us, through good report and ill,
Our daily cross to bear,
Like Thee to do our Father's will,
Our brethren's griefs to share.

3 Let grace our selfishness expel,
Our earthliness refine,

And kindness in our bosoms dwell,
As free and true as Thine.

4 Should friends misjudge, or foes defame,
Or brethren faithless prove,
Then, like Thine own, be all our aim
To conquer them by love.

5 Kept peaceful in the midst of strife,
Forgiving and forgiven,
O may we lead the pilgrim's life,
And follow Thee to heaven !
JOHN HAMPDEN GURNEY.

HAMBURG. L. M.

O Thou that hear'st when sin-ners cry, Tho' all my crimes be-fore Thee lie,

Be-hold them not with an-gry look, But blot their memory from Thy book.

296 *"The sacrifices of God are a broken spirit."*

O Thou that hear'st when sinners cry,
Though all my crimes before Thee lie,
Behold them not with angry look,
But blot their memory from Thy book.

2 Create my nature pure within,
And form my soul averse to sin ;
Let Thy good Spirit ne'er depart,
Nor hide Thy presence from my heart.

3 I cannot live without Thy light,
Cast out and banished from Thy sight ;
Thine holy joys, my God, restore,
And guard me that I fall no more.

4 A broken heart, my God, my King,
Is all the sacrifice I bring ;
The God of grace will ne'er despise
A broken heart for sacrifice.

5 O may Thy love inspire my tongue !
Salvation shall be all my song ;
And all my powers shall join to bless
The Lord, my Strength and Righteousness.
ISAAC WATTS.

297 *"My soul waiteth upon God."*

O THAT my load of sin were gone !
O that I could at last submit
At Jesus' feet to lay it down,
To lay my soul at Jesus' feet !

2 Rest for my soul I long to find ;
Saviour of all, if mine Thou art,
Give me Thy meek and lowly mind,
And stamp Thine image on my heart.

3 Break off the yoke of inbred sin,
And fully set my spirit free ;

I cannot rest till pure within,
Till I am wholly lost in Thee.

4 Fain would I learn of Thee, my God ;
Thy light and easy burden prove,
The cross all stained with hallowed blood,
The labor of Thy dying love.

5 I would, but Thou must give me power,
My heart from every sin release ;
Bring near, bring near the joyful hour,
And fill me with Thy perfect peace.
CHARLES WESLEY.

298 *"Create in me a clean heart, O God."*

Show pity, Lord ; O Lord, forgive ;
Let a repenting rebel live ;
Are not Thy mercies large and free ?
May not a sinner trust in Thee ?

2 My crimes are great, but don't surpass
The power and glory of Thy grace :
Great God, Thy nature hath no bound ;
So let Thy pardoning love be found.

3 O, wash my soul from every sin,
And make my guilty conscience clean ;
Here on my heart the burden lies,
And great offences pain mine eyes.

4 My lips with shame my sins confess
Against Thy law, against Thy grace ;
Lord, should Thy judgment grow severe,
I am condemned, but Thou art clear.

5 Yet save a trembling sinner, Lord,
Whose hope, still hovering round Thy word,
Would light on some sweet promise there,
Some sure support against despair.
ISAAC WATTS.

Christian Joy and Hope.

ANVERN. L. M.

The Lord is King! lift up thy voice, O earth, and, all ye heav'ns, re - joice! From world to world the joy shall ring, The Lord Om - ni - po-tent is King, The Lord Om - ni - po-tent is King.

299 *"God is King of all the earth ; sing ye praises with understanding."*

The Lord is King! lift up thy voice,
O earth, and, all ye heavens, rejoice!
From world to world the joy shall ring,
The Lord Omnipotent is King.

2 The Lord is King! who then shall dare
Resist His will, distrust His care,
Or murmur at His wise decrees,
Or doubt His royal promises?

3 The Lord is King! Child of the dust,
The Judge of all the earth is just:
Holy and true are all His ways:
Let every creature speak His praise.

4 He reigns! ye saints, exalt your strains;
Your God is King, your Father reigns:
And He is at the Father's side,
The Man of Love, the crucified.

5 Come, make your wants, your burdens
known,
He will present them at the throne;
And angel bands are waiting there
His messages of love to bear.

6 O when His wisdom can mistake,
His might decay, His love forsake,
Then may His children cease to sing,—
The Lord Omnipotent is King.

JOSIAH CONDER.

300 *"Mine eyes have seen Thy salvation."*

Lift up your heads, ye mighty gates!
Behold, the King of glory waits;
The King of kings is drawing near,
The Saviour of the world is here.

2 The Lord is just, a helper tried;
Mercy is ever at His side;
His kingly crown is holiness:
His scepter, pity in distress.

3 O blest the land, the city blest,
Where Christ the Ruler is confest!
O happy hearts and happy homes
To whom this King of triumph comes.

4 Fling wide the portals of your heart;
Make it a temple set apart
From earthly use for heaven's employ,
Adorned with prayer and love and joy.

5 Redeemer, come! I open wide
My heart to Thee; here, Lord, abide;
Let me Thine inner presence feel,
Thy grace and love in me reveal.

6 So come, my Sovereign, enter in;
Let new and nobler life begin;
Thy Holy Spirit guide us on,
Until the glorious crown is won!

GEORGE WEISSEL.

HEBER. C. M.

How sweet the name of Jesus sounds In a believ - er's ear! It soothes his sorrows, heals his wounds, And drives away his fear.

CHORAL. P. M.

Now thank we all our God, With heart and hand and voi - ces, }
Who wondrous things hath done, In whom His world rejoi - ces; } Who from our mother's arms

Hath blest us on our way, With countless gifts of love, And still is ours to - day.

301 *"This God is our God for ever and ever."*

Now thank we all our God,
 With heart and hand and voices,
Who wondrous things hath done,
 In whom His world rejoices;
Who from our mother's arms
Hath blest us on our way
With countless gifts of love,
And still is ours to-day.

2 O may this bounteous God
 Through all our life be near us,
With ever joyful hearts
 And blessed peace to cheer us;

And keep us in His grace,
 And guide us when perplexed,
And free us from all ills
 In this world and the next.

3 All praise and thanks to God
 The Father now be given,
The Son, and Him who reigns
 With them in highest heaven !
The One Eternal God
 Whom heaven and earth adore ;
For thus it was, is now,
 And shall be evermore !

MARTIN RINKART.

302 *"Unto you which believe He is precious."*

How sweet the name of Jesus sounds
 In a believer's ear !
It soothes his sorrows, heals his wounds,
 And drives away his fear.

2 It makes the wounded spirit whole,
 And calms the troubled breast ;
'T is manna to the hungry soul,
 And to the weary, rest.

3 Dear name ! the rock on which I build,
 My shield and hiding-place,
My never-failing treasury, filled
 With boundless stores of grace !

4 By Thee my prayers acceptance gain,
 Although with sin defiled ;

Satan accuses me in vain,
 And I am owned a child.

5 Jesus ! my Shepherd, Guardian, Friend,
 My Prophet, Priest, and King ;
My Lord, my Life, my Way, my End,
 Accept the praise I bring !

6 Weak is the effort of my heart,
 And cold my warmest thought ;
But when I see Thee as Thou art,
 I'll praise Thee as I ought.

7 Till then, I would Thy love proclaim,
 With every fleeting breath ;
And may the music of Thy name
 Refresh my soul in death.

JOHN NEWTON.

HARWELL. 8s, 7s. D.

Hark! ten thousand harps and voi - ces Sound the note of praise a - bove; }
Je - sus reigns, and heaven re - joi - ces; Je - sus reigns, the God of love: } See, He sits on yonder throne;
See, He sits

Je - sus rules the world a - lone. Hal - le - lu - jah, Hal-le - lu - jah, Hal - le - lu - jah, A - men.
Je - sus rules

303 *"And I heard the voice of many angels round about the throne."*

Hark ! ten thousand harps and voices
Sound the note of praise above ;
Jesus reigns, and heaven rejoices ;
Jesus reigns, the God of love :
See, He sits on yonder throne ;
Jesus rules the world alone.

2 King of glory, reign for ever !
Thine an everlasting crown :

Nothing from Thy love shall sever
Those whom Thou hast made Thine own ;
Happy objects of Thy grace,
Destined to behold Thy face.

3 Saviour, hasten Thine appearing ;
Bring, O bring the glorious day,
When, the awful summons hearing,
Heaven and earth shall pass away :
Then, with golden harps, we'll sing,—
'Glory, glory to our King.'

THOMAS KELLY.

DUKE STREET. L. M.

What e - qual hon - ors shall we bring, To Thee, O Lord our God, the Lamb;

When all the notes that an - gels sing Are far in - fe - rior to Thy Name ?

WALDHORN. C. M.

Through all the changing scenes of life, In trou-ble, and in joy,

The prais - es of my God shall still My heart and tongue em - ploy.

304 *"The angel of the Lord encampeth round about them that fear Him."*   **305** *"I shall not want."*

THROUGH all the changing scenes of life,
In trouble, and in joy,
The praises of my God shall still
My heart and tongue employ.

2 O magnify the Lord with me,
With me exa't His name ;
When in distress to Him I called,
He to my rescue came.

3 The hosts of God encamp around
The dwellings of the just ;
Deliverance He affords to all,
Who on His succor trust.

4 O make but trial of His love ;
Experience will decide
How blest are they, and only they,
Who in His truth confide.

5 Fear Him, ye saints, and you will then
Have nothing else to fear ;
Make you His service your delight,
Your wants shall be His care.

TATE AND BRADY.

My Shepherd is the living Lord,
I therefore nothing need ;
In pastures fair, near pleasant streams,
He setteth me to feed.

2 He shall convert and glad my soul,
And bring my mind in frame
To walk in paths of righteousness,
For His most holy name.

3 Yea, though I walk the vale of death,
Yet will I fear no ill :
Thy rod and staff do comfort me,
And Thou art with me still.

4 And in the presence of my foes,
My table Thou shalt spread ;
Thou wilt fill full my cup, and Thou
Anointed hast my head.

5 Through all my life Thy favor is
So frankly shown to me,
That in Thy house for evermore
My dwelling-place shall be.

THOMAS STERNHOLD.

306 *"Thou art worthy, O Lord, to receive glory and honor and power."*

WHAT equal honors shall we bring,
To Thee, O Lord our God, the Lamb,
When all the notes that angels sing
Are far inferior to Thy name?

2 Worthy is He that once was slain,
The Prince of Peace that groaned and died,
Worthy to rise, and live, and reign
At His Almighty Father's side.

3 Honor immortal must be paid
Instead of scandal and of scorn :
While glory shines around His head,
And a bright crown without a thorn.

4 Blessings for ever on the Lamb,
Who bore the curse for wretched men ;
Let angels sound His sacred name,
And every creature say, 'Amen.'

ISAAC WATTS.

ASHFORD. L. M.

Re - deem'd from guilt, redeem'd from fears, My soul en - larged, and dried my tears,

What can I do, O Lord Divine, What, to re - pay such gifts as Thine?

307 *"The Lord hath dealt bountifully with thee."*

REDEEMED from guilt, redeemed from fears,
My soul enlarged, and dried my tears,
What can I do. O Lord Divine,
What, to repay such gifts as Thine?

2 What can I do, so poor, so weak,
But from Thy hands new blessings seek,
A heart to feel Thy mercies more,
A soul to know Thee and adore?

3 O teach me at Thy feet to fall,
And yield Thee up myself, my all!
Before Thy saints my debts to own,
And live and die to Thee alone!

4 Thy Spirit, Lord, at large impart,
Expand and raise and fill my heart!
So may I hope my life shall be
Some faint return, O Lord, to Thee.
HENRY FRANCIS LYTE.

308 *"Because I live, ye shall live also."*

WHEN sins and fears prevailing rise,
And fainting hope almost expires,
To Thee, O Lord, I lift mine eyes,
To Thee I breathe my soul's desires.

2 Art Thou not mine, my living Lord?
And can my hope, my comfort die—
Fixed on Thine everlasting word,
That word which built the earth and sky?

3 If my immortal Saviour lives,
Then my immortal life is sure;
His word a firm foundation gives;
Here let me build, and rest secure.

4 Here let my faith unshaken dwell;
For ever sure the promise stands:
Not all the powers of earth or hell
Can e'er dissolve the sacred bands.

5 Here, O my soul, thy trust repose!
If Jesus is for ever mine,
Not death itself—that last of foes—
Shall break a union so divine.
ANNE STEELE.

309 *"Thy loving-kindness is better than life."*

O GOD, Thou art my God alone;
Early to Thee my soul shall cry;
A pilgrim in a land unknown,
A thirsty land whose springs are dry.

2 Yet through this rough and thorny maze,
I follow hard on Thee, my God:
Thine hand unseen upholds my ways;
I safely tread where Thou hast trod.

3 Thee, in the watches of the night,
When I remember on my bed,
Thy presence makes the darkness light,
Thy guardian wings are round my head.

4 Better than life itself Thy love,
Dearer than all beside to me;
For whom have I in heaven above,
Or what on earth compared with Thee?

5 Praise with my heart, my mind, my voice,
For all Thy mercy I will give;
My soul shall still in God rejoice;
My tongue shall bless Thee while I live.
JAMES MONTGOMERY.

OLMUTZ. S. M.

My soul, repeat His praise Whose mercies are so great; Whose anger is so slow to rise, So ready to a - bate.

310 *" Who crowneth thee with loving-kindness."*

My soul, repeat His praise
  Whose mercies are so great;
Whose anger is so slow to rise,
  So ready to abate.

2 God will not always chide;
  And, when His strokes are felt,
His strokes are fewer than our crimes,
  And lighter than our guilt.

3 High as the heavens are raised
  Above the ground we tread,
So far the riches of His grace
  Our highest thoughts exceed.

4 His power subdues our sins,
  And His forgiving love,
Far as the east is from the west,
  Doth all our guilt remove.

5 Our days are as the grass,
  Or like the morning flower:
If one sharp blast sweep o'er the field,
  It withers in an hour.

6 But Thy compassions, Lord,
  To endless years endure;
And children's children ever find
  Thy words of promise sure.
                    ISAAC WATTS.

MENDON. L. M.

Up to the Lord that reigns on high And views the na - tions from a - far,

Let ev - er - last - ing prais - es fly, And tell how large His boun - ties are.

311 *"Unto Thee, O Lord, do I lift up my soul."*

Up to the Lord that reigns on high
And views the nations from afar,
Let everlasting praises fly,
And tell how large His bounties are.

2 God, that must stoop to view the skies,
And bow to see what angels do,
Down to our earth He casts His eyes,
And bends His footsteps downward too.

3 He overrules all mortal things,
And manages our mean affairs;
On humble souls the King of kings
Bestows His counsels and His cares.

4 O, could our thankful hearts devise
A tribute equal to Thy grace,
To the third heaven our songs should rise,
And teach the golden harps Thy praise.
                    ISAAC WATTS.

ROCK OF AGES. 7s, 6 lines.

Rock of ages! cleft for me,   Let me hide myself in Thee!   Let the water and the blood, From Thy riven side which flow'd.
Be of sin the double cure, Cleanse me from its guilt and pow'r.

312   *"In the Lord Jehovah is everlasting strength."*

Rock of ages! cleft for me,
Let me hide myself in Thee!
Let the water and the blood,
From Thy riven side which flowed,
Be of sin the double cure,
Cleanse me from its guilt and power.

2 Not the labors of my hands
Can fulfil Thy laws' demands;
Could my zeal no respite know,
Could my tears for ever flow,
All for sin could not atone;
Thou must save, and Thou alone.

3 Nothing in my hand I bring;
Simply to Thy cross I cling;
Naked, come to Thee for dress;
Helpless, look to Thee for grace;
Foul, I to the Fountain fly;
Wash me, Saviour, or I die!

4 While I draw this fleeting breath,
When my eyelids close in death,
When I soar to worlds unknown,
See Thee on Thy judgment-throne;
Rock of ages, cleft for me,
Let me hide myself in Thee!

AUGUSTUS MONTAGUE TOPLADY.

WILMINGTON. C. M.

There is an eye that nev - er sleeps Beneath the wing of night;

There is an ear that nev - er shuts, When sink the beams of light.

313   *"If we ask anything according to His will, He heareth us."*

There is an eye that never sleeps
Beneath the wing of night;
There is an ear that never shuts,
When sink the beams of light.

2 There is an arm that never tires,
When human strength gives way;
There is a love that never fails,
When earthly loves decay.

3 That eye is fixed on seraph throngs;
That arm upholds the sky;

That ear is filled with angel songs;
That love is throned on high.

4 But there's a power which man can wield
When mortal aid is vain,
That eye, that arm, that love to reach,
That listening ear to gain.

5 That power is prayer, which soars on high,
Through Jesus, to the throne;
And moves the hand which moves the world,
To bring salvation down!

JOHN AIKMAN WALLACE.

Songs of praise the angels sang, Heaven with hal-le-lu-jahs rang, When Jehovah's work begun, When He spake and it was done.

314   *"Glory to God in the highest."*

Songs of praise the angels sang,
Heaven with hallelujahs rang,
When Jehovah's work begun,
When He spake and it was done.

2 Songs of praise awoke the morn,
When the Prince of Peace was born ;
Songs of praise arose when He
Captive led captivity.

3 Heaven and earth must pass away.—
Songs of praise shall crown that day :
God will make new heavens and earth,—
Songs of praise shall hail their birth.

4 And shall man alone be dumb,
Till that glorious kingdom come ?
No ! the church delights to raise
Psalms and hymns and songs of praise.

5 Saints below, with heart and voice,
Still in songs of praise rejoice ;
Learning here, by faith and love,
Songs of praise to sing above.

6 Borne upon their latest breath,
Songs of praise shall conquer death ;
Then, amid eternal joy,
Songs of praise their powers employ.
JAMES MONTGOMERY.

CONTENTMENT. S. M.

For all Thy saints, O Lord, Who strove in Thee to live, Who follow'd Thee, obey'd, ador'd,

Our grateful hymn receive. Who follow'd Thee, obey'd, ador'd, Our grateful hymn receive.

315   *"These all died in faith."*

For all Thy saints, O Lord,
Who strove in Thee to live,
Who followed Thee, obeyed, adored,
Our grateful hymn receive.

2 For all Thy saints, O Lord,
Accept our thankful cry,
Who counted Thee their great reward,
And strove in Thee to die.

3 They all in life and death,
With Thee, their Lord, in view,
Learned from Thy Holy Spirit's breath
To suffer and to do.

4 For this Thy name we bless,
And humbly pray that we
May follow them in holiness,
And live and die in Thee.
RICHARD MANT.

ORTONVILLE. C. M.

Ma - jes- tic sweetness sits enthron'd Upon the Saviour's brow; His head with radiant

glorics crown'd, His lips with grace o'erflow, His lips with grace o'erflow.

316   *"Looking unto Jesus."*

MAJESTIC sweetness sits enthroned
Upon the Saviour's brow ;
His head with radiant glories crowned,
His lips with grace o'erflow.

2 No mortal can with Him compare
Among the sons of men ;
Fairer is He than all the fair
That fill the heavenly train.

3 He saw me plunged in deep distress,
He flew to my relief ;
For me He bore the shameful cross,
And carried all my grief.

4 To Him I owe my life and breath
And all the joys I have :
He makes me triumph over death,
He saves me from the grave.

5 To heaven, the place of His abode,
He brings my weary feet ;
Shows me the glories of my God,
And makes my joy complete.

6 Since from His bounty I receive
Such proofs of love divine,
Had I a thousand hearts to give,
Lord, they should all be Thine !

SAMUEL STENNETT.

BEETHOVEN. L. M.

Trembling before Thine aw - ful throne, O Lord! in dust my sins I own:

Justice and mer - cy for my life Contend! O smile and heal the strife.

CALVARY.   7s.   6 lines, or 4 lines without repeat.

God of mer - cy, God of grace! Show the brightness of   Thy face: }
Shine up - on us, Saviour! shine; Fill Thy church with light di - vine; }

And Thy sav - ing health ex - tend Un - to earth's re - mot - est end.

317 *"God be merciful unto us, and bless us, and cause His face to shine upon us."*

GOD of mercy, God of grace !
Show the brightness of Thy face :
Shine upon us, Saviour ! shine ;
Fill Thy church with light divine ;
And Thy saving health extend
Unto earth's remotest end.

2 Let the people praise Thee, Lord !
Be by all that live adored ;
Let the nations shout and sing,
Glory to their Saviour King ;
At Thy feet their tribute pay,
And Thy holy will obey.

3 Let the people praise Thee, Lord !
Earth shall then her fruits afford ;
God to man His blessing give ;
Man to God devoted live ;
All below, and all above,
One in joy and light and love.
HENRY FRANCIS LYTE.

319 *"How shall we escape, if we neglect so great salvation."*

TREMBLING before Thine awful throne
O Lord ! in dust my sins I own ;
Justice and mercy for my life
Contend ! O smile and heal the strife !

2 The Saviour smiles ! upon my soul
New tides of hope tumultuous roll—
His voice proclaims my pardon found,
Seraphic transport wings the sound.

3 Earth has a joy unknown in heaven,
The new-born peace of sin forgiven !
Tears of such pure and sweet delight,
Ye angels ! never dimmed your sight.

318 *"I will make an everlasting covenant with you."*

THEY who seek the throne of grace,
Find that throne in every place :
If we live a life of prayer,
God is present every where.

2 In our sickness or our health,
In our want or in our wealth,
If we look to God in prayer,
God is present every where.

3 When our earthly comforts fail,
When the foes of life prevail,
'T is the time for earnest prayer ;—
God is present every where.

4 Then, my soul, in every strait
To thy Father come and wait ;
He will answer every prayer :
God is present every where.

4 Ye saw of old on chaos rise
The beauteous pillars of the skies ;
Ye know where morn exulting springs,
And evening folds her drooping wings.

5 Bright heralds of the eternal Will,
Abroad His errands ye fulfill ;
Or, throned in floods of beamy day,
Symphonious in His presence play.

6 But I amid your choirs shall shine,
And all your knowledge will be mine :
Ye on your harps must lean to hear
A secret chord that mine will bear.
AUGUSTUS LUCAS HILLHOUSE.

LOVING-KINDNESS. L. M.

Awake, my soul! in joyful lays, And sing thy great Redeemer's praise; He justly claims a song from me;

His loving-kind-ness, O how free! loving-kindness, lov-ing-kindness, His lov-ing-kind-ness, O how free!

320   *"Praise the Lord, O my soul."*

Awake, my soul, in joyful lays,
And sing thy great Redeemer's praise;
He justly claims a song from me;
His loving-kindness, O how free!

2 He saw me ruined in the fall,
Yet loved me notwithstanding all;
He saved me from my lost estate;
His loving-kindness, O how great!

3 Through mighty hosts of cruel foes
Where earth and hell my way oppose,
He safely leads my soul along;
His loving-kindness, O how strong!

4 When trouble, like a gloomy cloud,
Has gathered thick and thundered loud,
He near my soul has always stood;
His loving-kindness, O how good!

5 When I shall pass death's gloomy vale,
And life and mortal powers must fail,
O may my last expiring breath
His loving-kindness sing in death!

         SAMUEL MEDLEY.

STATE STREET. S. M.

My spirit on Thy care, Blest Saviour, I re-cline; Thou wilt not leave me to despair, For Thou art Love divine.

321   *"Into Thine hand I commit my spirit."*

My spirit on Thy care,
  Blest Saviour, I recline;
Thou wilt not leave me to despair,
  For Thou art Love divine.

2 In Thee I place my trust,
  On Thee I calmly rest;
I know Thee good, I know Thee just,
  And count Thy choice the best.

3 Whate'er events betide,
  Thy will they all perform;
Safe in Thy breast my head I hide,
  Nor fear the coming storm.

4 Let good or ill befall,
  It must be good for me;
Secure of having Thee in all,
  Of having all in Thee.

         HENRY FRANCIS LYTE.

BELMONT. C. M.

Thou Grace Di - vine, en - cir - cling all,   A shore - less, sound - less sea,

Where - in at last our souls must fall,   O Love of God, most free!

---

322 *"We have known and believed the love that God hath to us."*

Thou Grace Divine, encircling all,
A shoreless, soundless sea,
Wherein at last our souls must fall,
O Love of God, most free!

2 When over dizzy hights we go,
A soft hand blinds our eyes,
And we are guided safe and slow ;
O Love of God, most wise!

3 And though we turn us from Thy face,
And wander wide and long,
Thou hold'st us still in kind embrace ;
O Love of God, most strong!

4 But not alone Thy care we claim,
Our wayward steps to win ;
We know Thee by a dearer name,
O Love of God, within !

5 And fill'd and quickened by Thy breath,
Our souls are strong and free,
To rise o'er sin and fear and death,
O Love of God, to Thee !

ELIZA SCUDDER.

323 *"We have not an High Priest which cannot be touched with the feeling of our infirmities."*

With joy we meditate the grace
Of our High Priest above ;
His heart is made of tenderness,
And yearns with faithful love.

2 Touched with a sympathy within,
He knows our feeble frame :
He knows what sore temptations mean,
For He hath felt the same.

3 He in the days of feeble flesh
Poured out His cries and tears,
And in His measure feels afresh
What every member bears.

4 Then let our humble faith address
His mercy and His power ;
We shall obtain delivering grace,
In the distressing hour.

ISAAC WATTS.

324 *"Delight thyself in the Lord."*

O LORD, I would delight in Thee,
And on Thy care depend ;
To Thee in every trouble flee,
My best, my only Friend.

2 When all created streams are dried,
Thy fulness is the same ;
May I with this be satisfied,
And glory in Thy name !

3 No good in creatures can be found,
But may be found in Thee ;
I must have all things, and abound,
While God is God to me.

4 O that I had a stronger faith,
To look within the veil ;
To credit what my Saviour saith,
Whose word can never fail !

5 O Lord, I cast my care on Thee ;
I triumph and adore ;
Henceforth my great concern shall be
To love and please Thee more.

JOHN RYLAND.

SABBATH EVE. 7s.

Al - way in the Lord re - joice, Lift, my soul, thy heart and voice,

Lift them ho - ly, high, and pure, For His mer - cies aye endure.

325 *"Rejoice in the Lord alway, and again I say, rejoice."*

ALWAY in the Lord rejoice,
Lift, my soul, thy heart and voice,
Lift them holy, high, and pure,
For His mercies aye endure.

2 Up to heaven where He doth live,
Through the world which He doth give,
Raise thy heart and lift thy voice,
'And again I say, rejoice.'

3 Gently all thy trials take:
They are thine for Jesus' sake,
Meekly 'mid thy mercies move;
They are thine through Jesus' love.

4 All thou hast and all thou art
Own as His with thankful heart,
Use as His with heedful care,
For His coming to prepare.

5 Live in faith and live in prayer,
In His presence everywhere;
Live as angels, though on earth,
Children of the second birth.
JOHN SAMUEL BEWLEY MONSELL.

326 *"Sing unto the Lord and praise His name."*

Now begin the heavenly theme,
Sing aloud in Jesus' name;
Ye who Jesus' kindness prove,
Triumph in redeeming love.

2 Ye who see the Father's grace
Beaming in the Saviour's face,
As to Canaan on ye move,
Praise and bless redeeming love.

3 Mourning souls, dry up your tears;
Banish all your guilty fears;

See your guilt and curse remove,
Canceled by redeeming love.

4 Welcome, all by sin opprest,
Welcome to His sacred rest;
Nothing brought Him from above,
Nothing but redeeming love.

5 Hither, then, your music bring,
Strike aloud each joyful string;
Mortals, join the host above,
Join to praise redeeming love.
JOHN LANGFORD.

327 *"Heirs of God, and joint-heirs with Christ."*

CHILDREN of the heavenly King,
As ye journey, sweetly sing;
Sing your Saviour's worthy praise,
Glorious in His works and ways.

2 We are traveling home to God
In the way the fathers trod;
They are happy now, and we
Soon their happiness shall see.

3 Shout, ye little flock, and blest!
You on Jesus' throne shall rest;
There your seat is now prepared;
There your kingdom and reward.

4 Fear not, brethren; joyful stand
On the borders of your land;
Jesus Christ, your Father's Son,
Bids you undismayed go on.

5 Lord, obediently we go,
Gladly leaving all below;
Only Thou our leader be,
And we still will follow Thee.
JOHN CENNICK.

ABBE VOGLER. C. M.

O for a heart to praise my God, A heart from sin set free!
MELODY IN 1ST BASS.

A heart that al-ways feels Thy blood, So free-ly spilt for me!

---

328 *"Unite my heart to fear Thy Name."*

O FOR a heart to praise my God,
  A heart from sin set free!
A heart that always feels Thy blood,
  So freely spilt for me!

2 A heart resigned, submissive, meek,
  My dear Redeemer's throne :
Where only Christ is heard to speak,
  Where Jesus reigns alone.

3 A humble, lowly, contrite heart,
  Believing, true, and clean ;
Which neither life nor death can part
  From Him that dwells within.

4 A heart in every thought renewed,
  And full of love divine ;
Perfect, and right, and pure, and good,
  A copy, Lord, of Thine.

5 Thy nature, gracious Lord, impart ;
  Come quickly from above ;
Write Thy new name upon my heart,
  Thy new, best name of love.
                     CHARLES WESLEY.

329 *"My soul thirsteth for God."*

As pants the hart for cooling streams,
  When heated in the chase,
So longs my soul, O God, for Thee
  And Thy refreshing grace.

2 For Thee, my God, the living God,
  My thirsty soul doth pine ;

O when shall I behold Thy face,
  Thou Majesty Divine !

3 Why restless, why cast down, my soul?
  Trust God, who will employ
His aid for thee, and change these sighs
  To thankful hymns of joy.

4 Why restless, why cast down, my soul?
  Hope still, and thou shalt sing
The praise of Him, who is thy God,
  Thy health's eternal spring.
                     TATE AND BRADY.

330 *"I will never leave thee nor forsake thee."*

O HELP us, Lord ! each hour of need,
  Thy heavenly succor give ;
Help us in thought and word and deed,
  Each hour on earth we live !

2 O help us when our spirits bleed
  With contrite anguish sore ;
And when our hearts are cold and dead,
  O help us, Lord, the more !

3 O help us through the prayer of faith,
  More firmly to believe ;
For still, the more the servant hath,
  The more shall he receive.

4 O help us, Jesus, from on high !
  We know no help but Thee :
O help us so to live and die,
  As Thine in heaven to be.
                     HENRY HART MILMAN.

AUTUMN. 8s, 7s. D.

Love Divine, all love excell - ing, Joy of heav'n, to earth come down! Fix in us Thy humble dwelling, All Thy faithful mercies crown; Jesus! Thou art all compassion, Pure, un- bounded love Thou art; Visit us with Thy salva - tion, Enter ev'ry trembling heart.

331   " We have known and believed the love that God hath to us."

Love Divine. all love excelling,
   Joy of heaven, to earth come down !
Fix in us Thy humble dwelling,
   All Thy faithful mercies crown ;
Jesus ! Thou art all compassion,
   Pure, unbounded love Thou art ;
Visit us with Thy salvation,
   Enter every trembling heart.

2 Breathe, O breathe Thy loving Spirit,
   Into every troubled breast !
Let us all in Thee inherit,
   Let us find Thy promised rest ;
Come, almighty to deliver.
   Let us all Thy life receive !
Speedily return, and never,
   Never more Thy temples leave.

3 Finish then Thy new creation,
   Pure and spotless let us be :
Let us see our whole salvation
   Perfectly secured by Thee !
Changed from glory into glory.
   Till in heaven we take our place ;
Till we cast our crowns before Thee,
   Lost in wonder, love, and praise.
                    CHARLES WESLEY.

332   "Because he hath set his love upon Me, therefore will I deliver him."

Call Jehovah thy salvation,
   Rest beneath the Almighty's shade ;
In His secret habitation
   Dwell. nor ever be dismayed :
There no tumult can alarm thee,
   Thou shalt dread no hidden snare ;
Guile nor violence can harm thee,
   In eternal safeguard there.

2 From the sword at noon-day wasting,
   From the noisome pestilence,
In the depth of midnight blasting,
   God shall be thy sure defence :
Fear not thou the deadly quiver,
   When a thousand feel the blow ;
Mercy shall thy soul deliver,
   Though ten thousand be laid low.

3 Since. with pure and firm affection,
   Thou on God hast set thy love,
With the wings of His protection.
   He wil l shield thee from above :
Thou shalt call on Him in trouble,
   He will hearken, He will save,
Here, for grief reward thee double,
   Crown with life beyond the grave.
                    JAMES MONTGOMERY.

CAMBRIDGE. C. M.

Come, let us join our cheerful songs With an-gels round the throne: Ten thousand thousand are their tongues,

But all their joys are one, But all their joys are one, But all their joys are one.

333 *"Worthy is the Lamb that was slain."*

Come, let us join our cheerful songs
With angels round the throne ;
Ten thousand thousand are their tongues,
But all their joys are one.

2 'Worthy the Lamb that died,' they cry,
'To be exalted thus : '
'Worthy the Lamb,' our lips reply,
'For He was slain for us.'

3 Jesus is worthy to receive
Honor and power divine ;
And blessings, more than we can give,
Be, Lord, for ever Thine.

4 Let all that dwell above the sky,
And air, and earth, and seas,
Conspire to lift Thy glories high,
And speak Thine endless praise.

5 The whole creation join in one,
To bless the sacred name
Of Him that sits upon the throne,
And to adore the Lamb.
                                    ISAAC WATTS.

334 *"My spirit hath rejoiced in God my Saviour."*

O for a thousand tongues to sing
My dear Redeemer's praise,
The glories of my God and King,
The triumphs of His grace !

2 My gracious Master and my God,
Assist me to proclaim,
To spread through all the earth abroad,
The honors of Thy name.

3 Jesus, the name that charms our fears,
That bids our sorrows cease ;
'T is music in the sinner's ears ;
'T is life, and health, and peace !

4 He breaks the power of canceled sin ;
He sets the prisoner free ;
His blood can make the foulest clean ;
His blood availed for me.

5 He speaks, and, listening to His voice,
New life the dead receive ;
The mournful, broken hearts rejoice ;
The humble poor believe.

6 Look unto Him, ye nations ! own
Your God, ye fallen race !
Look, and be saved through faith alone,
Be justified by grace !
                                    CHARLES WESLEY.

335 *"Make a joyful noise unto the Lord, all ye lands."*

O for a shout of sacred joy
To God, the sovereign King ;
Let all the lands their tongues employ
And hymns of triumph sing.

2 Jesus, our God, ascends on high ;
His heavenly guards around
Attend Him riding through the sky,
With trumpets' joyful sound.

3 While angels shout and praise their King,
Let mortals learn their strains ;
Let all the earth His honor sing ;—
O'er all the earth He reigns.
                                    ISAAC WATTS.

SOUTHPORT. C. M.

Je - sus, these eyes have never seen That radiant form of Thine! The veil of sense hangs dark between Thy blessed face and mine!

336
"Whom unseen, we love."

JESUS, these eyes have never seen
  That radiant form of Thine!
The veil of sense hangs dark between
  Thy blessèd face and mine!

2 I see Thee not, I hear Thee not,
  Yet art Thou oft with me;
And earth hath ne'er so dear a spot,
  As where I meet with Thee.

3 Like some bright dream that comes un-
When slumbers o'er me roll, [sought,

Thine image ever fills my thought,
  And charms my ravished soul.

4 Yet though I have not seen, and still
  Must rest in faith alone;
I love Thee, dearest Lord!—and will,
  Unseen, but not unknown.

5 When death these mortal eyes shall seal,
  And still this throbbing heart,
The rending veil shall Thee reveal
  All glorious as Thou art!

RAY PALMER.

GEER. C. M.

Do not I love Thee, O my Lord? Be-hold my heart and see;

And turn the dear-est i - dol out That dares to ri - val Thee.

337
"Thou knowest that I love Thee."

Do not I love Thee, O my Lord?
  Behold my heart and see;
And turn the dearest idol out
  That dares to rival Thee.

2 Is not Thy name melodious still
  To mine attentive ear?
Doth not each pulse with pleasure bound,
  My Saviour's voice to hear?

3 Hast Thou a lamb in all Thy flock
  I would disdain to feed?

Hast Thou a foe, before whose face
  I fear Thy cause to plead?

4 Would not my heart pour forth its blood
  In honor of Thy name,
And challenge the cold hand of death
  To damp the immortal flame?

5 Thou knowest that I love Thee, Lord;
  But O! I long to soar
Far from the sphere of mortal joys,
  And learn to love Thee more.

PHILIP DODDRIDGE.

CORONAE. S. M. D.

Thou art gone up on high To mansions in the skies, And round Thy throne unceas - ing - ly The songs of praise arise

But we are lingering here With sin and care op - prest; Lord, send Thy promis'd Comforter, And lead us to Thy rest!

338 *"Waiting for the coming of our Lord Jesus Christ."*

O Thou art gone up on high
To mansions in the skies,
And round Thy throne unceasingly
The songs of praise arise :
But we are lingering here
With sin and care opprest ;
Lord, send Thy promised Comforter,
And lead us to Thy rest !

2 Thou art gone up on high :
But Thou didst first come down
Through earth's most bitter agony
To pass unto Thy crown :

And girt with griefs and fears
Our onward course must be ;
But only let that path of tears
Lead us at last to Thee !

3 Thou art gone up on high :
But Thou shalt come again
With all the bright ones of the sky
Attendant in Thy train.
O by Thy saving power
So make us live and die,
That we may stand, in that dread hour,
At Thy right hand on high !
EMMA TOKE.

HOPE. S. M.

In true and patient hope, My soul on God attend; And calmly confi - dent look up, Till His sal - va - tion send

339 *"Hope thou in God."*

O In true and patient hope,
My soul, on God attend ;
And calmly confident look up,
Till He salvation send.

2 I shall His goodness see,
While on His name I call ;
He will defend and strengthen me,
And I shall never fall.

3 Jesus, to Thee I fly,
My refuge and my tower ;
Upon Thy faithful love rely,
And find Thy saving power.

4 Trust in the Lord alone,
Who aids us from above ;
In every strait surround His throne,
And hang upon His love.
CHARLES WESLEY.

AMSTERDAM.   7s, 6s, P. M.

Rise, my soul, and stretch thy wings, Thy bet-ter portion trace;
Rise from transi - to - ry things Tow'rd heav'n, thy native place: Sun and moon and stars de - cay;

Time shall soon this earth re-move; Rise, my soul, and haste a - way To seats prepar'd a - bove.

340   *"Strangers and pilgrims on the earth."*

RISE, my soul, and stretch thy wings,
   Thy better portion trace ;
Rise from transitory things
   Toward heaven, thy native place :
Sun and moon and stars decay ;
   Time shall soon this earth remove ;
Rise, my soul, and haste away
   To seats prepared above.

2 Rivers to the ocean run,
   Nor stay in all their course ;
Fire ascending seeks the sun ;
   Both speed them to their source :

So a soul derived from God.
   Pants to view His glorious face ;
Upward tends to His abode,
   To rest in His embrace.

3 Cease, ye pilgrims, cease to mourn,
   Press onward to the prize ;
Soon our Saviour will return
   Triumphant in the skies :
Yet a season, and you know
   Happy entrance will be given,
All our sorrows left below,
   And earth exchanged for heaven.
              ROBERT SEAGRAVE.

CHORAL. L. M.

O Christ, who hast prepar'd a place For us around Thy throne of grace,

We pray Thee, lift our hearts a - bove, And draw them with the cords of love.

O Thou that hear'st the pray'r of faith, Wilt Thou not save a soul from death, That casts it-self on Thee?

I have no refuge of my own, But fly to what my Lord hath done And suffer'd once for me.

341 *"The just shall live by faith."*

O Thou that hear'st the prayer of faith,
Wilt Thou not save a soul from death,
   That casts itself on Thee?
I have no refuge of my own,
But fly to what my Lord hath done
   And suffered once for me.

2 Slain in the guilty sinner's stead,
His spotless righteousness I plead,
   And His availing blood:
Thy merit, Lord, my robe shall be,
Thy merit shall atone for me
   And bring me near to God.

3 Then save me from eternal death,
The Spirit of adoption breathe,
   His consolations send:
By Him some word of life impart,
And sweetly whisper to my heart,—
   'Thy Maker is thy Friend.'

4 The king of terrors then would be
A welcome messenger to me,
   To bid me come away:
Unclogged by earth or earthly things,
I'd mount, I'd fly, with eager wings,
   To everlasting day.
AUGUSTUS MONTAGUE TOPLADY.

342 *"I go to prepare a place for you."*

O Christ, who hast prepared a place
For us around Thy throne of grace,
We pray Thee, lift our hearts above
And draw them with the cords of love!

2 Source of all good, Thou Gracious Lord,
Art our exceeding great reward;
How transient is our present pain,
How boundless our eternal gain!

3 With open face and joyful heart,
We then shall see Thee as Thou art:
Our love shall never cease to glow,
Our praise shall never cease to flow.

4 Thy never-failing grace to prove,
A surety of Thine endless love,
Send down Thy Holy Ghost to be
The raiser of our souls to Thee.

5 O future Judge, Eternal Lord,
Thy name be hallowed and adored!

To God the Father, King of heaven,
And Holy Ghost, like praise be given.
JOHN CHANDLER.

343 *"The Spirit of God dwelleth in you."*

Come, ever-blessèd Spirit, come,
And make Thy servants' hearts Thy home:
May each a living temple be,
Hallowed for ever, Lord, to Thee!

2 Enrich that temple's holy shrine
With sevenfold gifts of grace divine:
With wisdom, light, and knowledge bless,
Strength, counsel, fear, and godliness.

3 O Trinity in Unity,
One only God and Persons Three!
In whom, through whom, by whom, we live,
To Thee we praise and glory give.

4 O grant us so to use Thy grace,
That we may see Thy glorious face,
And ever with the heavenly host
Praise Father, Son, and Holy Ghost!
CHRISTOPHER WORDSWORTH.

WILSON. 8s, 7s.

Light of those whose drear-y dwelling Bor-ders on the shades of death!

Rise on us, Thy-self re-veal-ing,— Dis-si-pate the clouds be-neath.

344 *"Arise, shine; for thy Light is come."*

LIGHT of those whose dreary dwelling
Borders on the shades of death!
Rise on us, Thyself revealing,—
Dissipate the clouds beneath.

2 Thou, of heaven and earth Creator!
In our deepest darkness rise;
Scattering all the night of nature,
Pouring day upon our eyes.

3 Still we wait for Thine appearing;
Life and joy Thy beams impart,

Chasing all our fears, and cheering
Every poor benighted heart.

4 Save us, in Thy great compassion,
O Thou mild, pacific Prince!
Give the knowledge of salvation,
Give the pardon of our sins.

5 By Thine all-restoring merit,
Every burdened soul release;
Every weary, wandering spirit
Guide into Thy perfect peace.

CHARLES WESLEY.

OFFERTORIUM. 6s, 5s. D.

Saviour, blessed Sav-iour, Lis-ten while we sing, Hearts and voi-ces rais-ing Praises to our King.

All we have we of-fer, All we hope to be, Bo-dy, soul, and spi-rit, All we yield to Thee.

INTEGER VITAE. 3s, 6s.

O Ho-ly Saviour, Friend un-seen, The faint, the weak, on Thee may lean:

Help me throughout life's varying scene, By faith to cling to Thee!

345 *" Who shall separate us from the love of Christ ?"*

O HOLY Saviour, Friend unseen,
The faint, the weak, on Thee may lean:
Help me throughout life's varying scene,
By faith to cling to Thee !

2 Though faith and hope awhile be tried,
I ask not, need not, aught beside ;
How safe, how calm, how satisfied,
The souls that cling to Thee !

3 They fear not life's rough storms to brave,
Since Thou art near, and strong to save :
Nor shudder e'en at death's dark wave ;
Because they cling to Thee !

4 Blest is my lot, whate'er befall :
What can disturb me, who appall,
While as my strength, my rock, my all,
Saviour ! I cling to Thee !

CHARLOTTE ELLIOTT.

346 *"Every day will I give thanks unto Thee: and praise Thy name for ever and ever."*

SAVIOUR, blessèd Saviour,
Listen while we sing,
Hearts and voices raising
Praises to our King.
All we have we offer,
All we hope to be,
Body, soul, and spirit,
All we yield to Thee.

2 Great and ever greater
Are Thy mercies here,
True and everlasting
Are the glories there,
Where no pain, or sorrow,
Toil, or care, is known,
Where the angel-legions
Circle round Thy throne.

3 Dark and ever darker
Was the wintry past,
Now a ray of gladness
O'er our path is cast.

Every day that passeth,
Every hour that flies,
Tells of love unfeigned,
Love that never dies.

4 Clearer still and clearer
Dawns the light from heaven,
In our sadness bringing
News of sin forgiven.
Life has lost its shadows,
Pure the light within ;
Thou hast shed Thy radiance
On a world of sin.

5 Onward, ever onward,
Journeying o'er the road
Worn by saints before us,
Journeying on to God ;
Leaving all behind us
May we hasten on,
Backward never looking
Till the prize is won.

GODFREY THRING.

THACHER. S. M.

Be - hold what won - drous grace The Fa - ther hath bestow'd

On sin - ners of a mor - tal race, To call them sons of God!

347 *"Now are we the sons of God."*
BEHOLD what wondrous grace
The Father hath bestowed
On sinners of a mortal race,
To call them sons of God!

2 'Tis no surprising thing
That we should be unknown ;
The Jewish world knew not their King,
God's Everlasting Son.

3 Nor doth it yet appear
How great we must be made ;
But when we see our Saviour here,
We shall be like our Head.

4 A hope so much divine
May trials well endure,
May purge our souls from sense and sin,
As Christ the Lord is pure.

5 If in my Father's love
I share a filial part,
Send down Thy Spirit like a dove,
To rest upon my heart.

6 We would no longer lie
Like slaves beneath the throne ;
Our faith shall Abba, Father, cry,
And Thou the kindred own.
ISAAC WATTS.

348 *"On Thee do I wait all the day."*
To God, in whom I trust,
I lift my heart and voice ;
O let me not be put to shame,
Nor let my foes rejoice.

2 To me Thy truth impart,
And lead me in Thy way :

For Thou art He that brings me help ;
On Thee I wait all day.

3 Thy mercies and Thy love,
O Lord, recall to mind ;
And graciously continue still,
As Thou wert ever, kind.

4 Let all my youthful crimes
Be blotted out by Thee ;
And for Thy wondrous goodness' sake,
In mercy think on me.

5 His mercy and His truth
The righteous Lord displays,
In bringing wandering sinners home,
And teaching them His ways.
TATE AND BRADY.

349 *"They shall see God."*
BLEST are the pure in heart,
For they shall see our God :
The secret of the Lord is theirs,
Their soul is Christ's abode.

2 The Lord, who left the heavens
Our life and peace to bring,
To dwell in lowliness with men,
Their Pattern and their King :

3 Still to the lowly soul
He doth Himself impart,
And for His dwelling and His throne
Chooseth the pure in heart.

4 Lord, we Thy presence seek ;
May ours this blessing be ;
Give us a pure and lowly heart,
A temple meet for Thee !
JOHN KEBLE.

While my Redeemer's near, My shepherd and my guide, I bid farewell to anxious fear: My wants are all supplied.

350 *"The Lord is my shepherd: I shall not want."*

WHILE my Redeemer's near,
My shepherd and my guide,
I bid farewell to anxious fear :
My wants are all supplied.

2 To ever-fragrant meads,
Where rich abundance grows,
His gracious hand indulgent leads,
And guards my sweet repose.

3 Dear Shepherd, if I stray,
My wandering feet restore ;
To Thy fair pastures guide my way,
And let me rove no more.
ANNE STEELE.

351 *"Your life is hid with Christ in God."*

STILL, still with Thee, my God,
I would desire to be :

By day, by night, at home, abroad,
I would be still with Thee.

2 With Thee, when dawn comes in,
And calls me back to care,
Each day returning to begin
With Thee, my God, in prayer.

3 With Thee, when day is done,
And evening calms the mind ;
The setting, as the rising sun
With Thee my heart would find.

4 With Thee, in Thee, by faith
Abiding I would be ;
By day, by night, in life, in death,
I would be still with Thee.
JAMES DRUMMOND BURNS.

SESSIONS. L. M.

Faith is a liv-ing pow'r from heav'n, Which grasps the promise God has giv'n,

Se-cure-ly fix'd on Christ a-lone, A trust that can-not be o'erthrown.

352 *"Without faith it is impossible to please God."*

FAITH is a living power from heaven
Which grasps the promise God has given ;
A trust that cannot be o'erthrown,—
Securely fixed on Christ alone.

2 Faith finds in Christ whate'er we need,
To save and strengthen, guide and feed ;
Strong in His grace it joys to share
His cross, in hope His crown to wear.

3 Faith to the conscience whispers peace,
And bids the mourner's sighing cease ;
By faith the children's right we claim,
And call upon our Father's name.

4 Such faith in us, O God, implant,
And to our prayers Thy favor grant ;
In Jesus Christ, Thy saving Son,
Who is our fount of health alone.

ST. GERTRUDE.   6s, 5s, D.

Onward, Christian sol - diers, Marching as to war, With the cross of Je - sus Go - ing on before.

Christ, the roy - al Mas - ter, Leads against the foe; Forward in - to bat - tle, See, His banners go.

CHORUS.

Onward, Christian sol - diers, Marching as to war, With the cross of Jesus Going on be - fore.

With the   cross of   Jesus

353   *"Of whom the whole family in Heaven and earth is named."*

ONWARD, Christian soldiers,
   Marching as to war,
With the cross of Jesus
   Going on before.
Christ, the royal Master,
   Leads against the foe ;
Forward into battle,
   See, His banners go.—CHO.

2 Like a mighty army,
   Moves the church of God ;
Brothers, we are treading
   Where the saints have trod ;
We are not divided,
   All one body we,
One in hope and doctrine,
   One in charity.—CHO.

3 Crowns and thrones may perish,
   Kingdoms rise and wane,
But the Church of Jesus
   Constant will remain ;
Gates of hell can never
   'Gainst that Church prevail ;
We have Christ's own promise,
   And that cannot fail.—CHO.

4 Onward, then, ye people,
   Join our happy throng ;
Blend with ours your voices
   In the triumph-song ;
Glory, laud, and honor,
   Unto Christ the King ;
This through countless ages,
   Men and angels sing.—CHO.

SAMUEL BARING GOULD.

MAIKAMMER. C. M.

My God, how wonderful Thou art, Thy majes - ty how bright, How beautiful Thy mercy seat, In depths of burning light.

TRUST. 8s, 7s.

God is love; His mer-cy brightens All the path in which we rove;

Bliss He wakes, and woe He light-ens: God is wis-dom, God is love.

354 *"With the Lord there is mercy."*

God is love ; His mercy brightens
All the path in which we rove ;
Bliss He wakes, and woe He lightens :
God is wisdom, God is love.

2 Chance and change are busy ever ;
Man decays, and ages move,
But His mercy waneth never :
God is wisdom, God is love.

3 E'en the hour that darkest seemeth
Will His changeless goodness prove ;
From the mist His brightness streameth :
God is wisdom, God is love.

4 He with earthly cares entwineth
Hope and comfort from above ;
Everywhere His glory shineth :
God is wisdom, God is love.

JOHN BOWRING

355 *"The High and Lofty One that inhabiteth eternity, whose name is Holy."*

My God, how wonderful Thou art,
Thy majesty how bright,
How beautiful Thy mercy-seat
In depths of burning light !

2 How dread are Thine eternal years,
O Everlasting Lord !
By prostrate spirits day and night
Incessantly adored !

3 How beautiful, how beautiful
The sight of Thee must be,
Thine endless wisdom, boundless power,
And awful purity !

4 O how I fear Thee, living God,
With deepest, tenderest fears,
And worship Thee with trembling hope
And penitential tears !

5 Yet I may love Thee too, O Lord !
Almighty as Thou art ;
For Thou hast stooped to ask of me
The love of this poor heart.

6 O then this worse than worthless heart
In pity deign to take,
And make it love Thee for Thyself
And for Thy glory's sake !

FREDERICK WILLIAM FABER.

356 *"Praise waiteth for Thee, O God, in Zion."*

Thy praise alone, O Lord, doth reign
In Zion Thine own hill ;
Their vows to Thee they there maintain
And promises fulfill.

2 For that Thou dost their prayers still hear
And dost thereto agree,
The people all, both far and near,
With trust shall come to Thee.

3 Our wicked life so far exceeds
That we shall fall therein ;
But, Lord, forgive our great misdeeds,
And purge us from our sin.

4 The man is blest whom Thou dost choose
Within Thy courts to dwell ;
Thy house and temple he shall use
With pleasures that excel.

STERNHOLD AND HOPKINS.

URANIA. 8s, 7s, 4s.

Guide me, O Thou great Je - ho - vah, Pil -grim through this barren land;

I am weak, but Thou art mighty, Hold me with Thy pow'rful hand;

Bread of heaven, Bread of heaven, Feed me till I want no more.

357   *"He hath remembered His covenant forever."*

GUIDE me, O Thou great Jehovah,
  Pilgrim through this barren land;
I am weak, but Thou art mighty,
  Hold me with Thy powerful hand;
    Bread of heaven,
  Feed me till I want no more.

2 Open now the crystal fountain,
  Whence the healing waters flow;
Let the fiery cloudy pillar

Lead me all my journey through:
    Strong Deliverer,
  Be Thou still my strength and shield.

3 When I tread the verge of Jordan,
  Bid the swelling stream divide;
Death of death, and hell's destruction,
  Land me safe on Canaan's side;
    Songs of praises
  I will ever give to Thee.

WILLIAM WILLIAMS.

HARTEL. L. M.

As when the weary traveler gains The hight of some o'erlook - ing hill,

His heart revives, if, 'cross the plains, He eyes his home tho' distant still;—

358   *"We walk by faith, not by sight."*

As when the weary traveler gains
  The hight of some o'erlooking hill,
His heart revives, if, 'cross the plains,
  He eyes his home though distant still;—

2 So when the Christian pilgrim views,
  By faith, his mansion in the skies;

The sight his fainting strength renews,
  And wings his speed to reach the prize.

3 'Tis there,' he says, 'I am to dwell
  With Jesus in the realms of day:
Then I shall bid my cares farewell,
  And He will wipe my tears away.'

JOHN NEWTON.

FELIX. 7s, 6s.

In heaven-ly love a-bid-ing, No change my heart shall fear; And safe is such con-fid-ing,

For nothing changes here. The storm may roar without me, My heart may low be laid, But God is round about me,

The storm may roar without me,

a-bout ...

And can I be dismay'd? But God is round a-bout me, And can I be dismay'd?

I be dismayed.

. me, But God is round a-bout me, And can I be dismay'd?

359 *"I will fear no evil, for Thou art with me."*

In heavenly love abiding,
  No change my heart shall fear;
And safe is such confiding,
  For nothing changes here.
The storm may roar without me,
  My heart may low be laid,
But God is round about me,
  And can I be dismayed?

2 Wherever He may guide me,
  No want shall turn me back;
My Shepherd is beside me,
  And nothing can I lack.
His wisdom ever waketh,
  His sight is never dim,
He knows the way He taketh,
  And I will walk with Him.

3 Green pastures are before me,
  Which yet I have not seen;
Bright skies will soon be o'er me,
  Where darkest clouds have been.

My hope I cannot measure,
  My path to life is free,
My Saviour has my treasure,
  And He will walk with me.
                    ANNA LÆTITIA WARING.

360 *"The Lord is my Light and my Salvation."*

God is my strong salvation,
  What foe have I to fear?
In darkness and temptation,
  My Light, my Help is near:
Though hosts encamp around me,
  Firm to the fight I stand;
What terror can confound me,
  With God at my right hand?

2 Place on the Lord reliance,
  My soul, with courage wait;
His truth be thine alliance,
  When faint and desolate:
His might thine heart shall strengthen,
  His love thy joy increase;
Mercy thy days shall lengthen;
  The Lord will give thee peace.
                    JAMES MONTGOMERY.

Christian Joy and Hope.

LAUDA SION. 8s, 7s.

Come, Thou Fount of ev - ery blessing, Tune my heart to sing Thy grace;
Streams of mer - cy nev - er ceasing, Call for songs of loudest praise.

361 *"Grace and truth came by Jesus Christ."*

COME, Thou Fount of every blessing,
Tune my heart to sing Thy grace;
Streams of mercy never ceasing,
Call for songs of loudest praise.

2 Teach me some melodious sonnet,
Sung by flaming tongues above;
Praise the mount. I'm fixed upon it,
Mount of God's unchanging love.

3 Jesus sought me, when a stranger,
Wandering from the fold of God;

He, to rescue me from danger,
Interposed His precious blood.

4 O! to grace how great a debtor,
Daily I'm constrained to be:
Let that grace now, like a fetter,
Bind my wandering heart to Thee!

5 Prone to wander, Lord, I feel it,
Prone to leave the God I love:
Here's my heart. O take and seal it,
Seal it from Thy courts above!

ROBERT ROBINSON.

MATILDA. C. M.

Far from the world, O Lord, I flee, From strife and tumult far; From scenes where Satan wages still His most successful war.

362 *"I flee unto Thee to hide me."*

FAR from the world, O Lord, I flee,
From strife and tumult far;
From scenes where Satan wages still
His most successful war.

2 The calm retreat, the silent shade,
With prayer and praise agree,
And seem by Thy sweet bounty made
For those who follow Thee.

3 There, if Thy Spirit touch the soul,
And grace her mean abode,

O with what peace, and joy, and love,
Does she commune with God!

4 Author and Guardian of my life;
Sweet Source of light divine;
And, all harmonious names in one,
My Saviour! Thou art mine!

5 What thanks I owe Thee, and what love,
A boundless, endless store,—
Shall echo through the realms above
When time shall be no more!

WILLIAM COWPER.

HEBER. C. M.

There is a safe and se-cret place Beneath the wings di-vine,

Re-serv'd for all the heirs of grace; O be that re-fuge mine!

363 *"Thou shalt hide them in the secret of Thy presence."*

O THERE is a safe and secret place
  Beneath the wings divine,
Reserved for all the heirs of grace;
  O be that refuge mine!

2 The least and feeblest there may bide,
  Uninjured and unawed ;
While thousands fall on every side.
  He rests secure in God.

3 He feeds in pastures large and fair
  Of love and truth divine :
O child of God, O glory's heir,
  How rich a lot is thine !

4 A hand almighty to defend,
  An ear for every call.
An honored life, a peaceful end.
  And heaven to crown it all !
               HENRY FRANCIS LYTE.

364 *"I have made a covenant with My chosen."*

O UNITE, my roving thoughts, unite
  In silence soft and sweet :
And thou, my soul, sit gently down
  At thy great Sovereign's feet.

2 Jehovah's awful voice is heard.
  Yet gladly I attend ;
For lo ! the Everlasting God
  Proclaims Himself my friend.

3 Harmonious accents to my soul
  The sounds of peace convey ;

The tempest at His word subsides,
  And winds and seas obey.

4 By all its joys, I charge my heart,
  To grieve His love no more ;
But charmed by melody divine,
  To give its follies o'er.
               PHILIP DODDRIDGE.

365 *"Whosoever shall call upon the name of the Lord shall be saved."*

APPROACH. my soul, the mercy-seat
  Where Jesus answers prayer ;
There humbly fall before His feet,
  For none can perish there.

2 Thy promise is my only plea,
  With this I venture nigh ;
Thou callest burdened souls to Thee,
  And such, O Lord, am I.

3 Bowed down beneath a load of sin,
  By Satan sorely prest,
By war without and fears within,
  I come to Thee for rest.

4 Be Thou my shield and hiding-place.
  That, sheltered near Thy side.
I may my fierce accuser face,
  And tell him Thou hast died !

5 O wondrous love ! to bleed and die,
  To bear the cross and shame,
That guilty sinners, such as I.
  Might plead Thy gracious name !
               JOHN NEWTON.

SEASONS. S. M.

Our Heavenly Father calls, And Christ invites us near; With both, our friendship shall be sweet, And our communion dear.

366 *"Our fellowship is with the Father, and with His Son Jesus Christ."*

Our Heavenly Father calls,
   And Christ invites us near ;
With both, our friendship shall be sweet,
   And our communion dear.

2 God pities all our griefs :
   He pardons every day ;
Almighty to protect our souls,
   And wise to guide our way.

3 How large His bounties are !
   What various stores of good,
Diffused from our Redeemer's hand,
   And purchased with His blood !

4 Jesus, our living Head,
   We bless Thy faithful care ;
Our Advocate before the throne,
   And our Forerunner there.

5 Here fix, my roving heart !
   Here wait, my warmest love !

Till the communion be complete,
   In nobler scenes above.
                  PHILIP DODDRIDGE.

367 *"And God said, Ask what I shall give thee."*
Behold the throne of grace !
   The promise calls us near :
There Jesus shows a smiling face,
   And waits to answer prayer.

2 That rich, atoning blood,
   Which sprinkled round we see,
Provides for those who come to God
   An all-prevailing plea.

3 Thine image, Lord ! bestow,
   Thy presence and Thy love :
We ask to serve Thee here below,
   And reign with Thee above.

4 Teach us to live by faith,
   Conform our will to Thine,
Let us victorious be in death,
   And then in glory shine.
                  JOHN NEWTON.

SHARON. C. M.

My God! the Spring of all my joys, The life of my de - lights,

The glo - ry of my bright - est days, And comfort of my nights.

The gold-en gates are lift-ed up, The doors are opened wide,

The King of glo-ry is gone in Un-to His Father's side.

---

368 *"I will come again and receive you unto Myself."*

The golden gates are lifted up,
The doors are opened wide,
The King of glory is gone in
Unto His Father's side.

2 Thou art gone up before us, Lord,
To make for us a place,
That we may be where now Thou art,
And look upon God's face.

3 And ever on Thine earthly path
A gleam of glory lies;
A light still breaks behind the cloud
That veiled Thee from our eyes.

4 Lift up our hearts, lift up our minds,
Let Thy dear grace be given,
That while we tarry here below,
Our treasure be in heaven!

5 That where Thou art, at God's right hand,
Our hope, our love may be;
Dwell Thou in us, that we may dwell
For evermore in Thee.
CECIL FRANCES ALEXANDER.

369 *"The Lord is thy Keeper."*

How are Thy servants blest, O Lord,
How sure is their defence!
Eternal Wisdom is their guide,
Their help, Omnipotence.

2 In foreign realms and lands remote,
Supported by Thy care,
Through burning climes they pass unhurt,
And breathe in tainted air.

3 When by the dreadful tempest borne
High on the broken wave,
They know Thou art not slow to hear,
Nor impotent to save.

4 The storm is laid, the winds retire,
Obedient to Thy will;
The sea, that roars at Thy command,
At Thy command is still.

5 In midst of dangers, fears, and deaths,
Thy goodness we'll adore;
And praise Thee for Thy mercies past,
And humbly hope for more.

6 Our life, while Thou preserv'st that life,
Thy sacrifice shall be;
And death, when death shall be our lot,
Shall join our souls to Thee.
JOSEPH ADDISON.

370 *"The Lord is my light and my salvation."*

My God! the Spring of all my joys,
The life of my delights;
The glory of my brightest days,
And comfort of my nights!

2 In darkest shades, if He appear,
My dawning is begun!
He is my soul's sweet morning star,
And He my rising sun.

3 The opening heavens around me shine
With beams of sacred bliss,
While Jesus shows His heart is mine,
And whispers I am His.

4 My soul would leave this heavy clay
At that transporting word,
Run up with joy the shining way,
To embrace my dearest Lord.

5 Fearless of hell and ghastly death,
I'd break through every foe;
The wings of love, and arms of faith,
Should bear me conqueror through.
ISAAC WATTS.

BRADFORD. C. M.

I know that my Re-deem-er lives, And ev-er prays for me;

A to-ken of His love He gives, A pledge of lib-er-ty.

---

371   *" Ye shall know the truth, and the truth shall make you free."*

I KNOW that my Redeemer lives,
  And ever prays for me ;
A token of His love He gives,
  A pledge of liberty.

2 I find Him lifting up my head ;
  He brings salvation near ;
His presence makes me free indeed,
  And He will soon appear.

3 He wills that I should holy be ;
  What can withstand His will?
The counsel of His grace in me
  He surely shall fulfill.

4 Jesus, I hang upon Thy word ;
  I steadfastly believe
Thou wilt return, and claim me, Lord,
  And to Thyself receive.

5 When God is mine, and I am His.
  Of paradise possest,
I taste unutterable bliss
  And everlasting rest.

                  CHARLES WESLEY.

372   *"If thou canst believe, all things are possible."*

LORD, I believe ; Thy power I own,
  Thy word I would obey ;
I wander comfortless and lone,
  When from Thy truth I stray.

2 Lord, I believe ; but gloomy fears
  Sometimes bedim my sight ;

I look to Thee with prayers and tears,
  And cry for strength and light.

3 Lord, I believe ; but oft, I know,
  My faith is cold and weak :
My weakness strengthen, and bestow
  The confidence I seek !

4 Yes ! I believe ; and only Thou
  Can give my soul relief :
Lord ! to Thy truth my spirit bow ;
  Help Thou mine unbelief!

           JOHN REYNELL WREFORD.

373   *"God is our Refuge and Strength."*

MY God, 't is to Thy mercy-seat
  My soul for shelter flies :
'T is here I find a safe retreat,
  When storms and tempests rise.

2 My cheerful hope can never die,
  If Thou, my God, art near ;
Thy grace can raise my comforts high,
  And banish every fear.

3 My great Protector and my Lord,
  Thy constant aid impart ;
And let Thy kind, Thy gracious word
  Sustain my trembling heart.

4 O never let my soul remove
  From this divine retreat ;
Still let me trust Thy power and love,
  And dwell beneath Thy feet.

                  ANNE STEELE.

PRAYER. C. M.

Pray'r is the soul's sincere desire, Un-utter'd, or exprest; The motion of a hidden fire That trembles in the breast.

374 *"Continuing instant in prayer."*

PRAYER is the soul's sincere desire,
Unuttered, or exprest;
The motion of a hidden fire
That trembles in the breast.

2 Prayer is the burden of a sigh,
The falling of a tear;
The upward glancing of the eye,
When none but God is near.

3 Prayer is the simplest form of speech
That infant lips can try;
Prayer the sublimest strains that reach
The Majesty on high.

4 Prayer is the contrite sinner's voice,
Returning from his ways;
While angels in their songs rejoice,
And cry—'Behold, he prays.'

5 Prayer is the Christian's vital breath,
The Christian's native air,
His watchword at the gates of death;
He enters heaven with prayer.

6 The saints, in prayer, appear as one
In word and deed and mind;
While with the Father and the Son
Sweet fellowship they find.

7 Nor prayer is made by man alone:
The Holy Spirit pleads;
And Jesus, on the eternal throne,
For sinners intercedes.

8 O Thou, by whom we come to God—
The Life, the Truth, the Way;
The path of prayer Thyself hast trod;
Lord, teach us how to pray.
JAMES MONTGOMERY.

375 *"The just shall live by faith."*

FAITH adds new charms to earthly bliss,
And saves us from its snares;
Its aid in every duty brings,
And softens all our cares.

2 It heals the deadly thirst of sin;
It lights the sacred fire
Of love to God and heavenly things,
And feeds the pure desire.

3 The wounded conscience knows its power,
The healing balm to give;
That balm the saddest heart can cheer,
And make the dying live.

4 It shows the precious promise, sealed
With the Redeemer's blood;
And helps our feeble hope to rest
Upon a faithful God.

5 Wide it unveils celestial worlds,
Where deathless pleasures reign;
And bids us seek our portion there,
Nor bids us seek in vain.
DANIEL TURNER.

376 *"A broken and contrite heart, O God, Thou wilt not despise."*

LORD, when we bend before Thy throne,
And our confessions pour,
Teach us to feel the sins we own,
And hate what we deplore.

2 Our broken spirits, pitying, see;
True penitence impart;
And let a kindling glance from Thee
Beam hope upon the heart.

3 When we disclose our wants in prayer,
May we our wills resign;
And not a thought our bosom share
Which is not wholly Thine.

4 Let faith each weak petition fill,
And waft it to the skies,
And teach our hearts 'tis goodness still
That grants it, or denies.
JOSEPH DACRE CARLYLE.

BRATTLE STREET. C. M. D.

While Thee I seek, protecting Pow'r, Be my vain wishes still'd; And may this con - se - cra - ted hour With bet - ter hopes be fill'd. Thy love the pow'rs of tho't bestow'd! To Thee my tho'ts would soar; Thy mercy o'er my life has flow'd; That mercy I adore.

377 *"His mercy endureth for ever."*

WHILE Thee I seek, protecting Power,
　Be my vain wishes stilled;
And may this consecrated hour
　With better hopes be filled.
Thy love the powers of thought bestowed!
　To Thee my thoughts would soar;
Thy mercy o'er my life has flowed;
　That mercy I adore.

2 In each event of life, how clear
　Thy ruling hand I see!
Each blessing to my soul more dear,
　Because conferred by Thee.

In every joy that crowns my days,
　In every pain I bear,
My heart shall find delight in praise,
　Or seek relief in prayer.

3 When gladness wings my favored hour,
　Thy love my thoughts shall fill;
Resigned, when storms of sorrow lower,
　My soul shall meet Thy will.
My lifted eye, without a tear,
　The gathering storm shall see;
My steadfast heart shall know no fear;
　That heart shall rest on Thee.
　　　　　　　　　HELEN MARIA WILLIAMS.

ARLINGTON. C. M.

When I can read my title clear To mansions in the skies, I bid farewell to every fear, And wipe my weeping eyes.

SEMPER FIDELIS. C. M. D.

Thou art my hiding-place, O Lord! In Thee I put my trust, . . . Encouraged by Thy

ho - ly word,—A feeble child of dust. I have no ar - gu - ment be - side, I

urge no other plea; And 't is enough the Saviour died, The Saviour died for me!

378 *" Who loved me and gave Himself for me."*

Thou art my hiding-place, O Lord!
  In Thee I put my trust,
Encouraged by Thy holy word,
  A feeble child of dust.
I have no argument beside,
  I urge no other plea;
And 't is enough the Saviour died,
  The Saviour died for me!

2 When storms of fierce temptation beat
  And furious foes assail,
My refuge is the mercy-seat,
  My hope within the veil.

From strife of tongues and bitter words,
  My spirit flies to Thee;
Joy to my heart the thought affords,
  ' My Saviour died for me !'

3 And when Thine awful voice commands
  This body to decay,
And life, in its last lingering sands,
  Is ebbing fast away ;—
Then, though it be in accents weak,
  My voice shall call on Thee,
And ask for strength in death to speak,
  ' My Saviour died for me !'

THOMAS RAFFLES.

379 *" Your joy no man taketh from you."*

When I can read my title clear
  To mansions in the skies,
I bid farewell to every fear,
  And wipe my weeping eyes.

2 Should earth against my soul engage,
  And hellish darts be hurled,
Then I can smile at Satan's rage,
  And face a frowning world.

3 Let cares like a wild deluge come,
  And storms of sorrow fall ;
May I but safely reach my home,
  My God, my heaven, my all :—

4 There shall I bathe my weary soul
  In seas of heavenly rest ;
And not a wave of trouble roll
  Across my peaceful breast.

ISAAC WATTS.

SELDON. C. M.

O Gift of gifts! O grace of faith! My God, how can it be That Thou who

hast discerning love Dost give that gift to me! Dost give that gift to me!

---

380 *"Who is he that overcometh the world, but he that believeth that Jesus is the Son of God?"*

O GIFT of gifts! O grace of faith!
My God, how can it be
That Thou who hast discerning love
Dost give that gift to me!

2 How many hearts Thou mightst have had
More innocent than mine!
How many souls more worthy far
Of that sweet touch of Thine!

3 Ah Grace! into unlikeliest hearts
It is thy boast to come,
The glory of thy light to find
In darkest spots a home.

4 How can they live, how will they die,
How bear the cross of grief,
Who have not got the light of faith,
The courage of belief!

5 The crowd of cares, the weightiest cross,
Seem trifles less than light;
Earth looks so little and so low,
When faith shines full and bright.

6 O happy, happy that I am!
If thou canst be, O Faith,
The treasure that thou art in life,
What wilt thou be in death!

7 Thy choice, O God of goodness, then,
I lovingly adore;
O give me grace to keep Thy grace,
And grace to merit more.
FREDERICK WILLIAM FABER.

381 *"Come ye, and let us walk in the light of the Lord."*

WALK in the light! so shalt thou know
That fellowship of love
His Spirit only can bestow
Who reigns in light above.

2 Walk in the light! and thou shalt own
Thy darkness past away,
Because in thee that light hath shone,
Which grows to perfect day.

3 Walk in the light! and thine shall be
A path, though thorny, bright;
For God by grace shall dwell in thee,
And God Himself is light!
BERNARD BARTON.

382 *"My soul, wait thou only upon God."*

AUTHOR of good! to Thee we turn:
Thine ever-wakeful eye
Alone can all our wants discern,
Thine hand alone supply.

2 O let Thy love within us dwell,
Thy fear our footsteps guide;
That love shall vainer loves expel,
That fear, all fears beside.

3 And since, by passion's force subdued,
Too oft, with stubborn will,
We blindly shun the latent good,
And grasp the specious ill;—

4 Not what we wish, but what we want,
Let mercy still supply:
The good we ask not, Father, grant!
The ill we ask, deny!
JAMES MERRICK.

ERIE. 8s, 7s. D.

What a Friend we have in Jesus, All our sins and griefs to bear! What a priv-i-lege to car-ry
All because we do not car-ry

Fine.   *Dal Segno.*

Ev - 'ry thing to God in pray'r! O, what peace we of-ten forfeit, O, what needless pain we bear,
Ev - 'ry thing to God in pray'r!

383 *"There is a friend that sticketh closer than a brother."*

WHAT a Friend we have in Jesus,
   All our sins and griefs to bear!
What a privilege to carry
   Every thing to God in prayer!
O, what peace we often forfeit,
   O, what needless pain we bear,
All because we do not carry
   Every thing to God in prayer!

2 Have we trials and temptations?
   Is there trouble anywhere?
We should never be discouraged,—
   Take it to the Lord in prayer.
Can we find a friend so faithful,
   Who will all our sorrows share?
Jesus knows our every weakness—
   Take it to the Lord in prayer.
      HORATIUS BONAR.

384 *"The mercy of the Lord is from everlasting to everlasting."*

THERE's a wideness in God's mercy,
   Like the wideness of the sea:
There's a kindness in His justice,
   Which is more than liberty.
There is welcome for the sinner,
   And more graces for the good:
There is mercy with the Saviour;
   There is healing in His blood.

2 There is no place where earth's sorrows
   Are more felt than up in heaven;
There is no place where earth's failings
   Have such kindly judgment given.

There is plentiful redemption
   In the blood that has been shed;
There is joy for all the members
   In the sorrows of the Head.

3 For the love of God is broader
   Than the measure of man's mind;
And the heart of the Eternal
   Is most wonderfully kind.
If our love were but more simple,
   We should take Him at His word;
And our lives would be all sunshine
   In the sweetness of our Lord.
      FREDERICK WILLIAM FABER.

385 *"Thou wilt keep him in perfect peace whose heart is stayed on Thee."*

GENTLY, Lord, O gently lead us
   Through this lonely vale of tears:
Thro' the changes Thou'st decreed us,
   Till our last great change appears.
When temptation's darts assail us,
   When in devious paths we stray,
Let Thy goodness never fail us,
   Lead us in Thy perfect way.

2 In the hour of pain and anguish,
   In the hour when death draws near,
Suffer not our hearts to languish,—
   Suffer not our souls to fear.
And, when mortal life is ended,
   Bid us on Thy bosom rest,
Till, by angel-bands attended,
   We awake among the blest.
      THOMAS HASTINGS.

ALLELUIA. 8s, 7s, D.

Mighty God! while angels bless Thee, May a mortal lisp Thy name? Lord of men, as well as angels! Thou art ev'ry creature's theme:

Lord of every land and nation! Ancient of e - ternal days! Sounded thro' the wide creation, Be Thy just and awful praise.

386   *"God hath highly exalted Him."*

MIGHTY God! while angels bless Thee,
  May a mortal lisp Thy name?
Lord of men, as well as angels!
  Thou art every creature's theme:
Lord of every land and nation!
  Ancient of eternal days!
Sounded through the wide creation,
  Be Thy just and awful praise.

2 For the grandeur of Thy nature,—
  Grand, beyond a seraph's thought;
For the wonders of creation,
  Works with skill and kindness wrought;
For Thy providence, that governs
  Through Thine empire's wide domain,
Wings an angel, guides a sparrow;
  Blessèd be Thy gentle reign.

·3 For Thy rich, Thy free redemption,
  Bright, tho' veiled in darkness long,
Thought is poor, and poor expression;
  Who can sing that wondrous song?
Brightness of the Father's glory!
  Shall Thy praise unuttered lie?
Break, my tongue, such guilty silence,
  Sing the Lord who came to die:—

4 From the highest throne of glory,
  To the cross of deepest woe, .
Came to ransom guilty captives!—
  Flow, my praise! forever flow:
Re-ascend, immortal Saviour!
  Leave Thy footstool, take Thy throne ·
Thence return and reign forever;—
  Be the kingdom all Thine own!
                    ROBERT ROBINSON.

MEAR. C. M.

O could I find, from day to day, A nearness to my God, Then would my hours glide sweet away While leaning on His word.

387   *"Our conversation is in heaven."*

O COULD I find, from day to day,
  A nearness to my God,
Then would my hours glide sweet away
  While leaning on His word.

2 Lord, I desire with Thee to live
  Anew from day to day,
In joys the world can never give,
  Nor ever take away.

3 Blest Jesus, come and rule my heart,
  And make me wholly Thine,
That I may never more depart,
  Nor grieve Thy love divine.

4 Thus, till my last, expiring breath,
  Thy goodness I'll adore;
And when my frame dissolves in death,
  My soul shall love Thee more.
                    BENJAMIN CLEVELAND.

OLIVET. 6s, 4s.

My faith looks up to Thee, Thou Lamb of Calvary, Saviour divine: Now hear me while I pray;

Take all my guilt away; O let me from this day Be wholly Thine.

388 *"Behold the Lamb of God!"*

My faith looks up to Thee,
Thou Lamb of Calvary,
  Saviour divine :
Now hear me while I pray;
Take all my guilt away;
O let me from this day
  Be wholly Thine.

2 May Thy rich grace impart
Strength to my fainting heart,
  My zeal inspire ;
As Thou hast died for me,
O may my love to Thee,
Pure, warm, and changeless be—
  A living fire.

3 While life's dark maze I tread,
And griefs around me spread,
  Be Thou my guide ;
Bid darkness turn to day,
Wipe sorrow's tears away,
Nor let me ever stray
  From Thee aside.

4 When ends life's transient dream,
When death's cold, sullen stream
  Shall o'er me roll ;
Blest Saviour, then, in love,
Fear and distrust remove ;
O bear me safe above—
  A ransomed soul.

RAY PALMER.

NIMBUS. C. M.

Eternal Sun of righteousness, Display Thy beams di - vine, And cause the glory of Thy face Up - on my heart to shine!

389 *"Lord, lift Thou up the light of Thy countenance upon us."*

Eternal Sun of righteousness,
  Display Thy beams divine,
And cause the glory of Thy face
  Upon my heart to shine !

2 Light, in Thy light, O may I see,
  Thy grace and mercy prove,
Revived, and cheered, and blest by Thee,
  The God of pardoning love.

3 Lift up Thy countenance serene,
  And let Thy happy child
Behold, without a cloud between,
  The Father reconciled.

4 On me Thy promised peace bestow,
  The peace by Jesus given ;—
The joys of holiness below,
  And then the joys of heaven.

CHARLES WESLEY.

ERNAN.   L. M.

'Tis by the faith of joys to come, We walk thro' de - serts dark as night;

Till we arrive at heav'n, our home, Faith is our guide, and faith our light.

390   *"Faith, the evidence of things not seen."*

'T is by the faith of joys to come,
  We walk thro' deserts dark as night;
Till we arrive at heaven, our home,
  Faith is our guide, and faith our light.

2 The want of sight she well supplies;
  She makes the pearly gates appear;
Far into distant worlds she pries,
  And brings eternal glories near.

3 Cheerful we tread the desert through,
  While faith inspires a heavenly ray;
Though lions roar, and tempests blow,
  And rocks and dangers fill the way.

4 So Abra'm by divine command
  Left his own house to walk with God;
His faith beheld the promised land
  And fired his zeal along the road.
               ISAAC WATTS.

391   *"If ye shall ask anything in My name, I will do it."*

JESUS! our best belovèd Friend,
  On Thy redeeming name we call;
Jesus! in love to us descend,
  Pardon and sanctify us all.

2 Our souls and bodies we resign,
  To fear and follow Thy commands;
O take our hearts—our hearts are Thine;
  Accept the service of our hands.

3 Firm, faithful, watching unto prayer,
  Thy blessèd will may we obey,
Toil in Thy vineyard here and bear
  The heat and burden of the day.

4 Yet, Lord! for us a resting place,
  In heaven, at Thy right hand, prepare,
And, till we see Thee face to face,
  Be all our conversation there.
            JAMES MONTGOMERY.

392   *"Seek ye first the Kingdom of God, and His righteousness."*

AND dost Thou say 'Ask what thou wilt?'
  Lord, I would seize the golden hour:
I pray to be released from guilt,
  And freed from sin and Satan's power.

2 More of Thy presence, Lord, impart;
  More of Thine image let me bear;
Erect Thy throne within my heart,
  And reign without a rival there.

3 Give me to read my pardon sealed,
  And from Thy joy to draw my strength;
O be Thy boundless love revealed,
  In all its hight, and breadth, and length.

4 Grant these requests—I ask no more;
  But to Thy care the rest resign:
Sick or in health, or rich or poor,
  All shall be well, if Thou art mine.
            JOHN NEWTON.

GUIDE. 7s.

Steal - ing from the world a - way, We are come to seek Thy face;

Kind - ly meet us, Lord, we pray, Grant us Thy re - viv - ing grace.

393 *"Our eyes wait upon the Lord our God."*

STEALING from the world away,
We are come to seek Thy face;
Kindly meet us, Lord, we pray,
Grant us Thy reviving grace.

2 Yonder stars that gild the sky
Shine but with a borrowed light;
We, unless Thy light be nigh
Wander, wrapt in gloomy night.

3 Sun of Righteousness! dispel
All our darkness, doubts, and fears:
May Thy light within us dwell,
Till eternal day appears.

4 Warm our hearts in prayer and praise,
Lift our every thought above;
Hear the grateful songs we raise,
Fill us with Thy perfect love.

RAY PALMER.

394 *"Hitherto hath the Lord helped us."*

LORD! I cannot let Thee go
Till a blessing Thou bestow;
Do not turn away Thy face,
Mine's an urgent, pressing case.

2 Once a sinner, near despair,
Sought Thy mercy-seat by prayer;
Mercy heard and set him free—
Lord! that mercy came to me.

3 Many days have passed since then,
Many changes I have seen;
Yet have been upheld till now:
Who would hold me up but Thou?

4 Thou hast helped in every need—
This emboldens me to plead:

After so much mercy past,
Canst Thou let me sink at last?

5 No—I must maintain my hold;
'T is Thy goodness makes me bold;
I can no denial take,
Since I plead for Jesus' sake.

JOHN NEWTON.

395 *"If we ask anything according to His will, He heareth us."*

COME, my soul, thy suit prepare,
Jesus loves to answer prayer;
He Himself has bid thee pray,
Therefore will not say thee nay.

2 Thou art coming to a King,
Large petitions with thee bring:
For His grace and power are such,
None can ever ask too much.

3 With my burden I begin:
Lord, remove this load of sin!
Let Thy blood, for sinners spilt,
Set my conscience free from guilt!

4 Lord, I come to Thee for rest;
Take possession of my breast;
There Thy blood-bought right maintain,
And without a rival reign.

5 While I am a pilgrim here,
Let Thy love my spirit cheer;
As my Guide, my Guard, my Friend,
Lead me to my journey's end.

6 Show me what I have to do;
Every hour my strength renew;
Let me live a life of faith,
Let me die Thy people's death.

JOHN NEWTON.

ST. AGNES. C. M.

O for a closer walk with God, A calm and heav'nly frame! A light to shine upon the road That leads me to the Lamb.

396   *" Walk as children of light."*

1 O FOR a closer walk with God,
A calm and heavenly frame!
A light to shine upon the road
That leads me to the Lamb!

2 Where is the blessedness I knew
When first I saw the Lord?
Where is the soul-refreshing view
Of Jesus and His word?

3 What peaceful hours I once enjoyed!
How sweet their memory still!
But they have left an aching void
The world can never fill.

4 Return. O holy Dove! return,
Sweet Messenger of rest!
I hate the sins that made Thee mourn,
And drove Thee from my breast.

5 The dearest idol I have known,
Whate'er that idol be,
Help me to tear it from Thy throne,
And worship only Thee!

6 So shall my walk be close with God,
Calm and serene my frame ;
So purer light shall mark the road
That leads me to the Lamb !

WILLIAM COWPER.

397   *"There am I in the midst of them."*

WHEREVER two or three may meet,
To worship in Thy name,
Bending beneath Thy mercy-seat,
This promise they may claim :—

2 Jesus in love will condescend
To bless the hallowed place ;
The Saviour will Himself attend,
And show His smiling face.

3 How bright the assurance ! gracious Lord,
Fountain of peace and love,
Fulfill to us Thy precious word,
Thy loving-kindness prove.

4 Now to our God—the Father, Son,
And Holy Spirit, sing !
With praise to God, the Three in One,
Let all creation ring.

THOMAS HASTINGS.

398   *"I know whom I have believed."*

I'M not ashamed to own my Lord,
Or to defend His cause ;
Maintain the honor of His word,
The glory of His cross.

2 Jesus, my God !—I know His name—
His name is all my trust ;
Nor will He put my soul to shame,
Nor let my hope be lost.

3 Firm as His throne, His promise stands,
And He can well secure
What I've committed to His hands,
Till the decisive hour.

4 Then will He own my worthless name
Before His Father's face,
And in the new Jerusalem
Appoint my soul a place.

ISAAC WATTS.

DALTON. C. M.

Lord, teach us how to pray aright, With rev'rence and with fear, Tho' dust and ashes in Thy sight, We may, we must draw near.

LUX BENIGNA. 10s. 4s.

Lead, kind-ly Light, a - mid th'en-circling gloom, Lead Thou me on!

The night is dark, and I am far from home—Lead Thou me on! Keep Thou my

feet; I do not ask to see The dis - tant scene,—one step enough for me.

399 *"A pillar of fire, to give them light."*

LEAD, kindly Light, amid the encircling
   Lead Thou me on! [gloom,
The night is dark, and I am far from home—
   Lead Thou me on!
Keep Thou my feet; I do not ask to see
The distant scene,—one step enough for me.

2 I was not ever thus, nor prayed that Thou
   Should lead me on;
I loved to choose and see my path, but now
   Lead Thou me on!

I loved the garish day, and spite of fears,
Pride ruled my will; remember not past
   years.

3 So long Thy power hath blest me, sure it
   Will lead me on, [stil'
O'er moor and fen, o'er crag and torrent,
   The night is gone; [till
And with the morn those angel faces smile
Which I have loved long since, and lost
   awhile.

      JOHN HENRY NEWMAN.

400 *"Lord, teach us to pray."*

LORD, teach us how to pray aright,
  With reverence and with fear:
Though dust and ashes in Thy sight,
  We may, we must, draw near.

2 God of all grace, we come to Thee,
  With broken, contrite hearts;
Give what Thine eye delights to see,—
  Truth in the inward parts.

3 Give deep humility; the sense
  Of godly sorrow give;

A strong, desiring confidence
  To hear Thy voice and live;—

4 Patience, to watch and wait and weep,
  Though mercy long delay;
Courage, our fainting souls to keep,
  And trust Thee, though Thou slay.

5 Give these, and then Thy will be done;
  Thus strengthened with all might.
We, through Thy Spirit and Thy Son,
  Shall pray, and pray aright.

      JAMES MONTGOMERY.

DALKEITH. 10s.

As pants the wearied hart for cooling springs,That sinks exhausted in the summer's chase,

So pants my soul for Thee,great King of kings,So thirsts to reach Thy sacred dwelling-place.

401   *"So longeth my soul after Thee, O God."*

As pants the wearied hart for cooling springs,
That sinks exhausted in the summer's
    chase,
So pants my soul for Thee,O King of kings,
So thirsts to reach Thy sacred dwelling-
    place.

2 Why throb, my heart? why sink, my sad-
    dening soul?
Why droop to earth with various woes
    opprest?
My years shall yet in blissful circles roll,
And peace be yet an inmate of my breast.

3 Lord,Thy sure mercies,ever in my sight,
My heart shall gladden thro' the tedious
    day ;
And 'midst the dark and gloomy shades of
    night,
To Thee,my God,I'll tune the grateful lay.

4 Why faint,my soul,why doubt Jehovah's
    aid?
Thy God the God of mercy still shall
    prove ;   [paid.
Within His courts thy thanks shall yet be
Unquestioned be His faithfulness and love.

ROBERT LOWTH.

WOODWORTH. L. M.

Just as I am, without one plea, But that Thy blood was shed for me,

And that Thou bid'st me come to Thee, O Lamb of God, I come, I come.

CREDO. L. M.

No more, my God! I boast no more, Of all the du - ties I have done;

I quit the hopes I held before, To trust the mer - its of Thy Son.

402 *"The righteousness which is of God by faith."*

No more, my God! I boast no more,
  Of all the duties I have done;
I quit the hopes I held before,
  To trust the merits of Thy Son.

2 Now, for the love I bear His name,
  What was my gain I count my loss;
My former pride I call my shame,
  And nail my glory to His cross.

3 Yes,—and I must and will esteem
  All things but loss for Jesus' sake;
O may my soul be found in Him,
  And of His righteousness partake!

4 The best obedience of my hands
  Dares not appear before Thy throne;
But faith can answer Thy demands,
  By pleading what my Lord has done.
                      ISAAC WATTS.

403   *"A very present help."*

How do Thy mercies close me round!
  Forever be Thy name adored;
I blush in all things to abound;
  The servant is above his Lord.

2 I rest beneath the Almighty's shade,
  My griefs expire, my troubles cease:
Thou, Lord, on whom my soul is stayed,
  Wilt keep me still in perfect peace.

3 Me for Thine own Thou lov'st to take,
  In time and in eternity;
Thou never, never wilt forsake
  A helpless soul that trusts in Thee.

4 Jesus protects! my fears begone!
  What can the Rock of Ages move!
Safe in Thine arms I lay me down,—
  Thine everlasting arms of love.
                      CHARLES WESLEY.

404 *"Him that cometh to Me, I will in no wise cast out."*

Just as I am, without one plea
But that Thy blood was shed for me,
And that Thou bidd'st me come to Thee,
  O Lamb of God, I come!

2 Just as I am, and waiting not
To rid my soul of one dark blot,
To Thee whose blood can cleanse each spot,
  O Lamb of God, I come!

3 Just as I am, though tost about
With many a conflict, many a doubt,
Fightings and fears, within, without,
  O Lamb of God, I come!

4 Just as I am, poor, wretched, blind,
Sight, riches, healing of the mind,
Yea, all I need, in Thee to find,
  O Lamb of God, I come!

5 Just as I am, Thou wilt receive,
Wilt welcome, pardon, cleanse, relieve;
Because Thy promise I believe,
  O Lamb of God, I come!

6 Just as I am,—Thy love unknown
Has broken every barrier down,—
Now to be Thine, yea, Thine alone,
  O Lamb of God, I come!
                    CHARLOTTE ELLIOTT.

RETREAT. L. M.

From ev'ry stormy wind that blows,From ev'ry swelling tide of woes,There is a calm,a sure retreat;—'Tis found beneath the mercy-seat.

405 *"In the secret of His tabernacle shall He hide me."*

FROM every stormy wind that blows,
From every swelling tide of woes,
There is a calm, a sure retreat ;—
'T is found beneath the mercy-seat.

2 There is a place where Jesus sheds
The oil of gladness on our heads ;
A place than all beside more sweet,—
It is the blood-bought mercy-seat.

3 There is a scene where spirits blend ;
Where friend holds fellowship with friend ;

Though sundered far, by faith they meet
Around one common mercy-seat.

4 There, there on eagle wings we soar,
And sin and sense molest no more :
And heaven comes down,our souls to greet,
And glory crowns the mercy-seat.

5 O may my hand forget her skill,
My tongue be silent, cold, and still,
This bounding heart forget to beat,
If I forget the mercy-seat !

HUGH STOWELL.

CHANT. P. M,

A - - men.

406

1 From the recesses of a lowly spirit. Our humble prayer ascends ; O | Father, |
hear it, ‖ Upsoaring on the wings of awe and meekness ! For- | give its | weakness. ‖

2 We see Thy hand ; it leads us, it supports us : We hear Thy voice ; it | counsels
and it | courts us :‖ And then we turn away ; and still Thy kindness For- | gives
our | blindness. ‖

3 O how long-suffering, Lord ! but Thou delightest To win with | love the | wander-
ing ;‖ Thou invitest By smiles of mercy, not by frowns or terrors,— | Ma.
from his | errors. ‖

4 Father and Saviour ! plant within each bosom the | seeds of | holiness.‖ and bid
them blossom In fragrance and in beauty bright and vernal, And | Spring e- |
ternal. ‖

5 Then place them in Thine everlasting gardens, Where angels walk and | Seraphs
are the | wardens :‖ Where every flower escaped through death's dark portal
Be- | comes im- | mortal.‖ A- |.- | men. ‖

JOHN BOWRING.

Christian Duty and Trial.

189

DORRNANCE. 8s, 7s.

Take my heart, O Father, take it; Make and keep it all Thine own;

Let Thy Spi - rit melt and break it—This proud heart of sin and stone.

407 *"O Lord, my strength and my refuge."*

TAKE my heart, O Father, take it;
Make and keep it all Thine own;
Let Thy Spirit melt and break it—
This proud heart of sin and stone.

2 Father, make me pure and lowly,
Fond of peace and far from strife;
Turning from the paths unholy
Of this vain and sinful life.

3 Ever let Thy grace surround me,
Strengthen me with power divine,
Till Thy cords of love have bound me:
Make me to be wholly Thine.

4 May the blood of Jesus heal me,
And my sins be all forgiven;
Holy Spirit, take and seal me,
Guide me in the path to heaven.

408 *"And they forsook all, and followed Him."*

JESUS calls us, o'er the tumult
Of our life's wild, restless sea;
Day by day His sweet voice soundeth,
Saying, Christian, follow Me!

2 Jesus calls us—from the worship
Of the vain world's golden store;
From each idol that would keep us,—
Saying, Christian, love Me more!

3 In our joys and in our sorrows,
Days of toil and hours of ease,
Still He calls, in cares and pleasures,
Christian, love Me more than these!

4 Jesus calls us! by Thy mercies,
Saviour, may we hear Thy call;
Give our hearts to Thy obedience,
Serve and love Thee best of all!

CECIL FRANCES ALEXANDER.

QUARTETT. 8s, 7s.

STEPHANOS. P. M.

Art thou weary, art thou languid, Art thou sore distrest? 'Come to me,' saith One, 'and coming, Be at rest.'

409 *"Come unto Me all ye that labor and are heavy laden!"*

Art thou weary, art thou languid,
Art thou sore distrest?' —
'Come to me,' saith One, 'and coming,
    Be at rest.'

2 Hath He marks to lead me to Him,
    If He be my Guide? —
'In His feet and hands are wound-prints,
    And His side.'

3 Is there diadem, as Monarch,
    That His brow adorns! —
'Yea, a crown, in very surety;
    But of thorns.'

4 If I find Him, if I follow,
    What His guerdon here? —

'Many a sorrow, many a labor,
    Many a tear.'

5 If I still hold closely to Him,
    What hath He at last? —
'Sorrow vanquisht, labor ended,
    Jordan past.'

6 If I ask Him to receive me,
    Will He say me nay? —
'Not till earth, and not till heaven
    Pass away.'

7 Finding, following, keeping, struggling,
    Is He sure to bless? —
'Saints, apostles, prophets, martyrs,
    Answer, 'Yes'.'

JOHN MASON NEALE.

ELIAS. P. M.

Art thou weary, art thou languid, Art thou sore distrest? 'Come to me, 'saith One, 'and coming, Be at rest.'

PLEYEL'S HYMN. 7s.

Who, O Lord, when life is o'er, Shall to heav'nly mansions soar? Who, an ev - er-welcome guest, In Thy holy place shall rest!

410   *"Lord, who shall abide in Thy tabernacle?"*

Who, O Lord, when life is o'er,
Shall to heavenly mansions soar?
Who, an ever-welcome guest,
In Thy holy place shall rest?

2 He whose heart Thy love has warmed;
He whose will, to Thine conformed,
Bids his life unsullied run;
He whose words and thoughts are one;

3 He who shuns the sinner's road,
Loving those who love their God;
Who, with hope, and faith unfeigned,
Treads the path by Thee ordained.

4 He who trusts in Christ alone,
Not in aught himself hath done;
He, great God, shall be Thy care,
And Thy choicest blessings share.

JAMES MERRICK.

GERMANY. L. M.

Be with me, Lord, where'er I go; Teach me what Thou wouldst have me do;

Suggest whate'er I think or say; Di-rect me in Thy nar-row way.

411 *"I will run the way of Thy commandments."*

Be with me, Lord, where'er I go ;
Teach me what Thou wouldst have me do ;
Suggest whate'er I think or say ;
Direct me in Thy narrow way.

2 Prevent me lest I harbor pride.
Lest I in mine own strength confide ;
Show me my weakness, let me see
I have my power, my all from Thee.

3 Enrich me always with Thy love ;
My kind protection ever prove :
Thy signet put upon my breast,
And let Thy Spirit on me rest.

4 O may I never do my will,
But Thine and only Thine fulfill :
Let all my time and all my ways
Be spent and ended to Thy praise.

JOHN CENNICK.

SHARON. C. M.

O that the Lord would guide my ways To keep His statutes still!

O that my God would grant me grace To know and do His will!

412 *"Make me to go in the path of Thy commandments."*

O THAT the Lord would guide my ways
To keep His statutes still !
O that my God would grant me grace
To know and do His will !

2 O send Thy Spirit down to write
Thy law upon my heart !
Nor let my tongue indulge deceit,
Nor act the liar's part.

4 From vanity turn off mine eyes ;
Let no corrupt design,

Nor covetous desire, arise
Within this soul of mine.

4 Order my footsteps by Thy word,
And make my heart sincere ;
Let sin have no dominion, Lord,
But keep my conscience clear.

5 Make me to walk in Thy commands,—
'Tis a delightful road ;
Nor let my head, or heart, or hands,
Offend against my God.

ISAAC WATTS.

LABAN. S. M.

A charge to keep I have, A God to glo-ri-fy, A never-dying soul to save, And fit it for the sky.

413   *"Be ye also ready."*

A CHARGE to keep I have,
A God to glorify,
A never-dying soul to save,
And fit it for the sky.

2 To serve the present age,
My calling to fulfill;
O may it all my powers engage
To do my Master's will.

3 Arm me with jealous care,
As in Thy sight to live;
And O, Thy servant, Lord, prepare,
A strict account to give.

4 Help me to watch and pray,
And on Thyself rely,
Assured, if I my trust betray
I shall forever die.

CHARLES WESLEY.

414   *"Take ye heed; watch and pray."*

MY soul, be on thy guard;
Ten thousand foes arise;
The hosts of sin are pressing hard
To draw thee from the skies.

2 O watch, and fight, and pray;
The battle ne'er give o'er;
Renew it boldly every day,
And help divine implore.

3 Ne'er think the victory won,
Nor lay thine armor down:
Thine arduous work will not be done,
Till thou obtain thy crown.

4 Fight on, my soul, till death
Shall bring thee to thy God;
He'll take thee, at thy parting breath,
To His divine abode.

GEORGE HEATH.

GIDEON. S. M.

Soldiers of Christ, a-rise, And put your ar-mor on, Strong in the strength which God supplies Thro' His E-ter-nal Son.

415   *"Be strong in the Lord, and in the power of His might."*

SOLDIERS of Christ, arise,
And put your armor on,
Strong in the strength which God supplies
Through His Eternal Son.

2 Strong in the Lord of Hosts,
And in His mighty power,
Who in the strength of Jesus trusts,
Is more than conqueror.

3 Stand, then, in His great might,
With all His strength endued;

And take, to arm you for the fight,
The panoply of God:—

4 That having all things done,
And all your conflicts past,
Ye may o'ercome through Christ alone,
And stand entire at last.

5 From strength to strength go on,
Wrestle, and fight, and pray;
Tread all the powers of darkness down,
And win the well-fought day.

CHARLES WESLEY.

VIA UNA. S. M. D.

Je-sus, my Strength, my Hope, On Thee I cast my care, With humble confidence look up, And know Thou hear'st my pray'r.

Give me on Thee to wait, Till I can all things do, On Thee, Al - mighty to create! Almight-y to re - new!

416 *"I can do all things through Christ which strengtheneth me."*

Jesus, my Strength, my Hope,
On Thee I cast my care,
With humble confidence look up,
And know Thou hear'st my prayer.
Give me on Thee to wait
Till I can all things do,
On Thee, Almighty to create!
Almighty to renew!

2 I want a sober mind.
A self-renouncing will,
That tramples down and casts behind
The baits of pleasing ill:
A soul inured to pain,
To hardship, grief, and loss;
Bold to take up, firm to sustain,
The consecrated cross.

3 I want a godly fear,
A quick-discerning eye,
That looks to Thee when sin is near,
And sees the tempter fly; .
A spirit still prepared,
And armed with jealous care,
For ever standing on its guard,
And watching unto prayer.

4 I want a true regard,
A single, steady aim,
Unmoved by threatening or reward,
To Thee and Thy great name;

A jealous, just concern
For Thine immortal praise;
A pure desire that all may learn
And glorify Thy grace.

5 I rest upon Thy word;
Thy promise is for me;
My succor and salvation, Lord,
Shall surely come from Thee,
But let me still abide,
Nor from my hope remove,
Till Thou my patient spirit guide
Into Thy perfect love!
CHARLES WESLEY.

417 *"Blessed are those servants whom the Lord when He cometh shall find watching."*

Ye servants of the Lord,
Each in his office wait,
Observant of His heavenly word,
And watchful at His gate.
Let all your lamps be bright,
And trim the golden flame;
Gird up your loins, as in His sight,
For awful is His name.

2 Watch! 'Tis your Lord's command;
And, while we speak, He's near;
Mark the first signal of His hand,
And ready all appear.
O happy servant he,
In such a posture found!
He shall his Lord with rapture see,
And be with honor crowned.
PHILIP DODDRIDGE.

WEBB. 7s, 6s. D.

Stand up, stand up for Jesus, Ye soldiers of the cross; Lift high His royal banner, It must not suffer loss: From vict'ry unto vict'ry His army shall He lead, Till ev-'ry foe is vanquish'd, And Christ is Lord in-deed.

418   *"Be thou faithful unto death, and I will give thee a crown of life."*

STAND up, stand up for Jesus,
  Ye soldiers of the cross;
Lift high His royal banner,
  It must not suffer loss:
From victory unto victory
  His army shall He lead,
Till every foe is vanquished,
  And Christ is Lord indeed.

2 Stand up, stand up for Jesus,
  The trumpet call obey;
Forth to the mighty conflict
  In this His glorious day:

'Ye that are men, now serve Him'
  Against unnumbered foes;
Let courage rise with danger,
  And strength to strength oppose.

3 Stand up, stand up for Jesus,
  The strife will not be long;
This day the noise of battle,
  The next the victor's song:
To Him that overcometh,
  A crown of life shall be;
He with the King of glory
  Shall reign eternally.

GEORGE DUFFIELD.

ABERDEEN. 7s.

Soldiers who to Christ belong, Trust ye in His word, be strong; For His prom-i-ses are sure, His rewards for aye endure.

419   *"Now they do it to obtain a corruptible crown, but we an incorruptible."*

SOLDIERS who to Christ belong,
Trust ye in His word, be strong;
For His promises are sure,
His rewards for aye endure.

2 His no crowns that pass away;
His no palm that sees decay;
His the joy that shall not fade;
His the light that knows no shade.

3 Here on earth ye can but clasp
Things that perish in the grasp:
Lift your hearts then to the skies,
God Himself shall be your prize.

4 Praise we now with saints at rest
Father, Son, and Spirit blest;
For His promises are sure,
His rewards shall aye endure.

CAMBRIDGE. C. M.

Am I a soldier of the cross, A follower of the Lamb? And shall I fear to own His cause, Or blush to speak His name? Or blush to speak His name? Or blush to speak His name?

420 *"Fight the good fight of faith."*

✗ Am I a soldier of the cross,
A follower of the Lamb?
And shall I fear to own His cause,
Or blush to speak His name?

ⱽ 2 Are there no foes for me to face?
Must I not stem the flood?
Is this vile world a friend to grace,
To help me on to God?

3 Sure I must fight, if I would reign;
Increase my courage, Lord:
I'll bear the toil, endure the pain,
Supported by Thy word.

4 Thy saints in all this glorious war
Shall conquer, though they die;
They view the triumph from afar,
And seize it with their eye.

5 When that illustrious day shall rise,
And all Thy armies shine
In robes of victory through the skies,
The glory shall be Thine.
ISAAC WATTS.

421 *"So run, that ye may obtain."*

✗ Awake, my soul, stretch every nerve,
And press with vigor on;
A heavenly race demands thy zeal,
And an immortal crown.

2 A cloud of witnesses around
Hold thee in full survey;
Forget the steps already trod,
And onward urge thy way.

3 'Tis God's all-animating voice,
That calls thee from on high:
'Tis His own hand presents the prize
To thine uplifted eye.

4 Blest Saviour, introduced by Thee,
Have I my race begun;
And, crowned with victory, at Thy feet
✗ I'll lay my honors down.
PHILIP DODDRIDGE.

422 *"What I do, thou knowest not now."*

God moves in a mysterious way
His wonders to perform;
He plants His footsteps in the sea,
And rides upon the storm.

2 Deep in the unfathomable mines
Of never-failing skill,
He treasures up His bright designs,
And works His sovereign will.

3 Judge not the Lord by feeble sense,
But trust Him for His grace;
Behind a frowning Providence
He hides a smiling face.

4 His purposes will ripen fast,
Unfolding every hour;
The bud may have a bitter taste,
But sweet will be the flower.

5 Blind unbelief is sure to err,
And scan His work in vain;
God is His own interpreter,
And He will make it plain.
WILLIAM COWPER.

HAMBURG L. M.

O Thou, to whose all-search - ing sight The darkness shin-eth as the light,

Search, prove my heart, it pants for Thee; O, burst these bonds and set it free!

423 *"Search me, O God, and know my heart."*

O Thou, to whose all-searching sight
The darkness shineth as the light,
Search, prove my heart—it pants for Thee;
O, burst these bonds and set it free!

2 Wash out its stains, refine its dross;
Nail my affections to the cross;
Hallow each thought; let all within
Be clean, as Thou, my Lord, art clean.

3 If in this darksome wild I stray,
Be Thou my light—be Thou my way;
No foes nor danger will I fear,
While Thou, my Saviour God, art near.

4 Saviour, where'er Thy steps I see,
Dauntless, untired, I follow Thee:
O let Thy hand support me still,
And lead me to Thy holy hill.

5 If rough and thorny be the way,
My strength proportion to my day,
Till toil and grief and pain shall cease,
Where all is calm and joy and peace.

GERHARD TERSTEEGEN.

424 *"I will not leave you comfortless."*

O Love Divine, that stooped to share
Our sharpest pang, our bitterest tear,
On Thee we cast each earth-born care,
We smile at pain while Thou art near!

2 Though long the weary way we tread,
And sorrow crowns each lingering year,

No path we shun, no darkness dread,
Our hearts still whispering, Thou art near!

3 When drooping pleasure turns to grief,
And trembling faith is changed to fear,
The murmuring wind, the quivering leaf,
Shall softly tell us Thou art near!

4 On Thee we fling our burdening woe,
O Love Divine, for ever dear,
Content to suffer while we know,
Living and dying, Thou art near!

OLIVER WENDELL HOLMES.

425 *"Casting all your care upon Him."*

Thrice happy he whose tranquil mind,
Whate'er, O Lord, his lot may be,
His truest source of peace can find
In casting all his care on Thee:

2 Who ever strives from day to day,
With earnest faith through toil and pain,
To tread the strait and narrow way
Till Thou shalt claim Thine own again:

3 Content to live, content to die,
Content, O Lord, through good or ill;
Content—without the asking why—
Whate'er befall, to do Thy will.

4 So may we strive, and striving win
The prize of those who die forgiven,
Content to live, till freed from sin,
We reach Thy mansions, King of heaven.

GODFREY THRING.

MISSIONARY CHANT. L. M.

So let our lips and lives express The holy gospel we profess,

So let our works and virtues shine To prove the doctrine all divine.

426 "*Denying ungodliness and worldly lusts, we should live soberly, righteously, and godly, in this present world.*"

So let our lips and lives express
The holy gospel we profess:
So let our works and virtues shine,
To prove the doctrine all divine.

2 Thus shall we best proclaim abroad
The honors of our Saviour God;
When His salvation reigns within,
And grace subdues the power of sin.

3 Our flesh and sense must be denied,
Passion and envy, lust and pride:
While justice, temperance, truth, and love,
Our inward piety approve.

4 Religion bears our spirits up,
While we expect that blessed hope,
The bright appearance of the Lord,
And faith stands leaning on His word.
                 ISAAC WATTS.

427 "*Let us labor, therefore, to enter into that rest.*"

Go, labor on; spend and be spent,
Thy joy to do the Father's will;
It is the way the Master went;
Should not the servant tread it still?

2 Go, labor on; 'tis not for naught;
Thine earthly loss is heavenly gain;
Men heed thee, love thee, praise thee not;
The Master praises:—what are men?

3 Go, labor on, while it is day;
The world's dark night is hastening on;

Speed, speed thy work, cast sloth away;
It is not thus that souls are won.

4 Toil on, faint not, keep watch, and pray;
Be wise the erring soul to win;
Go forth into the world's highway,
Compel the wanderer to come in.

5 Toil on, and in thy toil rejoice;
For toil comes rest, for exile home;
Soon shalt thou hear the Bridegroom's voice,
The midnight cry, 'Behold, I come!'
               HORATIUS BONAR.

428 "*Endure hardness, as a good soldier of Jesus Christ.*"

STAND up, my soul, shake off thy fears,
And gird the gospel armor on;
March to the gates of endless joy,
Where Jesus, thy great Captain's gone.

2 Hell and thy sins resist thy course;
But hell and sin are vanquished foes;
Thy Jesus nailed them to the cross,
And sung the triumph when He rose.

3 Then let my soul march boldly on,—
Press forward to the heavenly gate;
There peace and joy eternal reign,
And glittering robes for conquerors wait.

4 There shall I wear a starry crown,
And triumph in almighty grace,
While all the armies of the skies
Join in my glorious Leader's praise.
          ISAAC WATTS.

NAOMI. C. M.

Fa - ther! whate'er of earth - ly bliss Thy sov - 'reign hand de - nies,

Ac - cept - ed at Thy throne of grace, Let this pe - ti - tion rise;—

429   *"My meat is to do the will of Him that sent me."*

FATHER! whate'er of earthly bliss
  Thy sovereign hand denies,
Accepted at Thy throne of grace,
  Let this petition rise :—

2 'Give me a calm, a thankful heart,
  From every murmur free !
The blessings of Thy grace impart,
  And let me live to Thee.

3 'Let the sweet hope that Thou art mine
  My path of life attend :
Thy presence through my journey shine,
  And bless my journey's end.'
            ANNE STEELE.

430   *"Not as I will, but as Thou wilt."*

I WORSHIP Thee, sweet Will of God !
  And all Thy ways adore,
And every day I live, I seem
  To love Thee more and more.

2 I have no cares, O blessèd Will,
  For all my cares are Thine :
I live in triumph, Lord, for Thou
  Hast made Thy triumphs mine.

3 He always wins who sides with God,
  To him no chance is lost ;
God's will is sweetest to him when
  It triumphs at his cost.

4 Ill that He blesses, is our good,
  And unblest good is ill ;
And all is right that seems most wrong,
  If it be His sweet will.
          FREDERICK WILLIAM FABER.

431   *"Thy will be done."*

THY holy will, my God, be mine ;
  I yield my all to Thee ;
No more shall thought or wish repine,
  Whate'er my lot shall be.

2 Thy wisdom is a mighty deep,
  Beyond my thought Thy grace ;
My soul shall lay her fears asleep,
  Secure in Thine embrace.

3 When clouds and darkness rule the hour,
  Thy bow on high I see ;
And e'en the rending tempest's power
  Shall work but good for me.

4 At every step mine eyes shall turn
  To watch Thy guiding hand ;
My dearest wish shall be to learn
  And do Thy pure command.

5 On Thee I rest my trusting soul ;
  Thou wilt not let me fall ;
Though surging billows o'er me roll,
  I shall be safe through all.

6 Grant me, my God, at last to hear,
  Well pleased, the call to die ;
And 'mid the shades, with vision clear,
  To see my Saviour nigh.

7 Then when Thy glory breaks on me,
  All radiant as the sun,
Be this the joy of heaven,—to see
  Thy will for ever done.
         RAY PALMER.

JEWETT. 6s. D.

My Je-sus, as Thou wilt! O, may Thy will be mine; In-to Thy hand of love
I would my all resign; Through sor-row, or thro' joy, Con-duct me
as Thine own, And help me still to say, My Lord, Thy will be done!

432 *"I seek not mine own will."*

O My Jesus, as Thou wilt!
O, may Thy will be mine;
Into Thy hand of love
I would my all resign;
Through sorrow or through joy,
Conduct me as Thine own,
And help me still to say,
·My Lord, Thy will be done!'

2 My Jesus, as Thou wilt!
Though seen through many a tear,
Let not my star of hope
Grow dim or disappear.
Since Thou on earth hast wept,
And sorrowed oft alone,
If I must weep with Thee,
·My Lord, Thy will be done!'

3 My Jesus, as Thou wilt!
All shall be well for me;
Each changing future scene
I gladly trust with Thee:
Straight to my home above
I travel calmly on,
And sing, in life or death,
·My Lord, Thy will be done!'
JANE BORTHWICK.

433 *"Make Thy way straight before my face."*

O Thy way, not mine, O Lord,
However dark it be!
Lead me by Thine own hand,
Choose out the path for me.
I dare not choose my lot:
I would not, if I might;
Choose Thou for me, my God,
So shall I walk aright.

2 The kingdom that I seek
Is Thine: so let the way
That leads to it be Thine,
Else I must surely stray.
Take Thou my cup, and it
With joy or sorrow fill,
As best to Thee may seem;
Choose Thou my good and ill.

3 Choose Thou for me my friends,
My sickness or my health;
Choose Thou my cares for me,
My poverty or wealth.
Not mine, not mine the choice,
In things or great or small;
Be Thou my guide, my strength,
My wisdom and my all.
HORATIUS BONAR.

MARTYN. 7s, D.   Fine.   D.C. al Fine.

Jesus, lover of my soul, Let me to Thy bosom fly, } { Hide me, O my Saviour, hide, }
While the nearer waters roll, While the tempest still is high! } { Till the storm of life is past; }
Safe into the haven guide; O receive my soul at last !

434   *"Thou art my Refuge and my Portion in the land of the living."*

Jesus, lover of my soul,
   Let me to Thy bosom fly,
While the nearer waters roll,
   While the tempest still is high !
Hide me, O my Saviour, hide,
   Till the storm of life is past ;
Safe into the haven guide ;
   O receive my soul at last !

2 Other refuge have I none ;
   Hangs my helpless soul on Thee ;
Leave, ah ! leave me not alone,
   Still support and comfort me !
All my trust on Thee is stayed, ·
   All my help from Thee I bring :
Cover my defenceless head
   With the shadow of Thy wing !

3 Thou, O Christ, art all I want ;
   More than all in Thee I find ;
Raise the fallen, cheer the faint,
   Heal the sick, and lead the blind !
Just and holy is Thy name,—
   I am all unrighteousness ;
False and full of sin I am,—
   Thou art full of truth and grace.

4 Plenteous grace with Thee is found—
   Grace to pardon all my sin ;
Let the healing streams abound,
   Make and keep me pure within :
Thou of life the fountain art,
   Freely let me take of Thee ;
Spring Thou up within my heart,—
   Rise to all eternity.

CHARLES WESLEY.

SHELTER. 7s, D. (For Quartette.)

Jesus, lover of my soul, Let me to Thy bosom fly, While the nearer waters

roll, While the tempest still is high ! Hide me, O my Saviour, hide,

Till the storm of life is past ; Safe into the haven guide ; O receive my soul at last !

PHRYGIA. 7s, 6s.

O Lamb of God, still keep me Near to Thy wounded side; 'Tis only there in safety And peace I can abide. What foes and snares surround me,

What doubts and fears within! The grace that sought and found me, Alone can keep me clean.

435 "Looking unto Jesus, the Author and Finisher of our faith."

O LAMB of God, still keep me
Near to Thy wounded side;
'Tis only there in safety
And peace I can abide.
What foes and snares surround me,
What doubts and fears within!
The grace that sought and found me,
Alone can keep me clean.

2 'Tis only in Thee hiding,
I know my life secure;
Only in Thee abiding,
The conflict can endure:

Thine arm the victory gaineth
O'er every hateful foe;
Thy love my heart sustaineth
In all its care and woe.

3 Soon shall my eyes behold Thee
With rapture face to face;
One half hath not been told me
Of all Thy power and grace;
Thy beauty, Lord, and glory,
The wonders of Thy love,
Shall be the endless story
Of all Thy saints above.

JAMES GEORGE DECK.

SPANISH HYMN. 7s, D.

Sovereign Ruler of the skies, Ever gracious, ever wise, All my times are in Thy hand, All events at Thy command. Times of sickness, times of health, Times of penu-ry and wealth; Times of tri-al and of grief, Times of triumph and relief.

436 "My times are in Thy hand."

SOVEREIGN Ruler of the skies,
Ever gracious, ever wise,
All my times are in Thy hand,
All events at Thy command.
Times of sickness, times of health
Times of penury and wealth;
Times of trial and of grief,
Times of triumph and relief.

2 O Thou Gracious, Wise, and Just!
In Thy hands my life I trust:
Have I something dearer still?
I resign it to Thy will.
May I always own Thy hand;
Still to the surrender stand;
Know that Thou art God alone:
I and mine are all Thy own.

JOHN RYLAND.

HOLLEY. 7s.

Oft in sor-row, oft in woe, Onward, Christians, onward go;

Fight the fight, main-tain the strife, Strengthen'd with the Bread of Life.

437   *"Fight the good fight of faith."*

Oft in sorrow, oft in woe,
Onward, Christians, onward go;
Fight the fight, maintain the strife,
Strengthened with the Bread of Life.

2 Let not sorrow dim your eye,
Soon shall every tear be dry;
Let not fears your course impede;
Great your strength if great your need.

3 Let your drooping hearts be glad;
March, in heavenly armor clad;
Fight, nor think the battle long,
Soon shall victory wake your song.

4 Onward then to battle move,
More than conquerors ye shall prove;
Though opposed by many a foe,
Christian soldiers, onward go.

HENRY KIRKE WHITE. (Altered.)

HORTON. 7s.

'Tis my hap-pi-ness be-low, Not to live with-out the cross,

But the Sa-viour's pow'r to know, Sanc-ti-fy-ing ev-'ry loss.

438   *"The Lord is nigh unto all them that call upon Him."*

'Tis my happiness below,
Not to live without the cross,
But the Saviour's power to know,
Sanctifying every loss.

2 Trials must and will befall;
But, with humble faith to see

Love inscribed upon them all,—
This is happiness to me.

3 Trials make the promise sweet;
Trials give new life to prayer;
Trials bring me to His feet,
Lay me low, and keep me there.

WILLIAM COWPER.

ST. ANDREW OF CRETE. 6s, 5s. D.

In the hour of trial, Jesus, pray for me; Lest by base de-ni-al, I depart from Thee;

When Thou seest me waver, With a look re-call, Nor for fear or fa-vor, Suf-fer me to fall.

439 *"I pray for them."*

In the hour of trial,
Jesus, pray for me;
Lest by base denial,
I depart from Thee;
When Thou seest me waver,
With a look recall,
Nor, for fear or favor,
Suffer me to fall.

2 Should Thy mercy send me
Sorrow, toil, and woe;
Or should pain attend me
On my path below;

Grant that I may never
Fail Thy hand to see;
Grant that I may ever
Cast my care on Thee.

3 When my last hour cometh,
Fraught with strife and pain,
When my dust returneth
To the dust again,—
On Thy truth relying
Through that mortal strife,
Jesus, take me, dying,
To eternal life.

JAMES MONTGOMERY.

ST. AGNES. C. M.

Dear Refuge of my weary soul, On Thee, when sorrows rise—On Thee, when waves of trouble roll, My fainting hope relies.

440 *"Preserve me, O God: for in Thee do I put my trust."*

Dear Refuge of my weary soul,
On Thee, when sorrows rise—
On Thee, when waves of trouble roll,
My fainting hope relies.

2 To Thee I tell each rising grief,
For Thou alone canst heal;
Thy word can bring a sweet relief
For every pain I feel.

3 But O! when gloomy doubts prevail,
I fear to call Thee mine;

The springs of comfort seem to fail,
And all my hopes decline.

4 Yet, gracious God, where shall I flee?
Thou art my only trust;
And still my soul would cleave to Thee,
Though prostrate in the dust.

5 Thy mercy-seat is open still;
Here let my soul retreat,
With humble hope attend Thy will,
And wait beneath Thy feet.

ANNE STEELE.

HUMILITY.   7s. 6 lines.

Quiet, Lord, my froward heart, Make me teachable and mild, Upright, simple, free from art,

Make me as a weanèd child, From distrust and envy free, Pleas'd with all that pleases Thee.

441 *"Except ye be converted, and become as little children,*
ye shall not enter into the kingdom."

QUIET, Lord, my froward heart,
  Make me teachable and mild,
Upright, simple, free from art,
  Make me as a weanèd child,
From distrust and envy free,
Pleased with all that pleases Thee.

2 What Thou shalt to-day provide,
  Let me as a child receive;
What to-morrow may betide

Calmly to Thy wisdom leave:
'Tis enough that Thou wilt care;
Why should I the burden bear?

3 As a little child relies
  On a care beyond his own,
Knows he's neither strong nor wise,
  Fears to stir a step alone:
Let me thus with Thee abide.
As my Father, Guard, and Guide.

JOHN NEWTON.

REPOSE.   7s. 6 lines.

Quiet, Lord, my froward heart, Make me teach-a-ble and mild, Upright, sim-ple, free from art,

Make me as a weaned child, From distrust and en-vy free, Pleased with all that pleas-es Thee.

CARLTON. S. M.

If, thro' unruffled seas, Toward heav'n we calmly sail, With grateful hearts,O

God, to Thee, We'll own the favoring gale, We'll own the fa - - v'ring gale.

442 *"A man can receive nothing, except it be given him from heaven."*

If, through unruffled seas,
Toward heaven we calmly sail,
With grateful hearts, O God, to Thee,
We'll own the favoring gale.

2 But should the surges rise,
And rest delay to come,
Blest be the sorrow—kind the storm,
Which drives us nearer home.

3 Soon shall our doubts and fears,
All yield to Thy control:
Thy tender mercies shall illume
The midnight of the soul.

4 Teach us, in every state,
To make Thy will our own ;
And when the joys of sense depart
To live by faith alone.

CALVARY. 7s. 6 lines, or 4 lines without repeat.

Now, O God, Thine own I am !
Freedom,friends,and health,and fame, Now I give Thee back Thine own :
Con - se - crate to Thee a - lone :

Thine I live, thrice hap - py I ! Happier still if Thine I die.

443 *"Ye are not your own."*

Now, O God, Thine own I am !
Now I give Thee back Thine own :
Freedom, friends, and health, and fame,
Consecrate to Thee alone:
Thine I live, thrice happy I !
Happier still if Thine I die.

2 Take me, Lord, with all my powers ;
Take my mind, and heart, and will ;
All my goods, and all my hours,
All I know, and all I feel,
All I think, or speak, or do—
Take my soul and make it new !

PORTUGUESE HYMN. 11s.

How firm a foundation, ye saints of the Lord, Is laid for your faith in His excellent word; What more can He say than to

you He hath said,— To you who for refuge to Je - sus have fled, To you who for refuge to Jesus have fled?

444   *"None of them that trust in Him shall be desolate."*

How firm a foundation, ye saints of the Lord,
Is laid for your faith in His excellent word ;
What more can He say than to you He
  hath said,—
To you who for refuge to Jesus have fled?

2 Fear not, He is with thee, O be not
  dismayed ;   [aid ;
For He is thy God, and will give thee His
He'll strengthen thee, help thee, and cause
  thee to stand,
Upheld by His gracious, omnipotent hand.

3 When through the deep waters He calls
  thee to go,
The rivers of sorrow shall ne'er overflow ;
His presence shall guide thee, His mercy
  shall bless,
And sanctify to thee thy deepest distress.

4 When through fiery trials thy pathway is
  laid,   [aid ;
His grace all-sufficient shall lend thee its
The flame shall not hurt thee ; He does but
  design   refine.]
Thy dross to consume, and thy gold to

5 His people through life shall abundantly
  prove
His sovereign, eternal, unchangeable love ;
When age with gray hairs shall their tem-
  ples adorn,   [borne.
Like lambs they shall still in His bosom be

6 The soul that on Jesus hath leaned for
  repose,
He will not—He will not desert to its foes :
That soul—though all hell should endeavor
  to shake,
He'll never,—no, never—no, never forsake.

GEORGE KEITH.

CARINTHIA. 11s.

How firm a foundation, ye saints of the Lord, Is laid for your faith in His ex-cel-lent word ; What more can He say than to

you He hath said,— To you who for refuge to Jesus have fled? To you who for refuge to Jesus have fled?

My God and Father, while I stray Far from my home, on life's rough way,

O teach me from my heart to say 'Thy will be done!'

445   *"The will of the Lord be done."*

My God and Father, while I stray
Far from my home, on life's rough way,
O teach me from my heart to say,
    'Thy will be done!'

2 Though dark my path and sad my lot,
Let me be still and murmur not,
Or breathe the prayer divinely taught,
    'Thy will be done!'

3 Though Thou hast called me to resign
What most I prized, it ne'er was mine,
I have but yielded what was Thine;
    'Thy will be done!'

4 Let but my fainting heart be blest
With Thy sweet Spirit for its guest,
My God, to Thee I leave the rest;
    'Thy will be done!'

5 Renew my will from day to day;
Blend it with Thine; and take away
All that now makes it hard to say,
    'Thy will be done!'

6 Then, when on earth I breathe no more,
The prayer, oft mixed with tears before,
I'll sing upon a happier shore,
    'Thy will be done!'

                       CHARLOTTE ELLIOTT.

OSWALD. 8s, 7s.

Be that goeth forth with weeping, Bearing precious seed in love, Never tiring, never sleeping, Findeth mercy from a-bove.

446   *"They that sow in tears shall reap in joy."*

He that goeth forth with weeping,
Bearing precious seed in love,
Never tiring, never sleeping,
Findeth mercy from above.

2 Soft descend the dews of heaven,
Bright the rays celestial shine;
Precious fruits will thus be given,
Through an influence all divine.

3 Sow thy seed, be never weary,
Let no fears thy soul annoy;
Be the prospect ne'er so dreary,
Thou shalt reap the fruits of joy.

4 Lo, the scene of verdure brightening!
See the rising grain appear;
Look again! the fields are whitening,
For the harvest-time is near.

                       THOMAS HASTINGS.

WORK SONG. P. M.

Work, for the night is coming; Work thro' the morning hours; Work, while the dew is sparkling,
Work, for the night is coming,

Fine.   *D.S.*

Work 'mid springing flow'rs; Work when the day grows brighter, Work in the glowing sun;
When man's work is done.

X **447** *"Always abounding in the work of the Lord."*

WORK, for the night is coming;
  Work, through the morning hours;
Work, while the dew is sparkling;
  Work, 'mid springing flowers;
Work, when the day grows brighter,
  Work, in the glowing sun;
Work, for the night is coming,
  When man's work is done.

2 Work, for the night is coming,
  Work through the sunny noon;
Fill brightest hours with labor,
  Rest comes sure and soon.

Give every flying minute
  Something to keep in store:
Work, for the night is coming,
  When man works no more.

3 Work, for the night is coming,
  Under the sunset skies;
While their bright tints are glowing,
  Work, for daylight flies.
Work till the last beam fadeth,
  Fadeth to shine no more;
Work while the night is darkening,
  When man's work is o'er.

ANNA L. WALKER.

WARE. L. M.

Awake our souls, away our fears, Let every trembling thought be gone;

Awake and run the heav'nly race, And put a cheerful cour - age on.

EIN FESTE BURG. P. M.

A mighty fortress is our God, A bulwark never fail - ing:
Our Helper He a - mid the flood Of mortal ills pre - vail - ing. For still our ancient foe

Doth seek to work our woe; His craft and pow'r are great, And, arm'd with cruel hate, On earth is not his e - qual.

448 *"The Lord of hosts is with us."*

A MIGHTY fortress is our God,
A bulwark never failing:
Our Helper He amid the flood
Of mortal ills prevailing.
For still our ancient foe
Doth seek to work our woe;
His craft and power are great,
And, armed with cruel hate,
On earth is not his equal.

2 Did we in our own strength confide,
Our striving would be losing,—
Were not the right Man on our side,
The Man of God's own choosing.
Dost ask who that may be?
Christ Jesus, it is He,
Lord Sabaoth His name,
From age to age the same,
And He must win the battle.

3 And though this world, with devils filled,
Should threaten to undo us.
We will not fear, for God hath willed
His truth to triumph through us.
The Prince of darkness grim,
We tremble not for him,
His rage we can endure,
For lo! his doom is sure,
One little word shall fell him.

4 That word above all earthly powers,
No thanks to them, abideth,
The Spirit and the gifts are ours
Through Him that with us sideth.
Let goods and kindred go,
This mortal life also;
The body they may kill,
God's truth abideth still,
His kingdom is for ever.

MARTIN LUTHER.

449 *"They that wait upon the Lord shall renew their strength."*

AWAKE our souls, away our fears,
Let every trembling thought be gone;
Awake and run the heavenly race,
And put a cheerful courage on.

2 True, 't is a strait and thorny road,
And mortal spirits tire and faint;
But they forget the mighty God,
That feeds the strength of every saint:—

3 The mighty God, whose matchless power
Is ever new and ever young,

And firm endures, while endless years
Their everlasting circles run.

4 From Thee, the overflowing Spring,
Our souls shall drink a fresh supply,
While such as trust their native strength
Shall melt away, and droop, and die.

5 Swift as an eagle cuts the air,
We'll mount aloft to Thine abode;
On wings of love our souls shall fly,
Nor tire amid the heavenly road.

ISAAC WATTS.

ELLESDIE. 8s, 7s. D.

Je - sus, I my cross have ta - ken, All to leave and fol-low Thee: Des - ti - tute, despised, for-sak-en,
Yet how rich is my con-di-tion!

Fine.   *D.S.*

Thou, from hence, my all shalt be: Per - ish ev - 'ry fond am - bi - tion, All I've sought, or hoped, or known:
God and heav'n are still my own!

450   *"Behold, we have forsaken all and followed Thee."*

JESUS, I my cross have taken,
   All to leave and follow Thee :
Destitute, despised, forsaken,
   Thou, from hence, my all shalt be :
Perish every fond ambition,
   All I've sought, or hoped, or known ;
Yet how rich is my condition !
   God and heaven are still my own !

2 Take, my soul, thy full salvation ;
   Rise o'er sin, and fear, and care ,
Joy to find in every station,
   Something still to do or bear :

Think what Spirit dwells within thee !
   What a Father's smile is thine !
What a Saviour died to win thee !
   Child of heaven, shouldst thou repine?

3 Haste thee on from grace to glory,
   Armed by faith, and winged by prayer ;
Heaven's eternal day's before thee !
   God's own hand shall guide thee there !
Soon shall close thine earthly mission,
   Swift shall pass thy pilgrim days ;
Hope soon change to glad fruition,
   Faith to sight, and prayer to praise !

HENRY FRANCIS LYTE.

SEYMOUR. 7s.

Cast thy bur - den on the Lord, On - ly lean up - on His word;

Thou wilt soon have cause to bless, His un - chang - ing faith - ful - ness.

DENNIS. S. M.

How gen - tle God's commands! How kind His pre - cepts are!

'Come, cast your bur - dens on the Lord, And trust His con - stant care.'

451 *"He careth for you."*

How gentle God's commands!
How kind His precepts are!
'Come, cast your burdens on the Lord,
And trust His constant care.'

2 Beneath His watchful eye
His saints securely dwell;
That hand which bears all nature up
Shall guard His children well.

3 Why should this anxious load
Press down your weary mind?
Haste to your heavenly Father's throne,
And sweet refreshment find.

4 His goodness stands approved
Through each succeeding day:
I'll drop my burden at His feet,
And bear a song away.
PHILIP DODDRIDGE.

452 *"Commit thy way unto the Lord."*

Commit thou all thy griefs
And ways into His hands,
To His sure truth and tender care,
Who earth and heaven commands.

2 Who points the clouds their course,
Whom winds and seas obey,
He shall direct thy wandering feet;
He shall prepare thy way.

3 Thou on the Lord rely;
So safe shalt thou go on;
Fix on His work thy steadfast eye,
So shall thy work be done.

4 No profit canst thou gain
By self-consuming care;
To Him commend thy cause; His ear
Attends the softest prayer.

5 Give to the winds thy fears.
Hope and be undismayed;
God hears thy sighs and counts thy tears,
God shall lift up thy head.

6 What though thou rulest not?
Yet heaven and earth and hell
Proclaim, 'God sitteth on the throne
And ruleth all things well.'
PAUL GERHARDT.

453 *"A very present help."*

1 Cast thy burden on the Lord,
Only lean upon His word:
Thou wilt soon have cause to bless
His unchanging faithfulness.

2 He sustains thee by His hand,
He enables thee to stand;
Those whom Jesus once hath loved,
From His grace are never moved.

3 Heaven and earth may pass away,
God's free grace shall not decay;
He hath promised to fulfill
All the pleasure of His will.

4 Jesus, guardian of Thy flock,
Be Thyself our constant rock;
Make us by Thy powerful hand,
Firm as Zion's mountain stand.
WILLIAM HAMMOND.

PATER. P. M.

O Thou, the con-trite sin-ners' Friend, Who lov-ing, lov'st them to the end,

On this a-lone my hopes depend, That Thou wilt plead for me!

454   *"If any man sin, we have an Advocate with the Father."*

1 O Thou, the contrite sinners' Friend,
Who loving, lov'st them to the end,
On this alone my hopes depend,
   That Thou wilt plead for me!

2 When, weary in the Christian race,
Far off appears my resting-place,
And fainting I mistrust Thy grace,
   Then, Saviour, plead for me!

3 When I have erred and gone astray
Afar from Thine and wisdom's way,
And see no glimmering guiding ray,
   Still, Saviour, plead for me!

4 When Satan, by my sins made bold,
Strives from Thy cross to loose my hold,
Then with Thy pitying arms enfold,
   And plead, O plead for me!

5 And when my dying hour draws near,
Darkened with anguish, guilt, and fear,
Then to my fainting sight appear,
   Pleading in heaven for me!

6 When the full light of heavenly day
Reveals my sins in dread array,
Say Thou hast washed them all away:
   O say Thou plead'st for me!

CHARLOTTE ELLIOTT.

SUBMISSION. P. M.

Whate'er my God ordains is right, Holy His will abi - deth: I will be still, whate'er He doth, And follow where He guid - eth.

ff

He is my God, though dark my road, He holds me that I shall not fall, Wherefore to Him I leave it all.

SANCTUS L. M. 6 lines.

Jesus, my Lord, my God, my all! Blest Saviour, hear me when I call; O hear, and from Thy dwelling-place

Pour down the riches of Thy grace: Jesus, my Lord, I Thee a-dore—O make me love Thee more and more!

455 *"Whom having not seen ye love."*

Jesus, my Lord, my God, my all!
Blest Saviour, hear me when I call;
O hear, and from Thy dwelling-place
Pour down the riches of Thy grace:
Jesus, my Lord, I Thee adore—
O make me love Thee more and more!

2 Jesus, alas! too coldly sought,
How can I love Thee as I ought?
And how extol Thy matchless fame,
The glorious beauty of Thy name?
Jesus, my Lord, I Thee adore—
O make me love Thee more and more!

3 Jesus! of Thee shall be my song;
To Thee my heart and soul belong;
All that I am or have is Thine,
And Thou, my Saviour, Thou art mine!
Jesus, my Lord, I Thee adore—
O make me love Thee more and more!
HENRY COLLINS.

456 *"Lo, I am with you alway."*

When gathering clouds around I view,
And days are dark and friends are few,
On Him I lean, who not in vain

457 *"The ways of the Lord are right."*

Whate'er my God ordains is right
Holy His will abideth;
I will be still, whate'er He doth,
And follow where He guideth.
He is my God, though dark my road:
He holds me that I shall not fall,
Wherefore to Him I leave it all.

2 Whate'er my God ordains is right,
He never will deceive me:
He leads me by the proper path,

Experienced every human pain;
He sees my wants, allays my fears,
And counts and treasures up my tears.

2 If aught should tempt my soul to stray
From heavenly wisdom's narrow way;
To fly the good I would pursue,
Or do the sin I would not do;
Still He, who felt temptation's power,
Shall guard me in that dangerous hour.

3 If vexing thoughts within me rise,
And, sore dismayed, my spirit dies;
Still He, who once vouchsafed to bear
The sickening anguish of despair,
Shall sweetly soothe, shall gently dry,
The throbbing heart, the streaming eye.

4 And O! when I have safely past
Through every conflict but the last;
Still, still unchanging, watch beside
My painful bed, for Thou hast died!
Then point to realms of cloudless day,
And wipe the latest tear away!
SIR RICHARD GRANT.

I know He will not leave me,
And take content what He hath sent:
His hand can turn my grief away,
And patiently I wait His day.

3 Whate'er my God ordains is right,
Here shall my stand be taken:
Though sorrow, need, or death be mine,
Yet am I not forsaken:
My Father's care is round me there:
He holds me that I shall not fall,
And so to Him I leave it all.
SAMUEL RODIGAST.

HENDON. 7s.

Christ, of all my hopes the ground, Christ, the spring of all my joy, Still in Thee may

I be found, Still for Thee my pow'rs em-ploy, Still for Thee my pow'rs employ.

458 *"To me to live is Christ, and to die is gain."*

CHRIST, of all my hopes the ground,
   Christ, the spring of all my joy,
Still in Thee may I be found,
   Still for Thee my powers employ.

2 Fountain of o'erflowing grace,
   Freely from Thy fulness give ;
Till I close my earthly race,
   May I prove it 'Christ to live !'

3 Firmly trusting in Thy blood,
   Nothing shall my heart confound ;

Safely shall I pass the flood,
   Safely reach Immanuel's ground.

4 When I touch the blessèd shore,
   Back the closing waves shall roll ;
Death's dark stream shall never more
   Part from Thee my ravished soul.

5 Thus, O thus, an entrance give
   To the land of cloudless sky ;
Having known it 'Christ to live,'
   Let me know it 'Gain to die.'

                RALPH WARDLAW.

ELYSIUM. L. M.

Where high the heavenly temple stands, The house of God not made with hands,

A great High Priest our na-ture wears, The guardian of mankind appears.

GLUCK. C. M.

God's glo - ry is a won - drous thing, Most strange in all its ways,

And, of all things on earth, least like What men a - gree to praise.

459 *"I am not ashamed, for I know whom I have believed."*

God's glory is a wondrous thing,
Most strange in all its ways,
And, of all things on earth, least like
What men agree to praise.

2 O, blest is he to whom is given
The instinct that can tell
That God is on the field, when He
Is most invisible!

3 And blest is he who can divine
Where real right doth lie,

And dares to take the side that seems
Wrong to man's blindfold eye!

4 O learn to scorn the praise of men!
O learn to lose with God!
For Jesus won the world through shame,
And beckons thee His road.

5 And right is right, since God is God;
And right the day must win;
To doubt would be disloyalty,
To falter would be sin!

                FREDERICK WILLIAM FABER.

460 *"He hath borne our griefs, and carried our sorrows."*

WHERE high the heavenly temple stands,
The house of God not made with hands,
A great High Priest our nature wears,
The guardian of mankind appears.

2 He who for man their Surety stood,
And poured on earth His precious blood,
Pursues in heaven His mighty plan,
The Saviour and the Friend of man.

3 Though now ascended up on high,
He bends to earth a brother's eye;

Partaker of the human name,
He knows the frailty of our frame.

4 Our fellow-sufferer yet retains
A fellow-feeling of our pains;
And still remembers, in the skies,
His tears, His agonies, and cries.

5 With boldness, therefore, at the throne,
Let us make all our sorrows known;
And ask the aid of heavenly power
To help us in the evil hour.

                JOHN LOGAN

BETHANY. 6s, 4s.   :S:

Near - er, my God, to Thee! Near - er   to Thee, E'en though it be   a cross
Near - er, my God to Thee,

Fine.   *D.C.*

That rais-eth me;   Still all my song shall be,   Near - er, my God, to Thee,
Near - er to Thee!

461. *"If thou seek Him, He will be found of thee."*

NEARER, my God, to Thee ! |
   Nearer to | Thee, |
E'en though it be a cross
   That raiseth | me ;
Still all my | song shall | be, ‖
Nearer, my | God, to | Thee, |
   Nearer to | Thee !‖

2 Though like the wanderer,
   The | sun gone | down, |
Darkness be over me,
   My | rest a | stone ; |
Yet in my | dreams I'd | be ‖
Nearer, my | God, to | Thee, |
   Nearer to | Thee !‖

3 There let the way appear |
   Steps unto | Heaven ; |
All that Thou sendest me
   In | mercy | given ; |

Angels to | beckon | me‖
Nearer, my | God to | Thee, |
   Nearer to | Thee !‖

4 Then with my waking thoughts |
   Bright with Thy | praise, |
Out of my stony griefs |
   Bethel I'll | raise ; |
So by my | woes to | be‖
Nearer, my | God, to | Thee, |
   Nearer to | Thee !‖

5 Or if on joyful wing |
   Cleaving the | sky, |
Sun, moon, and stars forgot, |
   Upward I | fly, |
Still all my | song shall | be,‖
Nearer, my | God, to | Thee, |
   Nearer to | Thee !‖

SARAH FLOWER ADAMS.

CHANT.

Time, Death, and Judgment.

ONIDO. 7s D.

Blessing, honor, thanks, and praise, Pay we, gracious God, to Thee; Thou in Thine a -
bun - dant grace Givest us the vic - to - ry. True and faith - ful to Thy word,
Thou hast glo - rified Thy Son: Jesus Christ our dying Lord Hath for us the vict'ry won.

462 *"Just and true are Thy ways, Thou King of saints."*

BLESSING, honor, thanks, and praise,
Pay we, gracious God, to Thee;
Thou in Thine abundant grace
Givest us the victory.
True and faithful to Thy word,
Thou hast glorified Thy Son:
Jesus Christ our dying Lord
Hath for us the victory won.

2 Happy are the faithful dead,
In the Lord who sweetly die;
They from all their toils are freed,
In God's keeping safely lie:
These the Spirit hath declared
Blest, unutterably blest;
Jesus is their great reward.
Jesus is their endless rest.

3 Followed by their works they go
Where their Head is gone before,
Reconciled by grace below;
Grace has opened mercy's door:
Fuller joys ordained to know,
Waiting for the last great day,
When the archangel's trump shall blow,
'Rise, to judgment come away.'

4 Absent from our loving Lord
We shall not continue long:
Join we then with one accord
In the new, the joyful song:
Blessing, honor, thanks, and praise
Triune God, we pay to Thee,
Who in Thine abundant grace
Givest us the victory.

CHARLES WESLEY.

DALLAS. 7s.

For Thy mercy and Thy grace, Faithful through an - oth - er year,

Hear our song of thankful - ness, Fa - ther, and Redeem - er, hear!

463 *"So teach us to number our days that we may apply our hearts unto wisdom."*

For Thy mercy and Thy grace,
Faithful through another year,
Hear our song of thankfulness,
Father, and Redeemer, hear!

2 In our weakness and distress,
Rock of strength! be Thou our stay!
In the pathless wilderness
Be our true and living way!

3 Who of us death's awful road
In the coming year shall tread?

With Thy rod and staff, O God,
Comfort Thou his dying head!

4 Keep us faithful, keep us pure,
Keep us evermore Thine own!
Help, O help us to endure!
Fit us for the promised crown!

5 So within Thy palace gate
We shall praise, on golden strings,
Thee, the only Potentate,
Lord of lords, and King of kings!

HENRY DOWNTON.

BENEVENTO. 7s, D.

While with ceaseless course the sun Hasted thro' the former year, Many souls their race have run, Never more to meet us here.

Fix'd in an e - ter-nal state, They have done with all below; We a little longer wait, But how little none can know.

O

BATTELL'S CHORAL. L. M.

Great God, we sing that mighty hand By which sup - port - ed still we stand;

The opening year Thy mer - cy shows; Let mer - cy crown it till it close.

464 *"Hitherto hath the Lord helped us."*

Great God, we sing that mighty hand
By which supported still we stand;
The opening year Thy mercy shows;
Let mercy crown it till it close.

2 By day, by night, at home, abroad,
Still are we guarded by our God;
By His incessant bounty fed,
By His unerring counsel led.

3 With grateful hearts the past we own;
The future, all to us unknown,

We to Thy guardian care commit,
And peaceful leave before Thy feet.

4 In scenes exalted or deprest,
Thou art our joy, and Thou our rest;
Thy goodness all our hopes shall raise,
Adored through all our changing days.

5 When death shall interrupt these songs,
And seal in silence mortal tongues,
Our Helper, God, in whom we trust,
In better worlds our souls shall boast.
PHILIP DODDRIDGE.

465 *"The day of the Lord so cometh as a thief in the night."*

While, with ceaseless course, the sun
Hasted through the former year,
Many souls their race have run,
Never more to meet us here:
Fixed in an eternal state,
They have done with all below;
We a little longer wait,
But how little—none can know.

2 As the wingèd arrow flies
Speedily the mark to find;
As the lightning from the skies
Darts, and leaves no trace behind,—

Swiftly thus our fleeting days
Bear us down life's rapid stream:
Upward, Lord, our spirits raise!
All below is but a dream.

3 Thanks for mercies past receive;
Pardon of our sins renew;
Teach us, henceforth, how to live
With eternity in view:
Bless Thy word to young and old;
Fill us with a Saviour's love;
And when life's short tale is told,
May we dwell with Thee above.
JOHN NEWTON.

CINCINNATI. C. M.

Awake, ye saints, and raise your eyes, And raise your voi - - ces high;

Awake and praise that sovereign love, That shows sal - va - - tion nigh.

466 *"Now is our salvation nearer than when we believed."*

Awake, ye saints, and raise your eyes,
And raise your voices high;
Awake and praise that sovereign love,
That shows salvation nigh.

2 On all the wings of time it flies,
Each moment brings it near;
Then welcome each declining day!
Welcome each closing year!

3 Not many years their round shall run,
Nor many mornings rise,
Ere all its glories stand revealed
To our admiring eyes.

4 Ye wheels of nature. speed your course!
Ye mortal powers, decay!
Fast as ye bring the night of death,
Ye bring eternal day!
PHILIP DODDRIDGE.

467 *"Awake to righteousness, and sin not."*

Thee we adore, Eternal Name!
And humbly own to Thee,
How feeble is our mortal frame,
What dying worms are we!

2 The year rolls round, and steals away
The breath that first it gave;
Whate'er we do, whate'er we be,
We're traveling to the grave.

3 Great God! on what a slender thread
Hang everlasting things!
The eternal state of all the dead
Upon life's feeble strings.

4 Infinite joy, or endless wo,
Attends on every breath,
And yet, how unconcerned we go
Upon the brink of death!

5 Waken, O Lord, our drowsy sense,
To walk this dangerous road;
And if our souls are hurried hence,
May they be found with God.
ISAAC WATTS.

468 *"My times are in Thy hand."*

Our Father, through the coming year
We know not what shall be;
But we would leave without a fear
Its ordering all to Thee.

2 It may be we shall toil in vain
For what the world holds fair;
And all the good we thought to gain,
Deceive and prove but care.

3 It may be it shall darkly blend
Our love with anxious fears,
And snatch away the valued friend,
The tried of many years.

4 It may be it shall bring us days
And nights of lingering pain;
And bid us take a farewell gaze
Of these loved haunts of men.

5 But calmly, Lord, on Thee we rest;
No fears our trust shall move;
Thou knowest what for each is best,
And Thou art Perfect Love.
WILLIAM GASKELL.

BERA. L. M.

Be-hold the path that mor-tals tread Down to the regions of the dead!

Nor will the fleet-ing mo-ments stay, Nor can we measure back our way.

469. *"It is appointed unto men once to die, but after this the judgment."*

BEHOLD the path that mortals tread
Down to the regions of the dead!
Nor will the fleeting moments stay,
Nor can we measure back our way.

2 Our kindred and our friends are gone;
Know, O my soul, this doom thine own;
Feeble as theirs my mortal frame,
The same my way, my house the same.

3 And must I, from the cheerful light,
Pass to the grave's perpetual night,—
From scenes of duty, means of grace,
Must I to God's tribunal pass?

4 Awake, my soul, thy way prepare,
And lose, in this, each mortal care;
With steady feet that path be trod,
Which through the grave conducts to God.

REST. L. M.

Asleep in Jesus! blessed sleep, From which none ever wakes to weep, A calm and undisturbed repose, Unbroken by the last of foes

470. *"Them also which sleep in Jesus will God bring with Him."*

ASLEEP in Jesus! blessed sleep,
From which none ever wakes to weep,
A calm and undisturbed repose,
Unbroken by the last of foes!

2 Asleep in Jesus! O how sweet
To be for such a slumber meet!
With holy confidence to sing
That death hath lost his venomed sting.

3 Asleep in Jesus! peaceful rest,
Whose waking is supremely blest;
No fear, no woe, shall dim that hour
That manifests the Saviour's power.

4 Asleep in Jesus! O for me
May such a blissful refuge be,
Securely shall my ashes lie,
Waiting the summons from on high!

MARGARET MACKAY.

ETERNITY. S. M. D.

It is not death to die, To leave this weary road, And,'mid the brotherhood on high, To be at home with God.

It is not death to bear The wrench that sets us free From dungeon-chain, to breathe the air Of boundless lib - er - ty.

---

471   *"Death is swallowed up in victory."*

It is not death to die,
To leave this weary road,
And, 'mid the brotherhood on high,
To be at home with God.
It is not death to bear
The wrench that sets us free
From dungeon-chain, to breathe the air
Of boundless liberty.

2 It is not death to fling
Aside this sinful dust,
And rise on strong, exulting wing
To live among the just.
Jesus, Thou Prince of life!
Thy chosen cannot die;
Like Thee, they conquer in the strife,
To reign with Thee on high.

CÆSAR MALAN.

DEUX PONTS. L. M.

How blest the righteous when he dies; When sinks a wea - ry soul to rest;

How mildly beam the clos - ing eyes; How gently heaves th'ex-pir - ing breast!

---

472 *"Death is swallowed up in victory."*

How blest the righteous when he dies;
When sinks a weary soul to rest;
How mildly beam the closing eyes;
How gently heaves the expiring breast!

2 So fades a summer cloud away,
So sinks the gale when storms are o'er,
So gently shuts the eye of day,
So dies a wave along the shore.

3 A holy quiet reigns around,
A calm which life nor death destroys;
And naught disturbs that peace profound
Which his unfettered soul enjoys.

4 Life's labor done, as sinks the day,
Light from its load the spirit flies,
While heaven and earth combine to say,
'How blest the righteous when he dies!'

ANNA LÆTITIA BARBAULD.

DIES IRÆ. 8s, 7s, 4s.

Day of judgment, day of wonders! Hark '—the trumpet's awful sound, Louder than a

thousand thunders, Shakes the vast cre - a - tion round: How the summons Will the sinner's heart con - found!

473 *"The trumpet shall sound, and the dead shall be raised."*

Day of judgment, day of wonders !
Hark !—the trumpet's awful sound,
Louder than a thousand thunders,
Shakes the vast creation round :
How the summons
Will the sinner's heart confound !

2 See the Judge, our nature wearing,
Clothed in majesty divine !
You, who long for His appearing,
Then shall say.— 'This God is mine !'
Gracious Saviour,
Own me in that day for Thine.

3 At His call, the dead awaken,
Rise to life from earth and sea ;
All the powers of nature shaken
By His looks, prepare to flee :
Careless sinner,
What will then become of thee ?

4 But to those who have confessed,
Loved and served the Lord below,
He will say.—'Come near, ye blessèd !
See the kingdom I bestow :
You for ever
Shall My love and glory know.'

JOHN NEWTON.

NUREMBERG. 7s.

Christ will gather in His own To the place where He is gone, Where their heart and treasure lie, Where our life is hid on high.

474 *"The Lord hath need of him."*

Christ will gather in His own
To the place where He is gone,
Where their heart and treasure lie,
Where our life is hid on high.

2 Day by day the voice saith, 'Come,
Enter thine eternal home ;'
Asking not if we can spare
This dear soul it summons there.

3 Had He asked us, well we know
We should murmur, 'Spare this blow !'

Yes, with streaming tears should pray,
'Lord, we love him, let him stay.'

4 But the Lord doth naught amiss,
And, since He hath ordered this,
We have naught to do but still
Rest in silence on His will.

5 Many a heart no longer here
Ah ! was all too inly dear ;
Yet, O Love ! 'tis Thou dost call,
Thou wilt be our all in all.

NICHOLAS LOUIS ZINZENDORF.

JUDGMENT HYMN.   P. M.

Great God! what do I see and hear? The end of things crea - ted!
Behold the Judge of man appear, On clouds of glory   seat- ed! The trumpet sounds, the

graves restore The dead which they contain'd before! Prepare, my soul! to   meet Him.

475   *"Behold, the Bridegroom cometh: go ye out to meet Him."*

GREAT God! what do I see and hear?—
The end of things created!
Behold the Judge of man appear,
On clouds of glory seated!
The trumpet sounds—the graves restore
The dead which they contained before!
Prepare, my soul! to meet Him.

2 The dead in Christ shall first arise,
To greet the archangel's warning,
To meet the Saviour in the skies
On this auspicious morning:

No gloomy fears their souls dismay,
His presence sheds eternal day
On those prepared to meet Him.

3 Great God! what do I see and hear?—
The end of things created!
Behold the Judge of man appear,
On clouds of glory seated!
Beneath His cross I view the day
When heaven and earth shall pass away,
And thus prepare to meet Him!

WILLIAM BENGO COLLYER.

BOYLSTON.   S. M.

And will the Judge descend, And will the dead a - rise, And not a single soul escape His all-discerning eyes?

476   *"Every eye shall see Him."*

AND will the Judge descend,
And will the dead arise,
And not a single soul escape
His all-discerning eyes?

2 How will my heart endure
The terrors of that day,
When earth and heaven before His face
Astonished shrink away!

3 But ere that trumpet shakes
The mansions of the dead,

Hark, from the gospel's gentle voice
What joyful tidings spread!

4 Ye sinners, seek His grace
Whose wrath ye cannot bear;
Fly to the shelter of His cross,
And find salvation there.

5 So shall that curse remove,
By which the Saviour bled;
And the last awful day shall pour
His blessings on your head.

PHILIP DODDRIDGE.

NEARER HOME. S. M. D. (For Quartette.)

One sweetly solemn thought Comes to me o'er and o'er,—I'm nearer to my home to-day Than e'er I was before. Nearer my Father's house, Where many mansions be; Nearer the Saviour's great white throne, Nearer the crys-tal sea!

477 *"The night is far spent, the day is at hand."*

One sweetly solemn thought
Comes to me o'er and o'er.—
I'm nearer to my home to-day
Than e'er I was before.

2 Nearer my Father's house,
Where many mansions be;
Nearer the Saviour's great white throne,
Nearer the crystal sea!

3 Nearer the bound of life,
Where burdens we lay down;
Nearer to leave the heavy cross,
Nearer to wear the crown.

4 But, lying dark between,
And winding through the night,
There rolls the dim and unknown stream
That leads at last to light.

5 O if my mortal feet
Have almost joined the brink!
And I to-day am nearer home,
Nearer than now I think!

6 Father, perfect my trust!
And let me feel in death
My spirit's feet are firmly set
Upon the rock of faith!

PHŒBE CARY.

SOUTHWELL. S. M.

One sweetly solemn thought Comes to me o'er and o'er,—I'm nearer to my home to-day Than e'er I was before.

MOUNT ZION. 8s, 7s, 4s.

Lo! He comes, with clouds descending, Once for favor'd sin - ners slain: Thousand thousand saints at - tend-ing

Swell the triumph of His train: Hal - le - lu - jah! Hal - le - lu - jah! God ap-pears on earth to reign!

478   *"Surely I come quickly."*

Lo! He comes, with clouds descending,
Once for favored sinners slain:
Thousand thousand saints attending
Swell the triumph of His train:
   Hallelujah!
God appears, on earth to reign!

2 Every eye shall now behold H.m,
Robed in dreadful majesty;
Those who set at naught and sold Him,
Pierced and nailed Him to the tree,
   Deeply wailing,
Shall the true Messiah see.

3 Now redemption, long expected,
See in solemn pomp appear!

All His saints, by man rejected,
Now shall meet Him in the air;
   Hallelujah!
See the day of God appear!

4 Answer Thine own Bride and Spirit;
Hasten, Lord, the general doom;
The new Heaven and earth to inherit
Take Thy pining exiles home:
   All creation
Travails, groans, and bids Thee come!

5 Yea, Amen! let all adore Thee,
High on Thine eternal throne:
Saviour, take the power and glory;
Claim the kingdom for Thine own:
   O come quickly,
Everlasting God, come down!
             CHARLES WESLEY.

ELYSIUM. L. M.

That day of wrath! that dreadful day, When heav'n and earth shall pass a-way!

What power shall be the sin - ner's stay? How shall he meet that dread - ful day?

MERIBAH. C. P. M.

When Thou, my righteous Judge, shalt come To fetch Thy ransom'd peo-ple home, Shall I among them stand!

Shall such a worthless worm as I, Who sometimes am a-fraid to die, Be found at Thy right hand!

479 *"Behold the Judge standeth before the door."*

When Thou, my righteous Judge, shalt come
To fetch Thy ransomed people home,
　Shall I among them stand?
Shall such a worthless worm as I,
Who sometimes am afraid to die,
　Be found at Thy right hand?

2 Blest Saviour! grant it by Thy grace;
Be Thou, dear Lord, my hiding-place,
　In this the accepted day;
Thy pardoning voice O let me hear,
To still my unbelieving fear,
　Nor let me fall, I pray.

3 Among Thy saints let me be found,
Whene'er the archangel's trump shall sound,
　To see Thy smiling face;
Then in triumphant strains I'll sing,
While heaven's resounding mansions ring
　With shouts of sovereign grace.
　　　SELINA, COUNTESS OF HUNTINGDON.

480 *"Watch therefore, for ye know neither the day nor the hour."*

Lo! on a narrow neck of land,
'Twixt two unbounded seas I stand!
　Yet how insensible!

A point of time, a moment's space,
Removes me to you heavenly place,
　Or—shuts me up in hell!

2 O God! mine inmost soul convert,
And deeply on my thoughtful heart
　Eternal things impress;
Give me to feel their solemn weight,
And save me ere it be too late;
　Wake me to righteousness.

3 Before me place, in dread array,
The pomp of that tremendous day,
　When Thou with clouds shalt come
To judge the nations at Thy bar;
And tell me, Lord! shall I be there
　To meet a joyful doom?

4 Be this my one great business here,
With holy trembling, holy fear,
　To make my calling sure!
Thine utmost counsel to fulfill,
And suffer all Thy righteous will,
　And to the end endure!
　　　CHARLES WESLEY.

481 *"Dies iræ, dies illa."*

That day of wrath! that dreadful day,
When heaven and earth shall pass away!
What power shall be the sinner's stay?
How shall he meet that dreadful day?

2 When, shriveling like a parchèd scroll,
The flaming heavens together roll,
And louder yet, and yet more dread,
Swells the high trump that wakes the dead.

3 O, on that day, that wrathful day,
When man to judgment wakes from clay,
Be Thou, O Christ, the sinner's stay,
Though heaven and earth shall pass away.
　　　SIR WALTER SCOTT.

CANAAN. C. M.

Je - ru - sa - lem, my hap - py home, ... dear ... to me!

When shall my labors have ... end, In joy and peace and thee?

482. "..."

Jerusalem, my happy home,
  Name ever dear to me!
When shall my labors have an end,
  In joy and peace and thee?

2 Where shall these eyes thy heaven...
  And pearly gates behold?
Thy bulwarks with salvation strong,
  And streets of shining gold?

3 There happier ... than Eden's ...
  Nor sin ... ...
Blest ... thro' ... and storms...
  I onward press to you.

Why should I shrink from pain and woe,
  ...at death ...?
...'s ... bend to ...,
  And ... of endless day.

Apostles, martyrs, prophets, there
  ...my ... around.
All ... my friends in Christ below
  Will ... the glorious band.

Jerusalem, my happy home!
  My soul still pants for thee:
Then shall my labors have an end,
  When I thy joys shall see.

WIMBORNE. L. M.

When God is nigh my faith is ... Heaven is my ... ...

Be glad my heart, re joice ... ... My dying flesh shall rest in hope.

RHINE. C. M.

O mother dear, Je-ru-salem; When shall I come to thee? When shall my sorrows
have an end! Thy joys when shall I see? Thy joys when shall I see?

483 *"The city of the living God, the heavenly Jerusalem."*

O MOTHER dear, Jerusalem;
　When shall I come to thee?
When shall my sorrows have an end?
　Thy joys when shall I see?

2 O happy harbor of God's saints!
　O sweet and pleasant soil!
In thee no sorrow can be found,
　Nor grief, nor care, nor toil.

3 No dimming cloud o'ershadows thee,
　No gloom nor darksome night;
But every soul shines as the sun,
　For God Himself gives light.

4 Thy walls are made of precious stones,
　Thy bulwarks' diamond-square,
Thy gates are all of orient pearl;
　O God, if I were there!

5 O passing happy were my state,
　Might I be worthy found

To wait upon my God and King,
　His praises there to sound!
　　　　　　　　　　　DAVID DICKSON.

484 *"Whose builder and maker is God."*

THERE is a house not made with hands,
　Eternal, and on high:
And here my spirit waiting stands,
　Till God shall bid it fly.

2 Shortly this prison of my clay
　Must be dissolved and fall;
Then, O my soul, with joy obey
　Thy heavenly Father's call.

3 We walk by faith of joys to come;
　Faith lives upon His word;
But while the body is our home,
　We're absent from the Lord.

4 'T is pleasant to believe Thy grace,
　But we had rather see;
We would be absent from the flesh,
　And present, Lord, with thee.
　　　　　　　　　　　ISAAC WATTS.

485 *"Thou art with me."*

WHEN God is nigh, my faith is strong,
　His arm is my almighty prop:
Be glad my heart, rejoice my tongue,
　My dying flesh shall rest in hope.

2 Though in the dust I lay my head,
　Yet, gracious God, Thou wilt not leave
My soul forever with the dead,
　Nor lose Thy children in the grave.

3 My flesh shall Thy first call obey,
　Shake off the dust and rise on high;
Then shalt Thou lead the wondrous way
　Up to Thy throne above the sky.

4 There streams of endless pleasure flow;
　And full discoveries of Thy grace,
Which we but tasted here below,
　Spread heavenly joys thro' all the place.
　　　　　　　　　　　ISAAC WATTS.

Je - ru-sa-lem the golden, With milk and honey blest, Beneath thy con-tem-pla-tion Sink heart and voice opprest.

I know not, O, I know not What joys await us there; What radiancy of glo - ry, What bliss beyond compare.

486 *"The throne of God and the Lamb."*

JERUSALEM the golden,
　With milk and honey blest,
Beneath thy contemplation
　Sink heart and voice opprest.
I know not, O, I know not
　What joys await us there ;
What radiancy of glory,
　What bliss beyond compare.

2 They stand, those halls of Zion,
　Conjubilant with song,
And bright with many an angel,
　And all the martyr throng.
The Prince is ever with them ;
　The daylight is serene ;
The pastures of the blessèd
　Are decked in glorious sheen.

3 There is the throne of David ;
　And there, from care released,
The song of them that triumph,
　The shout of them that feast.
And they who with their Leader
　Have conquered in the fight,
For ever and for ever
　Are clad in robes of white.

JOHN MASON NEALE.

487 *"Here have we no continuing city, but we seek one to come."*

BRIEF life is here our portion,
　Brief sorrow, short-lived care ;
The life that knows no ending,
　The tearless life, is there.
O happy retribution !
　Short toil, eternal rest !
For mortals and for sinners
　A mansion with the blest !

2 And now we fight the battle,
　But then shall wear the crown
Of full and everlasting
　And passionless renown.

But He whom now we trust in
　Shall then be seen and known,
And they who know and see Him
　Shall have Him for their own.

3 The morning shall awaken,
　And shadows shall decay,
And each true-hearted servant
　Shall shine as does the day.
And God, our King and Portion,
　In fulness of His grace,
We then shall see for ever
　And worship face to face.

JOHN MASON NEALE.

488 *"They desire a better country, that is, a heavenly."*

FOR thee, O dear, dear country,
　Mine eyes their vigils keep ;
For very love, beholding
　Thy happy name, they weep.
O one, O only mansion !
　O Paradise of joy !
Where tears are ever banished,
　And smiles have no alloy.

2 Thine ageless walls are bonded
　With amethyst unpriced ;
The saints build up its fabric,
　The corner-stone is Christ.
Upon the Rock of ages
　They raise thy holy tower ;
Thine is the victor's laurel,
　And thine the golden dower.

3 O sweet and blessèd country,
　The home of God's elect !
O sweet and blessèd country,
　That eager hearts expect !
Jesus, in mercy bring us
　To that dear land of rest ;
Who art with God the Father
　And Spirit ever blest.

JOHN MASON NEALE.

THREE ANGELS. C. M.

There is a land of pure delight, Where saints im - mor - tal reign;

In - fi - nite day excludes the night, And pleas - ures ban - ish pain.

---

489 *"Thine eyes shall see the King in His beauty; they shall behold the land that is very far off."*

There is a land of pure delight,
  Where saints immortal reign;
Infinite day excludes the night,
  And pleasures banish pain.

2 There everlasting spring abides,
    And never-withering flowers:
  Death, like a narrow sea, divides
    This heavenly land from ours.

3 Sweet fields beyond the swelling flood
    Stand drest in living green;
  So to the Jews old Canaan stood,
    While Jordan rolled between.

4 But timorous mortals start and shrink
    To cross the narrow sea,
  And linger, shivering on the brink,
    And fear to launch away.

5 O could we make our doubts remove,
    These gloomy doubts that rise,
  And see the Canaan that we love,
    With unbeclouded eyes:—

6 Could we but climb where Moses stood,
    And view the landscape o'er,—
  Not Jordan's stream, nor death's cold flood,
    Should fright us from the shore.

ISAAC WATTS.

490 *"He that keepeth thee will not slumber."*

To heaven I lift my waiting eyes,
  There all my hopes are laid;
The Lord that built the earth and skies
  Is my perpetual aid.

2 Their feet shall never slide, nor fall,
    Whom He designs to keep;

His ear attends the softest call;
  His eyes can never sleep.

3 He will sustain our weakest powers
    With His almighty arm,
  And watch our most unguarded hours
    Against surprising harm.

4 Israel, rejoice, and rest secure;
    Thy keeper is the Lord:
  His wakeful eyes employ His power
    For thine eternal guard.

5 He guards thy soul, He keeps thy breath,
    Where thickest dangers come;
  Go and return, secure from death,
    Till God commands thee home.

ISAAC WATTS.

491 *"The things which are not seen are eternal."*

O could our thoughts and wishes fly,
  Above these gloomy shades,
To those bright worlds beyond the sky
  Which sorrow ne'er invades!

2 There joys, unseen by mortal eyes,
    Or reason's feeble ray,
  In ever blooming prospect rise,
    Unconscious of decay.

3 Lord, send a beam of light divine,
    To guide our upward aim!
  With one reviving touch of Thine
    Our languid hearts inflame.

4 Then shall, on faith's sublimest wing,
    Our ardent wishes rise
  To those bright scenes, where pleasures [spring,
    Immortal in the skies.

ANNE STEELE.

IVES. 7s. D.

What are these in bright array,   This innu - mer - able throng, Round the altar, night and day,
Wisdom, riches, to obtain,

Fine.

Hymning one triumphant song?'Worthy is the Lamb once slain, Blessing, honor, glory, pow'r,
New dominion   ev'ry hour.'

Fine.

492   *"He that overcometh, the same shall be clothed in white raiment."*

WHAT are these in bright array,
  This innumerable throng,
Round the altar, night and day,
  Hymning one triumphant song?—
'Worthy is the Lamb once slain,
  Blessing, honor, glory, power,
Wisdom, riches, to obtain,
  New dominion every hour.'

2 These through fiery trials trod!—
  These from great affliction came;
Now before the throne of God,
  Sealed with His almighty name,

Clad in raiment pure and white,
  Victor palms in every hand,
Through their dear Redeemer's might,
  More than conquerors they stand.

3 Hunger, thirst, disease, unknown,
  On immortal fruits they feed;
Them the Lamb amid the throne
  Shall to living fountains lead:
Joy and gladness banish sighs;
  Perfect love dispels all fear;
And for ever from their eyes,
  God shall wipe away the tear.

               JAMES MONTGOMERY.

BENISON. 7s, D.

What are these in bright array,   This innumer - able throng,   Round the altar night and day, Hymning one triumphant song!

'Worthy is the Lamb once slain, Blessing, honor, glory, pow'r, Wisdom, riches, to obtain, New dominion ev'ry hour.'

VOM HIMMEL HOCH. L. M.

Now let our souls, on wings sublime, Rise from the van-i-ties of time,

Draw back the part-ing veil, and see The glories of e-ter-ni-ty.

493 *"The spirit shall return unto God who gave it."*
Now let our souls, on wings sublime,
Rise from the vanities of time,
Draw back the parting veil, and see
The glories of eternity.

2 Born by a new celestial birth,
Why should we grovel here on earth?
Why grasp at vain and fleeting toys,
So near to heaven's eternal joys?

3 Shall aught beguile us on the road
While we are walking back to God?
For strangers into life we come,
And dying is but going home.

4 Welcome, sweet hour of full discharge,
That sets our longing souls at large;
Unbinds our chains, breaks up our cell;
And gives us with our God to dwell.

5 To dwell with God, to feel His love,
Is the full heaven enjoyed above;
And the sweet expectation now,
Is the young dawn of heaven below.
THOMAS GIBBONS.

494 *"I shall be satisfied, when I awake with Thy likeness."*
WHAT sinners value I resign;
Lord, 't is enough that Thou art mine:
I shall behold Thy blissful face,
And stand complete in righteousness.

2 This life 's a dream, an empty show;
But the bright world to which I go

Hath joys substantial and sincere;
When shall I wake and find me there?

3 O glorious hour! O blest abode!
I shall be near and like my God!
And flesh and sin no more control
The sacred pleasures of the soul.

4 My flesh shall slumber in the ground,
Till the last trumpet's joyful sound;
Then burst the chains with sweet surprise,
And in my Saviour's image rise.
ISAAC WATTS.

495 *"And there shall be no more death."*
How vain is all beneath the skies,
How transient every earthly bliss;
How slender all the fondest ties,
That bind us to a world like this.

2 The evening cloud, the morning dew,
The withering grass, the fading flower,
Of earthly hopes are emblems true,
The glory of a passing hour.

3 But though earth's fairest blossoms die,
And all beneath the sky is vain,
There is a land whose confines lie
Beyond the reach of care and pain.

4 Then let the hope of joys to come
Dispel our cares and chase our fears:
If God be ours, we're traveling home,
Though passing through a vale of tears.

MERIBAH. C. P. M.

There is a dwell-ing-place a-bove; Thith-er to meet the God of love, The poor in spi - rit go:

There is a par-a-dise of rest; For contrite hearts and souls distrest Its streams of com-fort flow.

496   *"Great is your reward in heaven."*

THERE is a dwelling-place above :
Thither to meet the God of love.
The poor in spirit go :
There is a paradise of rest ;
For contrite hearts and souls distrest
Its streams of comfort flow.

2 There is a voice to mercy true ;
To them who mercy's path pursue
That voice shall bliss impart :

There is a sight from man concealed ;
That sight, the face of God revealed,
Shall bless the pure in heart.

3 There is a name in heaven bestowed ;
That name, which hails them sons of God,
The friends of peace shall know :
There is a kingdom in the sky,
Where they shall reign with God on high,
Who serve Him here below.

RICHARD MANT.

HEXHAM. 11s.

I would not live al-way, I ask not to stay Where storm af-ter storm ri-ses dark o'er the way:

The few lurid mornings that dawn on us here, Are e-nough for life's woes, full e-nough for its cheer.

LANDSTUHL. C. M. 5 lines.

There is an hour of peaceful rest, To mourning wand'rers given; There is a joy for souls distrest, A balm for every wounded breast, 'Tis found above— in heav'n.

497   *"There the weary be at rest."*

THERE is an hour of peaceful rest,
To mourning wanderers given :
There is a joy for souls distrest,
A balm for every wounded breast,
'T is found above—in heaven.

2 There is a home for weary souls
By sin and sorrow driven ;
When tost on life's tempestuous shoals,
Where storms arise and ocean rolls,
And all is drear but heaven.

3 There, faith lifts up her cheerful eye.
To brighter prospects given ;
And views the tempest passing by,
The evening shadows quickly fly,
And all serene in heaven.

4 There, fragrant flowers immortal bloom.
And joys supreme are given ;
There, rays of light disperse the gloom ;—
Beyond the confines of the tomb
Appears the dawn of heaven.

WILLIAM BINGHAM TAPPAN.

498   *"O that I had wings like a dove! for then would I fly away, and be at rest."*

I WOULD not live alway : I ask not to stay
Where storm after storm rises dark o'er
     the way ;
The few lurid mornings that dawn on us
     here,
Are enough for life's woes, full enough
     for its cheer.

2 I would not live alway, thus fettered by
     sin,
Temptation without and corruption within :
E'en the rapture of pardon is mingled with
     fears,
And the cup of thanksgiving with penitent
     tears.

3 I would not live alway ; no—welcome
     the tomb ;
Since Jesus hath lain there, I dread not its
     gloom ;

There, sweet be my rest, till He bid me
     arise
To hail Him in triumph descending the
     skies.

4 Who, who would live alway, away from
     his God ;
Away from yon heaven, that blissful abode,
Where the rivers of pleasure flow o'er the
     bright plains,
And the noontide of glory eternally reigns :-

5 Where the saints of all ages in harmony
     meet,
Their Saviour and brethren transported to
     greet ;
While the anthems of rapture unceasingly
     roll,
And the smile of the Lord is the feast of
     the soul.

WILLIAM AUGUSTUS MUHLENBERG.

CHRISTMAS. C. M.

Give me the wings of faith, to rise Within the veil, and see The saints a-bove—how great their joys! How bright their glories be, How bright their glories be!

499 *"He that overcometh shall inherit all things."*

Give me the wings of faith, to rise
Within the veil, and see
The saints above—how great their joys!
How bright their glories be!

2 Once they were mourning here below,
And wet their couch with tears;
They wrestled hard, as we do now,
With sins, and doubts, and fears.

3 I ask them whence their victory came;
They, with united breath,
Ascribe their conquest to the Lamb,
Their triumph to His death.

4 They marked the footsteps that He trod,—
His zeal inspired their breast;
And, following their incarnate God,
Possess the promised rest.

5 Our glorious Leader claims our praise
For His own pattern given,
While the long cloud of witnesses
Shows the same path to heaven.
ISAAC WATTS.

500 *"To me to live is Christ, and to die is gain."*

Lord, it belongs not to my care
Whether I die or live;
To love and serve Thee is my share,
And this Thy grace must give.

2 If life be long, I will be glad,
That I may long obey;

If short, yet why should I be sad,
To soar to endless day?

3 Christ leads me through no darker rooms
Than He went through before;
He that unto God's kingdom comes
Must enter by this door.

4 Come, Lord, when grace hath made me meet
Thy blessed face to see;
For if Thy work on earth be sweet,
What will Thy glory be!

5 My knowledge of that life is small;
The eye of faith is dim;
But 't is enough that Christ knows all,
And I shall be with Him.
RICHARD BAXTER.

501 *"He that sitteth on the throne shall dwell among them."*

There, on a high, majestic throne,
The Almighty Father reigns,
And sheds His glorious goodness down
On all the blissful plains.

2 Bright, like a sun, the Saviour sits,
And spreads eternal noon;
No evenings there, nor gloomy nights,
To want the feeble moon.

3 Jesus, and when shall that dear day,
That joyful hour appear,
When I shall leave this house of clay,
To dwell among them there?
ISAAC WATTS.

St Edmund's.

HEAVEN IS MY HOME.   P. M.

I'm but a stranger here, Heav'n is my home; Earth is a desert drear, Heav'n is my home.

Danger and sorrow stand Round me on ev'ry hand; Heav'n is my fatherland, Heav'n is my home. Amen.

502   *"In My Father's house are many mansions."*

I'M but a stranger here;
Earth is a desert drear,
  Heaven is my home.
Danger and sorrow stand
Round me on every hand :
Heaven is my fatherland,
  Heaven is my home.

2 What though the tempest rage?
Short is my pilgrimage,
  Heaven is my home ;
And time's wild wintry blast
Soon will be overpast ;
I shall reach home at last,
  Heaven is my home.

3 There, at my Saviour's side,
I shall be glorified ;
  Heaven is my home ;
There with the good and blest,
Those I love most and best,
I shall for ever rest ;
  Heaven is my home.

4 Grant me to murmur not,
Whate'er my earthly lot ;
  Heaven is my home ;
Grant me to surely stand
There at my Lord's right hand ;
Heaven is my fatherland,
  Heaven is my home.
            THOMAS RAWSON TAYLOR.

503   *"Behold, the tabernacle of God is with men."*

LO ! what a glorious sight appears
  To our believing eyes !
The earth and seas are past away,
  And the old rolling skies.

2 From the third heaven, where God resides,
  That holy, happy place,
The new Jerusalem comes down,
  Adorned with shining grace.

3 Attending angels shout for joy,
  And the bright armies sing,—
'Mortals, behold the sacred seat
  Of your descending King.

4 'The God of glory down to men
  Removes His blest abode ;
Men, the dear objects of His grace,
  And He the loving God.

5 'His own kind hand shall wipe the tears
  From every weeping eye ;
And pains, and groans, and griefs, and fears,
  And death itself shall die.'

6 How long, dear Saviour, O how long
  Shall this bright hour delay?
Fly swiftly round, ye wheels of time,
  And bring the welcome day !
            ISAAC WATTS.

ONWARD. S. M.

CHORUS.

vv. I, V. For ev - er with the Lord!   Amen, so let it be!   Life from the dead is in that word, And im - mor-tal - i - ty!

SOLO.   *ril.*   D.C.

vv. II. Here in the bo - dy pent,   Absent from Him I roam, Yet nightly pitch my moving tent A day's march nearer home.
III. My Father's, etc.
IV. Ah! then my, etc.

SOLO.   *ril.*

v. VI. So when my la - test breath Shall rend the veil in twain, By death I shall escape from death, And life eternal gain.

CHORUS. *Tempo.*

v. VII. Knowing as I am known, How shall I love that word, And oft repeat before the throne,—'For ever with the Lord!' 'For ever with the Lord!"

504   *"And so shall we ever be with the Lord."*

' For ever with the Lord ! '
   Amen ! so let it be !
Life from the dead is in that word,
   And immortality !

2 Here in the body pent,
   Absent from Him I roam,
Yet nightly pitch my moving tent
   A day's march nearer home.

3 My Father's house on high,
   Home of my soul ! how near,
At times, to faith's foreseeing eye,
   Thy golden gates appear !

4 Ah ! then my spirit faints
   To reach the land I love,

The bright inheritance of saints,
   Jerusalem above !

5 ' For ever with the Lord ! '
   Saviour, if 't is Thy will,
The promise of that faithful word
   E'en here to me fulfil.

6 So when my latest breath
   Shall rend the veil in twain,
By death I shall escape from death,
   And life eternal gain.

7 Knowing as I am known,
   How shall I love that word,
And oft repeat before the throne,—
   ' For ever with the Lord ! '
           JAMES MONTGOMERY.

PARADISE. P. M.

O Paradise! O Paradise! Who doth not crave for rest? Who would not seek the happy land Where they that luv'd are blest;

loyal hearts and true

REF. Where loy - al hearts and true Stand ever in the light, All rapture thro' and thro,' In God's most ho - ly sight!

505 *"Behold. I come quickly, and My reward is with Me."*

O PARADISE! O Paradise!
Who doth not crave for rest?
Who would not seek the happy land,
Where they that loved are blest;
Where loyal hearts and true
Stand ever in the light,
All rapture through and through,
In God's most holy sight!

2 O Paradise! O Paradise!
'Tis weary waiting here:
I long to be where Jesus is,
To feel, to see Him near;—REF.

3 O Paradise! O Paradise!
I want to sin no more;
I want to be as pure on earth
As on Thy spotless shore!—REF.

FREDERICK WILLIAM FABER.

CANTUS FIRMUS.

For ev - er with the Lord! A - men, so let it be!

Life from the dead is in that word, And im - mor - ta - li - ty.

240   **Heaven.**

NEW JERUSALEM. P. M.

We are on our journey home,   Where Christ our Lord is gone;   We shall meet a-
vv. II. Tho' clouds   rise   dark between;
" III.   From the nev - er - set - ting Sun!
" IV.   Those mansions fair to see;

-round His throne, When He makes His people   one   In the new Je - ru - sa - lem.

506   *"And I saw heaven opened."*

We are on our journey home,
   Where Christ our Lord is gone;
We shall meet around His throne,
   When He makes His people one
     In the new Jerusalem.

2 We can see that distant home,
   Though clouds rise dark between;
Faith views the radiant dome,
   And a luster flashes keen
     From the new Jerusalem.

3 O glory shining far
   From the never-setting Sun!
O trembling morning-star!
   Our journey's almost done
     To the new Jerusalem!

4 Our hearts are breaking now
   Those mansions fair to see;
O Lord, Thy heavens bow,
   And raise us up with Thee
     To the new Jerusalem!

CHARLES BEECHER.

OLD MELODY. L. M. 6 lines.

The saints of God! their conflict past And life's long bat-tle   won   at   last, No more they need the shield or sword,

They cast them down before their Lord: O happy saints! for ev - er blest, At Je-sus' feet how safe you rest!

AMERICA. 6s, 4s.

My country, 'tis of thee, Sweet land of lib-er-ty, Of thee I sing; Land where my

fa-thers died, Land of the pilgrims' pride, From ev'ry mountain side Let freedom ring.

507 *"Thou shalt judge the people righteously, And govern the nations upon earth."*

My country, 'tis of thee,
Sweet land of liberty,
  Of thee I sing;
Land where my fathers died,
Land of the pilgrims' pride,
From every mountain side
  Let freedom ring.

2 My native country, thee—
Land of the noble free—
  Thy name I love;
I love thy rocks and rills,
Thy woods and templed hills;
Rapture my spirit thrills
  Like that above.

3 Let music swell the breeze,
And ring from all the trees
  Sweet freedom's song:
Let mortal tongues awake;
Let all that breathe partake;
Let rocks their silence break,—
  The sound prolong.

4 Our fathers' God, to Thee,
Author of liberty,
  To Thee we sing:
Long may our land be bright
With freedom's holy light;
Protect us by Thy might,
  Great God, our King.

SAMUEL FRANCIS SMITH.

508 *"Lord, if he sleep, he shall do well."*

THE saints of God! their conflict past
And life's long battle won at last,
No more they need the shield or sword,
They cast them down before their Lord:
  O happy saints! for ever blest,
  At Jesus' feet how safe you rest!

2 The saints of God! their wanderings done,
No more their weary course they run,
No more they faint, no more they fall,

No foes oppress, no fears appall:
  O happy saints! for ever blest,
  In that dear home how sweet your rest!

3 O God of saints! to Thee we cry;
O Saviour! plead for us on high;
O Holy Ghost! our Guide and Friend,
Grant us Thy grace till life shall end:
That with all saints our rest may be
In that bright Paradise with Thee!

GUARDIAN ANGELS. P. M. (For Quartette.)

At eve, when twilight's last greeting In shadows is lost in the west; When nature her dewdrops is

weep - ing, My soul longs for sleep then, and rest. The heav'nly gates now are lift - ed, And visions seraphic ap -

pear; With voice and wings they are gifted, With strains of sweet song they draw near. They watch o'er me while I am

They draw near and

At eve, when twilight's last greeting
  In shadows is lost in the west ;
When nature her dewdrops is weeping,
  My soul longs for sleep then and rest.—
  The heavenly gates now are lifted,
    And visions seraphic appear ;
  With voice and wings they are gifted,
    With strains of sweet song they draw
      near.

They watch o'er me while I am sleeping,
  And chant alleluias to God.
Secure I thus rest in their keeping,
  And dream of their heavenly abode.
  Sweet angels, when my call shall come,
    Outstretch then your wings—take
      me home !

GUSTAVE J. STOECKEL.

I will a-rise, I will a-rise and go to my fa

ther, And will say un-to him: Fa - ther! Fa - ther! I have

sin - ned, have sin-ned, I have sin-ned against heav'n and be-fore thee; I am

no more worthy to be call - ed thy son. I will a-rise!

I will a-rise and go to my fa - ther, my fa - ther.

Chants.

1.

Amen, A - men.

2.

3.

A - men.

1 Our Father who art in heaven,
Hallowed | be Thy | name : .

2 Thy Kingdom come ; Thy will be done
On | earth, ·· as it | is in | heaven.

3 Give us this day our | daily | bread :

4 And forgive us our trespasses,
As we for- | give · them that | trespass a- | gainst us.

5 And lead us not into temptation,
But de- | liver · us from | evil :

6 For Thine is the Kingdom.
And the power, and the | glory for | ever and | ever. Amen.

VENITE, EXULTEMUS DOMINO.

4.

5.

6.

1 O COME, let us sing | unto · the | Lord : ‖ let us heartily rejoice in the | strength · of | our · sal- | vation.
Let us come before His presence with | thanks- = | giving : ‖ and show ourselves | glad · in | Him · with | psalms.

2 For the Lord is a | great · = | God : ‖ and a great King a- | bove · = | all · = | gods.
In His hand are all the corners | of · the | earth : ‖ and the strength of the | hills · is | His · = | also.

3 The sea is His, | and · He | made it : ‖ and His hands pre- | par-ed the | dry · = | land.
O come, let us worship, | and · fall | down : ‖ and kneel be- | fore · the | Lord · our | Maker.

4 For He is the | Lord · our | God : ‖ and we are the people of His pasture, and the | sheep · of | His · = | hand.
O worship the Lord in the | beauty · of | holiness : ‖ let the whole earth | stand · in | awe · of | Him.

:8: 5 For He cometh, for He cometh to | judge · the | earth : ‖ and with righteous- ness to judge the world, and the | peo ple | with · His | truth.

6 Glory be to the Father, | and · to the | Son : ‖ and | to · the | Ho-ly | Ghost ;
As it was in the beginning, is now, and | ev-er | shall be : ‖ world | without | end.
A- | men.

Psalm xcv.

TE DEUM LAUDAMUS.

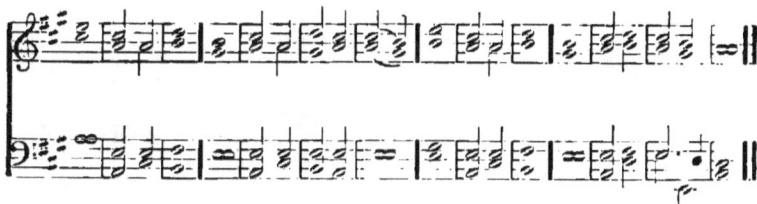

1 We praise | Thee · O | God : ‖ we acknowledge | Thee · to | be · the | Lord.
All the earth doth | wor-ship | Thee : ‖ the Father | ev-er | last= | ing.

2 To Thee all Angels | cry · a- | loud : ‖ the Heavens, and | all · the | powers · there- | in.
To Thee, Cherubim and | Se-raph- | im : ‖ con- | tin-ual- | ly · do | cry ;

3 Holy, | Ho-ly, | Holy : ‖ Lord | God · of | Sa-ba- | oth ;
Heaven and | earth · are | full : ‖ of the | Majes-ty | of · Thy | glory.

4 The glorious company of the Apostles | praise ·= | Thee : ‖
The goodly fellowship of the | Pro-phets | praise ·= | Thee.
The noble army of Martyrs | praise ·= | Thee : ‖
The holy Church throughout all the world | doth · ac- | know-ledge | Thee ;

5 The Father, of an | in-finite | Majesty : ‖
Thine adorable, | true · and | on-ly | Son ;
Also the | Ho-ly | Ghost : ‖
The | Com-= | = · fort- | er.

6 Thou | art · the | King : ‖ of | glo-ry, | O = | Christ.
Thou art the ever- | last-ing | Son : ‖ of | = · the | Fa- = | ther.

7 When Thou tookest upon Thee to de- | liv-er | man : ‖ Thou didst humble Thyself
to be | born · = | of · a | Virgin.
When Thou hadst overcome the | sharpness · of | death : ‖ Thou didst open the
kingdom of | Heaven · to | all · be- | lievers.

8 Thou sittest at the right | hand · of | God : ‖ in the | glo-ry | of · the | Father.
We believe that | Thou · shalt | come : ‖ to | be · = | our · = | Judge.

9 We therefore pray Thee | help · Thy | servants : ‖ whom Thou hast redeemed |
with · Thy | pre-cious | blood.
Make them to be numbered | with · Thy | saints : ‖ in glory | ev-er- | last- ·= |
ing.

10 O Lord, | save · Thy | people : ‖ and | bless · Thine | her-it- | age.
Gov- | = · ern | them : ‖ and | lift · them | up · for | ever.

11 Day | = · by | day : ‖ we | mag-ni- | fy = | Thee ;
And we | worship · Thy | Name : ‖ ever | world · with- | out = | end.

12 Vouch- | safe, O | Lord : ‖ to keep us | this · day | with-out | sin.
O Lord, have | mercy · up- | on us : ‖ have | mer-cy⌢up- | on · = | us.

13 O Lord, let Thy mercy | be · up- | on us : ‖ as our | trust = | is · in | Thee.
O Lord, in Thee | have · I | trusted : ‖ let me | nev-er | be · con- | founded.

BENEDICITE, OMNIA OPERA DOMINI.

1 O ALL ye works of the Lord, | bless · ye the | Lord : ‖ praise Him, and | magni-
fy | Him · for | ever.
  O ye Angels of the Lord, | bless · ye the | Lord : ‖ praise Him, and | magni-fy |
Him · for | ever.

2 O ye Heavens, | bless · ye the | Lord : ‖ praise Him, and | magni-fy | Him for |
ever.
  O ye Waters that be above the Firmament, | bless · ye the | Lord : ‖ praise Him,
and | magni-fy | Him · for | ever.

3 O all ye Powers of the Lord, | bless · ye the | Lord : ‖ praise Him, and | magni-
fy | Him · for | ever.
  O ye Sun and Moon, | bless · ye the | Lord : ‖ praise Him, and | magni-fy | Him ·
for | ever.

4 O ye Stars of Heaven, | bless · ye the | Lord : ‖ praise Him, and | magni-fy |
Him · for | ever.
  O ye Showers and Dew, | bless · ye the | Lord : ‖ praise Him, and | magni-fy |
Him · for | ever.

5 O ye Winds of God, | bless · ye the | Lord : ‖ praise Him, and | magni-fy |
Him · for | ever.
  O ye Fire and Heat, | bless ·· ye the | Lord : ‖ praise Him, and | magni-fy |
Him · for | ever.

6 O ye Winter and Summer, | bless · ye the | Lord : ‖ praise Him, and | magni-fy | Him · for | ever.

 O ye Dews and Frosts, | bless · ye the | Lord : ‖ praise Him, and | magni-fy | Him · for | ever.

7 O ye Frost and Cold, | bless · ye the | Lord : ‖ praise Him, and | magni-fy | Him · for | ever.

 O ye Ice and Snow, | bless · ye the | Lord : ‖ praise Him, and | magni-fy | Him · for | ever.

8 O ye Nights and Days, | bless · ye the | Lord : ‖ praise Him, and | magni-fy | Him · for | ever.

 O ye Light and Darkness, | bless · ye the | Lord : ‖ praise Him, and | magni-fy | Him · for | ever.

9 O ye Lightnings and Clouds, | bless · ye the | Lord : ‖ praise Him, and | magni-fy | Him · for | ever.

 O let the Earth, | bless ·—the | Lord : ‖ Yea, let it praise Him, and | magni-fy | Him · for | ever.

10 O ye Mountains and Hills, | bless · ye the | Lord : ‖ praise Him, and | magni-fy | Him · for | ever.

 O all ye Green Things upon the Earth, | bless · ye the | Lord : ‖ praise Him, and | magni-fy | Him · for | ever.

11 O ye Wells, | bless · ye the | Lord : ‖ praise Him, and | magni-fy | Him · for | ever.

 O ye Seas and Floods, | bless · ye the | Lord : ‖ praise Him, and | magni-fy | Him · for | ever.

12 O ye Whales, and all that move in the waters, | bless · ye the | Lord : ‖ praise Him, and | magni-fy | Him · for | ever.

 O all ye Fowls of the Air, | bless · ye the | Lord :‖ praise Him, and | magni-fy | Him · for | ever.

13 O all ye Beasts and Cattle, | bless · ye the | Lord : ‖ praise Him, and | magni-fy | Him · for | ever.

 O ye children of Men, | bless · ye the | Lord : ‖ praise Him, and | magni-fy | Him · for | ever.

14 O let Israel | bless·—the | Lord :‖ praise Him, and | magni-fy | Him · for | ever.

 O ye Priests of the Lord, | bless · ye the | Lord :‖ praise Him, and | magni-fy | Him · for | ever.

15 O ye Servants of the Lord, | bless · ye the Lord : ‖ praise Him, and | magni-fy | Him · for | ever.

 O ye Spirits and Souls of the Righteous, | bless · ye the | Lord : ‖ praise Him, and | magni-fy | Him · for | ever.

16 O ye holy and humble Men of Heart, | bless · ye the | Lord : ‖ praise Him, and | magni-fy | Him · for | ever.

17 Glory be to the Father, | and · to the | Son : ‖ and | to · the | Ho-ly | Ghost ; As it was in the beginning, is now, and | ev-er | shall be : ‖ world | without | end. A- | men.

Chants.

JUBILATE DEO.

11.

12.

13.

14.

1 O BE joyful in the Lord, | all · ye | lands : ‖ serve the Lord with gladness, and come before His | pre-sence | with · a | song.
  Be ye sure that the Lord, | He · is | God : ‖ it is He that hath made us, and not we ourselves ; we are His people, and the | sheep · of | His = | pasture.

2 O go your way into His gates with thanksgiving, and into His courts | with = | praise : ‖ be thankful unto Him. and | speak · good | of · His | Name.
  For the Lord is gracious, H's mercy is | ev-er- | lasting : ‖ and His truth endureth from generation to | gen-er- | a- = | tion.

3 Glo-ry be to the Father, | and · to the | Son : ‖ and | to · the | Ho-ly | Ghost ;
  As it was in the beginning, is now, and | ev·er | shall be : ‖ world | with-out | end. A- | men.

Psalm c.

BENEDICTUS.

15.

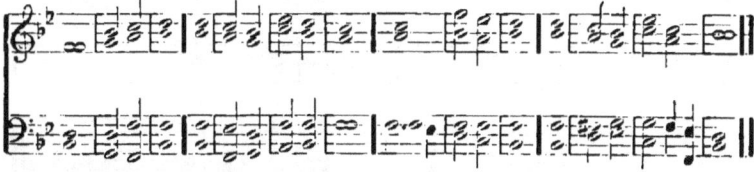

16.

17.

1 BLESSED be the Lord God of | Is-ra- | el : ‖ for He hath visited, | and · re- | deemed · His | people ;
And hath raised up a mighty salvation | for · ⸗ | us : ‖ in the house | of · His | servant | David ;

2 As He spake by the mouth of His | ho-ly | Prophets : ‖ which have been | since · the | world · be- | gan ;
That we should be saved | from· our | enemies :‖ and from the hand of | all · that | hate · ⸗ | us ;

3 Glo-ry be to the Father, | and · to the | Son : ‖ and | to · the | Ho-ly | Ghost ;
As it was in the beginning, is now, and | ev-er | shall be : ‖ world | without | end.
A- | men.

Luke i. 68 ff.

BENEDICTUS DOMINUS DEUS.

18.

Prais'd and | all for e - - - ver.
exalted above }

19.

20.

1 Blessed art Thou, O Lord | God of · our | fathers : || praised and exalted
above | all · for | e-| ver.
2 Blessed art Thou for the | Name · of Thy | Majesty :|| praised and exalted
above | all · for | e-| ver.

3 Blessed art Thou in the temple | of Thy | holiness : || praised and exalted
above | all · for | e-| ver.
4 Blessed art Thou that beholdest the depths, and dwellest be-| tween the |
cherubim : || praised and exalted above | all · for | e-| ver.

5 Blessed art Thou on the glorious | throne · of Thy | kingdom : || praised
and exalted above | all · for | e-| ver.
6 Blessed art Thou in the | firmament of | heaven : || praised and exalted
above | all · for | e-|ver.

Glory be to the Father, | and · to the | Son :|| and | to · the | Ho-ly | Ghost.
As it was in the beginning, is now, and | ev-er | shall be : || world | with-
out | end. A- | men.

CANTATE DOMINO.

1 O sing unto the Lord a | new · — | song : ‖ for He | hath · done | marvellous | things.
  With His own right hand, and with His | ho-ly | arm : ‖ hath He gotten Him- | self · the | vic-to- | ry.

2 The Lord declared | His · sal- | va-tion : ‖ His righteousness hath He openly showed | in · the | sight · of the | heathen.
  He hath remembered His mercy and truth toward the house of | Is-ra- | el : ‖ and all the ends of the world have seen the sal- | va-tion | of · our | God.

3 Show yourselves joyful unto the Lord, | all · ye | lands : ‖ sing, re- | joice, and | give · — | thanks.
  Praise the Lord up- | on · the | harp : ‖ sing to the harp with a | psalm · of | thanks- — | giving.

4 With trumpets | also · and | shawms : ‖ O show yourselves joyful be- | fore · the | Lord, · the | King.
  Let the sea make a noise, and all that | there-in | is : ‖ the round world, and | they · that | dwell · there- | in.

5 Let the floods clap their hands, and let the hills be joyful together be- | fore · the | Lord : ‖ for He | cometh · to | judge · the | earth.
  With righteousness shall He | judge · the | world : ‖ and the | peo-ple | with · — | equity.

6 Glory be to the Father. | and · to the | Son : ‖ and | to · the | Ho-ly | Ghost.
  As it was in the beginning, is now, and | ev-er | shall be : ‖ world | with-out | end.
  A- | men.

Psalm xcviii.

BONUM EST CONFITERI.

24.

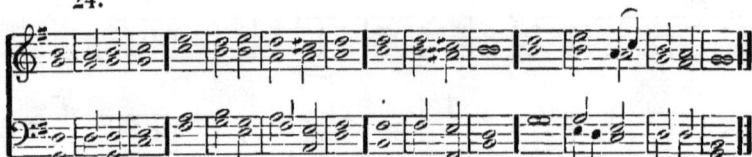

25.

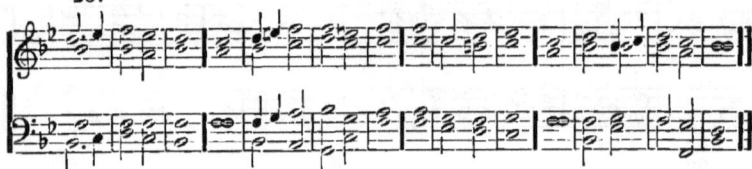

26.

27.

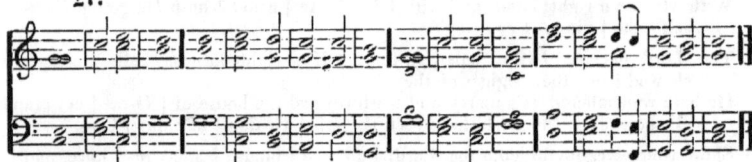

1 It is a good thing to give thanks | unto · the | Lord : ‖ and to sing.praises unto
Thy Name, | O · ═ | Most · ═ | Highest.
To tell of Thy loving-kindness early | in · the | morning : ‖ and of Thy truth | in ·
the | night · ═ | season.

2 Upon an instrument of ten strings, and up- | on · the | lute : ‖ upon a loud instru-
ment, | and · up- | on · the | harp.
For Thou, Lord, hast made me glad | through · Thy | works : ‖ and I will rejoice in
giving praise for the oper- | a-tions | of · Thy | hands.

Glory be to the Father, | and · to the | Son : ‖ and | to · the | Ho-ly | Ghost ;
As it was in the beginning, is now, and | ev-er | shall be : ‖ world | without |
end. A- | men.

Psalm xcii.

DEUS MISEREATUR.
28.

1. God be merciful unto us and bless us; And cause His face to shine up-on us; That Thy way may be known upon

earth, Thy saving health a - mong all nations. Let the peoples praise Thee O God; Let all the peoples praise Thee.
Let the peoples praise Thee O God; Let all the peoples praise Thee.

ff

O let the nations be glad and sing for joy; For Thou shalt judge the peoples with equity, } na - tions up - on earth.
and govern the
The earth hath yielded her increase; And God, even our own God shall bless us.

God shall bless us, And all the ends of the earth shall fear Him; God shall bless us And all the ends of the earth shall fear Him.

Glory be to the Father, and to the Son, and to the Holy Ghost; As it was in the begin- } shall be, world without end A - men. Amen.
ning, is now, and ever {

Psalm lxvii.

BENEDIC, ANIMA MEA.

29.

30.

31.

1 PRAISE the Lord, | O · my | soul : ‖ and all that is within me | praise · His | ho-
ly | Name.
Praise the Lord, | O · my | soul : ‖ and forget not | all · His | ben-e- | fits ;

2 Who forgiveth | all · thy | sin : ‖ and healeth all | thine · in | firm-i- | ties ;
Who saveth thy life | from · de- | struction : ‖ and crowneth thee with mercy
and | lov-ing- | kind- ꞊ | ness.

3 O praise the Lord, ye Angels of His, ye that ex- | cel · in | strength : ‖ ye that
fulfil His commandment, and hearken unto the | voice · of | His · ꞊ | word.
O praise the Lord, all | ye · His | hosts : ‖ ye servants of | His · that | do · His |
pleasure.

:8: 4 O speak good of the Lord, all ye works of His, in all places of | His · do- | min-
ion : ‖ praise thou the Lord, | O · ꞊ | my · ꞊ | soul.
Glory be to the Father, | and · to the | Son : ‖ and | to · the | Ho-ly | Ghost ;
As it was in the beginning, is now, and | ev-er | shall be : ‖ world | with-out |
end. A- | men.   Psalm ciii.

GLORIA IN EXCELSIS.

GLORY be to | God · on | high : ‖ and on earth | peace, · good- | will · towards | men.

We praise Thee, we bless Thee, we | wor-ship | Thee : ‖ we glorify Thee, we give thanks to | Thee · for | Thy · great | glory.

O Lord God, | heaven-ly | King : ‖ God the | Father | Al-— | mighty.
O Lord, the only-begotten Son | JE-SUS | CHRIST : ‖ O Lord God, Lamb of God, | Son · of the | Fa- — | ther.

That takest away the | sins · of ⌒ the | world : ‖ have mercy up- | on · — | us.
Thou that takest away the | sins · of ⌒ the | world : ‖ have mercy up- | on · — | us.
Thou that takest away the | sins · of ⌒ the | world : ‖ re- | ceive · our | prayer.
Thou that sittest at the right hand of | God · the | Father : ‖ have mercy up- | on · — | us.

For Thou only | art · — | holy : ‖ Thou | on-ly | art · the | Lord.
Thou only, O Christ, with the | Ho-ly | Ghost : ‖ art most high in the | glory · of | God · the | Father. ‖ A- | men.

A · men.

DOMINI EST TERRA

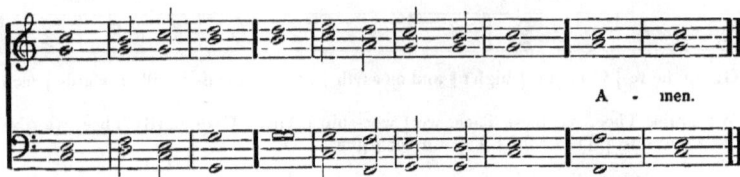

A - men.

1 THE earth is the Lord's, and the fulness thereof;
The world and they that | dwell there- | in ;‖
For He hath founded it upon the seas,
And es- | tablished ·· it up- | on the floods.

SOLO.

2 Who shall ascend into the hill of the Lord?
And who shall stand in His | holy | place?‖

CHORUS.

He that hath clean hands and a pure heart;
Who hath not lifted up his soul unto vanity,
And hath not | sworn⌒ | de-⌒ | ceitfully.

3 He shall receive a blessing from the Lord,
And righteousness from the God of | his sal- | vation.‖
This is the generation of them that seek after Him,
That seek Thy | face, O | God of | Jacob.

4 Lift up your heads, O ye gates ;
And be ye lift up, ye everlasting doors ;
And the King of Glory | shall come | in. ‖

SOLO.

Who is this King of Glory?

CHORUS.

The Lord, strong and mighty :
The | Lord⌒ | mighty ·· in | battle.

5 Lift up your heads, O ye gates ;
Yea, lift them up ye everlasting doors ;
And the King of Glory | shall come | in.‖

SOLO.

Who is this King of Glory?

CHORUS.

The Lord of hosts, | He ·· is the | King of | Glory.

Psalm xxiv.

EXALTABO TE, DEUS.

35.

36.

A - men.

1 I WILL extol Thee, my | God, O | King ; : ‖
And I will bless Thy | name for | ever · and | ever.

The Lord is | good to | all ; : ‖
And His tender mercies are | over | all His | works.

2 All Thy works shall give thanks unto | Thee, O | Lord ; : ‖
And Thy | saints shall | bless ⸗ | Thee.

Thy kingdom is an ever- | lasting | kingdom, : ‖
And Thy dominion endureth through- | out all | gene- | rations.

3 The Lord upholdeth | all that | fall, : ‖
And raiseth up all | those that | be bowed | down :

The eyes of | all · wait up- | on Thee : ‖
And Thou givest them their | meat in | due ⸗ | season.

4 Thou | openest · Thine | hand, : ‖
And satisfiest the desire of | every | living | thing.

The Lord is righteous in | all His | ways, : ‖
And | gracious in | all His | works.

5 The Lord is nigh unto all them that | call upon | Him, : ‖
To all that | call upon | Him in | truth.

My mouth shall speak the | praise of the | Lord ;
And let all flesh bless His holy | name for | ever and | ever.

Psalm cxlv.

MAGNIFICAT.

37.

INTONATION. CHANT.   *Allegro.*

Mag - ni - fi - cat anima mea Dominum. Hallelujah! Amen. Hallelujah! Amen.

Intonation.   *Chant.*

1 My soul doth ‖ magni- | fy the | Lord, ‖ and my spirit hath re- | joiced in | God my | Saviour.

2   For he hath looked upon the low estate of | His hand- | maiden : ‖ for behold, from henceforth all gene- | rations · shall | call me | blessed.

3   For He that is mighty hath done to me | great = | things, ‖ and | holy | is His | name.

4   And His mercy is unto generations and | gener- | ations ‖ on | them that | fear= | Him.

5   He hath showed strength | with His | arm, ‖ He hath scattered the proud in the imagi- | nation | of their | hearts ;

6   He hath put down princes | from their | thrones, ‖ and hath exalted | them of | low de- | gree.

7   The hungry He hath filled with | good = | things, ‖ and the rich He hath | sent = | empty · a- | way.

8   He hath holpen Israel His servant, that he might re- | member | mercy, ‖ As He spake unto our fathers, toward Abraham, | and his | seed for | ever.

9 Glory · be to the ‖ Father, and | to the | Son, ‖ and | to the | Holy | Ghost,

10   As it was in the beginning, is now, and | ever | shall be, ‖ world | with-out | end. A- | men. Hallelujah ! Amen.

Luke 1. 46.

38.

LEVAVI OCULOS MEOS.

39.

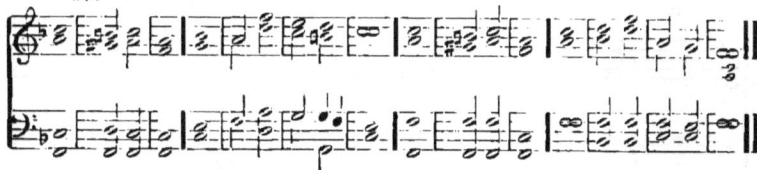

40.

41.

1 { I will lift up mine eyes unto the mountains :
{ From whence shall my | help = | come?

2 { My help cometh from the Lord,
{ Who | made = | heaven · and | earth.

3 { He will not suffer thy foot to be moved :
{ He that keepeth thee | will not | slumber.

4 { Behold He that keepeth Israel,
{ Shall | neither | slumber · nor | sleep.

5 { The Lord is thy keeper ;
{ The Lord is thy shade upon thy | right = | hand.

6 { The sun shall not smite thee by day, |
{ Nor the | moon by | night.

7 { The Lord shall keep thee from all evil ;
{ He shall | keep thy | soul.

8 { The Lord shall keep thy going out, and thy coming in.
{ From this time forth, | and for | ever | more.

Psalm cxxI.

DOMINUS REGIT ME.

42.

A   -   men.

43.

A   ·   men.

1 The Lord is my shepherd; I | shall not | want.

2 He maketh me to lie down in green pastures :
He leadeth me beside the | still = | waters.

3 He restoreth my soul :
He guideth me in the paths of righteousness for His | name's = | sake,

4 Yea though I walk through the valley of the shadow of death,
I will fear no evil; for Thou art with me ;
Thy rod and Thy | staff, they | comfort me.

5 Thou preparest a table before me in the presence of mine enemies :
Thou anointest my head with oil; my | cup · runneth | over.

6 Surely goodness and mercy shall follow me all the days of my life :
And I will dwell in the house of the | Lord for | ever.

Psalm xxiii.

44.

CONFITEMINI DOMINO.

45.

46.

1 O give thanks unto the Lord, call upon His name ;
Make known His doings a- | mong the | peoples.

2 Sing unto Him, sing praises unto Him ;
Talk ye of | all His | marvellous | works.

3 Glory ye in His holy name:
Let the heart of them rejoice that | seek the | Lord.

4 Seek ye the Lord and His strength ; |
Seek His | face · ever- | more.

5 Remember His marvellous works that He hath done ;
His wonders, and the judgments | of His | mouth.

6 He is the Lord our God :
His judgments | are in | all the | earth.

Psalm cv.

LAUDA, ANIMA MEA.

1 Praise | ye the | Lord,
Praise the Lord, | O my | soul.

2 While I live will I | praise the | Lord :
I will sing praises unto my God while I | have · any | being.

3 Who made | heaven and | earth,
The sea, and all that in them is ;
Who keepeth | truth for | ever :

4 Who executeth judgment | for the · op- | pressed ;
Who giveth food to the hungry :
The Lord looseth the | prison- | ers ;

5 The Lord openeth the | eyes · of the | blind ;
The Lord raiseth up them that are bowed down ;
The Lord | loveth · the | righteous :

6 The Lord shall reign for ever,
Thy God, O Zion, unto | all · gene- | rations.
Praise | ye the | Lord.

Psalm cxlvi.

DESCENDET SICUT PLUVIA.

47.

1 { He shall come down like rain upon the | mown grass ;
    As showers that water the | earth.

2 { In His days shall the righteous | flourish :
    And abundance of | peace, · till the | moon · be no | more.

3 { All kings shall fall down be- | fore Him ;
    All nations shall | serve Him.

4 { His name shall endure for | ever ;
    His name shall be continued as long as the sun ;
    And men shall be blessed in Him ;
    All | nations · shall | call Him | happy.

5 { Blessed be the Lord | God, ‖ the God of | Israel ;
    Who only doeth wondrous | things :

6 { And blessed be His glorious name for ever ;
    And let the whole | earth be | filled · with His | glory.

                                   Psalm lxxii.

CONSERVA ME, DOMINE.

1 Preserve me, O | God, ‖ for in Thee do I put my | trust.

2 { I have said unto the Lord, Thou art | my Lord :
    I have no | good be- | yond · ═ | Thee.

3 { The lines are fallen unto me in pleasant | places :
    Yea, I have a goodly | heritage.

4 { I will bless the Lord, who hath given me | counsel ;
    Yea, my reins in- | struct me · in the | night- ═ | seasons.

5 { I have set the Lord always be- | fore me ;
    Because He is at my right hand I shall not be | moved.

6 { Therefore my heart is glad, and my glory re- | joiceth ;
    My flesh | also · shall | dwell in | safety.

7 { Thou wilt show me the path of | life,—
    Thou wilt show me the path of | life.

8 { In Thy presence is fulness of | joy ;
    At Thy right hand there are | pleasures · for | ever | more.

                                   Psalm xvi.

ALLELUIA.

54.

Hal - le - lu - jah!

Alleluia : quoniam regnavit Dominus Deus.

Hallelujah !

1 For the Lord our God, the Al- | mighty, | reigneth !

Rev. xix. 6.

2 The kingdom of this world is become the kingdom of our Lord and of His
Christ ; and He shall | reign for | ever and | ever.

Rev. xi. 15.

3 King of kings and | Lord of | lords.

Rev. xix. 16.

4 Worthy art Thou. our Lord and our God. to receive the glory and the honor and
the power : for Thou didst create all things, and because of Thy will they |
were, and | were cre- | ated.

Rev. iv. 11.

5 Salvation and glory and power be- | long to our | God.

Rev. xix. 1.

6 Salvation to our God who sitteth upon the | throne and | unto · the | Lamb.

Rev. vii. 10.

7 Blessing. and glory. and wisdom, and thanksgiving, and honor, and | power, and
| might

8 Be unto our | God for | ever and | ever.

Rev. vii. 12.

Hallelujah ! Amen.

LAUDATE DOMINUM.

1 Praise | ye the | Lord ;

2 { For it is good to sing praises unto our God ;
{ For it is | pleasant · and | praise is comely.

3 { Great is our Lord. and | mighty · in | power :
{ His | under- | standing · is | infinite.

4 { Sing unto the Lord with | thanks · = | giving :
{ Sing praises upon the | harp | unto · our | God.

5 { Glory be to the Father. | and · to the | Son,
{ And | to the | Holy | Ghost,

6 { As it was in the beginning, is now, and | ever | shall be,
{ World | without | end. A- | men.

Psalm cxlvii.

Hal - - le - lu - jah! A - - men, A - - - - - men.

QUID RETRIBUAM DOMINO.

49.

A - - men.

50.

1 What shall I render unto the Lord for all His | bene- · fits | toward me?
2 I will take the cup of salvation, and | call up- · on the | name · of the | Lord.
3 I will pay my vows unto the Lord. yea, in the presence of | all His | people.
4 { O Lord, truly I am Thy servant ; I am Thy servant, the son of Thy handmaid,
   { Thou hast | loosed · my | bonds.
5 { I will offer to Thee the sacrifice of thanksgiving,
   { And will | call up- · on the | name · of the | Lord.
6 { In the courts of the Lord's house,
   { In the midst of thee, O Jerusalem. | Praise = | ye the | Lord.   Psalm cxvi. 12.

QUAM PULCHRI SUPER MONTES.

1 { How beautiful upon the mountains
  { Are the feet of him that bringeth good tidings, that | publish-eth | peace ;
2 { That bringeth good tidings of good, that publisheth salvation ;
  { That saith unto Zion. | Thy God | reign- == | eth.
3 { The voice of thy watchmen ! They lift up the voice,
  { Together | do they | sing :
4 { For they shall see eye to eye,
  { When the | Lord re- | turneth · to | Zion.
5 { Break forth into joy, sing together,
  { Ye waste | places · of Je- | rusalem !
6 { For the Lord hath comforted His people,
  { He | hath re- | deemed · Je- | rusalem !
7 { The Lord hath made bare His holy arm
  { In the eyes of | all the | nations ;
8 { And all the ends of the earth
  { Shall see the sal- | va-tion | of our | God.   Isa. lii. 7-10.

51.

LEX DOMINI IMMACULATA.

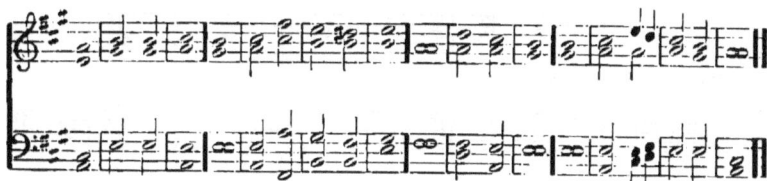

52.

1 The law of the Lord is perfect, re- | storing · the | soul :
The testimony of the Lord is sure, | making | wise the | simple.

The precepts of the Lord are right, re- | joicing · the | heart :
The commandment of the Lord is | pure, en- | lightening · the | eyes.

2 The fear of the Lord is clean, end- | uring · for | ever :
The judgments of the Lord are true and | righteous | alto- | gether.

More to be desired are they than gold, yea, than | much fine | gold :
Sweeter also than | honey · and the | honey- | comb.

3 Moreover by them is Thy | servant | warned :
In keeping of | them · there is | great re- | ward.

Who can dis- | cern his | errors?
Clear Thou | me from | hidden | faults.

4 Keep back Thy servant also from presumptuous sins ;
Let them not have dominion over me : then shall | I be | perfect,
And I shall be | clear from | great trans-| gression.

Let the words of my mouth and the meditation of my heart be acceptable |
in Thy | sight,
O Lord, my | Rock and | my Re- | deemer.

Psalm xix. 7-14.

QUAM DILECTA TABERNACULA TUA.

53.

[INTONATION.] [CHANT.]

1 .How ‖ amiable are Thy tabernacles, O | Lord of | hosts!

2 { My soul longeth, yea, even fainteth for the courts of the Lord ;
{ My heart and my flesh cry | out un · to the | living | God.

3 { Yea, the sparrow hath found her an house,
{ And the swallow a nest for herself, where she may lay her young,
{ Even Thine altars, O Lord of hosts, my | King and · my | God.

4 { Blessed are they that dwell in Thy house :
{ They | will be · still | praising | Thee.

5 { Blessed is the man whose strength is in Thee :
{ In whose heart are the | highways to | Zion.

6 { Passing through the valley of Weeping, they make it a place of springs ;
{ Yea, the | early · rain | covereth it with | blessings.

7 { They go from strength to strength ;
{ Every one of them appeareth before | God in | Zion.

8 { Lord God of hosts, hear my prayer :
{ Give | ear, O | God of | Jacob.

9 { Behold, O God our shield,
{ And look upon the face of | Thine an- | ointed.

10 { For a dây in Thy courts is better than a thousand.
{ I had rather be a door-keeper in the house of my God,
{ Than to | dwell · in the | tents of | wickedness.

11 { For the Lord God is a sun and a shield : the Lord will give grace
{   and glory :
{ No good thing will He withhold from them that | walk up- | rightly.

12   O Lord of hosts, blessed is the | man that | trusteth..in | Thee.

Psalm lxxxiv.

54.

55.

MAGNUS DOMINUS.

56.

57.

1 Great is the Lord, and highly to be praisèd,
   In the city of our God, in His | holy | mountain.

2 We have thought on Thy loving-kindness, O God,
   In the | midst · of | Thy = | temple.

3 As is Thy name, O God,

4 So is Thy praise unto the | ends · of the | earth : ‖
   Thy right | hand is | full of | righteousness.

5 Let Mount Zion be glad,
   Let the daughters of Judah rejoice,
   Be- | cause of · Thy | judgments.

6 Walk about Zion, and go round about her : |
   Tell · the | towers there- | of.

7 Mark ye well her bulwarks, consider her palaces ;
   That ye may tell it to the gene- | ration | following.

8 For this God is our God, for ever and ever ;
   He will be our | guide · even | unto | death.

Ps. xlviii.

VENITE AD ME OMNES QUI LABORATIS.

58.

A - men,   A - men.

1   ' Come unto me all ye that labor and are | heavy | laden,
2   ' Come unto me all ye that labor and are heavy laden,
     And | I will give you | rest.
3   ' Take my yoke upon you, and learn of me ;
     For I am meek and | lowly · in | heart :
4   ' And ye shall find | rest unto your | souls.
5   ' For my yoke is easy, and my | burden · is | light ;
6   ' For my yoke is easy, and my | burden is = | light.'   Matt. xi. 28.
7   And the Spirit and the bride say, · Come.'
     And let him that | beareth · say, | ' Come.'
8   And let him that is athirst, come :
     And whosoever will, let him take the | water of · life = | freely.
         Rev. xxii. 17.

CHRIST, AND IMMORTALITY.

59.

Maestoso:

Soon shall the trumpet sound, and we shall rise to im-mor-tal-i-ty.   A-men.

1 WE sing His love who once was slain, Who soon o'er death re- | viv'd a- | gain, ‖
That all His saints through Him might have Eternal | conquests | o'er the | grave. ‖
Soon shall the trumpet sound, and we Shall rise to immortality.

2 The saints who now in Jesus sleep, His own almighty | power shall | keep, ‖
Till dawns the bright illustrious day, When death it- | self shall | die a-way. ‖
Soon, etc.

3 How loud shall our glad voices sing, When Christ His risen | saints shall | bring ‖
From beds of dust and silent clay, To realms of | ever- | lasting | day. ‖
Soon, etc.

4 When Jesus we in glory meet,· Our utmost joys shall | be com- | plete : ‖
When landed on that heavenly shore, Death and the | curse shall | be no | more. ‖
Soon, etc.

         R. Hill's Coll.

MISERERE MEI DEUS.

60.

61.

62.

1 { Have mercy upon me, O God, according to Thy | loving- | kindness ;

2 { According to the multitude of Thy tender mercies blot out | my trans- | gres- = | sions.

3 { Wash me thoroughly from my iniquity, And cleanse me | from my | sin.

4 { For I acknowledge my transgressions ; And my | sin is | ever · be- | fore me.

5 { Against Thee, Thee only have I sinned, And done that which is evil | in Thy | sight.

6 { That thou mayest be justified when thou speakest, And be | clear when | Thou = | judgest.

7 { Create in me a clean heart, O God ; And renew a right | spirit · with- | in me.

8 { Cast me not away from Thy presence ; And take not Thy | Holy | Spirit | from me.

9 { Restore unto me the joy of Thy salvation, And uphold me with | a free | spirit :

10 { Then will I teach transgressors Thy ways ; And sinners shall be con- | verted | unto | Thee.

11 { O Lord, open | Thou my | lips ; And my | mouth · shall show | forth Thy | praise.

Psalm li.

Chants.

DE PROFUNDIS.

1 Out of the depths have I cried unto | Thee, O | Lord.

2 Lord, hear my voice;
Let Thine ears be attentive to the | voice of · my | suppli- | cations.

3 If Thou Lord shouldest mark iniquities,
O Lord, | who shall | stand.

4 But there is forgiveness with Thee,
That | Thou = | mayest · be | feared.

5 I wait for the Lord, my soul doth wait,
And in His | word · do I | hope.

6 My soul looketh for the Lord
More than watchmen look for the morning,
Yea, | more than · | watchmen · for the | morning.

7 O Israel, hope in the Lord:
For with the Lord there is mercy,
And with Him is | plenteous · re- | demption.

8 And He shall redeem Israel
From | all = | his in- | iquities.

Psalm cxxx.

DEUS NOSTER REFUGIUM.

66.

A

B

A
1 God is our refuge and strength, a very present | help in | trouble. ‖
Therefore will we not fear, though the earth do change, and though the mountains
be | moved · in the | heart · of the | seas. ‖

2 Though the waters thereof | roar · and be | troubled.
B Though the mountains | shake · with the | swelling · there- | of.

3 There is a river, the streams whereof make glad the | city · of | God ; ‖
The holy place of the tabernacles of the | Most ⌢ | ⌢ | High.

4 God is in the midst of her ; she shall | not be | moved. ‖
A God shall help her, and | that ⌢ | right ⌢ | early.

5 The nations raged, the kingdoms were moved ; He uttered His voice, the |
earth ⌢ | melted. ‖
The Lord of hosts is with us ; the God of | Jacob | is our | refuge.

6 Come behold the works of the Lord, what desolations He hath | made · in the | earth. ‖
He maketh wars to cease unto the end of the earth ; He breaketh the bow, and
B cutteth the spear in sunder ; He burneth the | chariots | in the | fire.

7 Be still, and know that | I am | God. ‖
I will be exalted among the heathen, I will be ex- | alted | in the | earth.

8 The Lord of hosts is with us ; the God of Jacob | is our | refuge. ‖
The Lord of hosts is with us ; The God of Jacob | is our | refuge.

Psalm xlvi.

A · · · · · men, A · · · men, A · · · · · men, A · · · · men.

DOMINE, REFUGIUM NOSTER.

67.

68.

1   Lord, Thou hast been our | dwelling- | place
In | all · gene- | ra- ═ | tions.

2   Before the mountains were brought forth,
Or ever Thou hadst formed the | earth · and the | world,
Even from everlasting to ever- | lasting, | Thou art | God.

3   Thou turnest | man · to de- | struction ;
And sayest, ' Re- | turn, ye | children · of | men.'

4   For a thousand years in Thy sight
Are but as yesterday | when it · is | past,
And | as a | watch · in the | night.

5   Thou carriest them away as with a flood ; they | are · as a | sleep ;
In the morning they are like | grass which | groweth | up.

6   In the morning it flourisheth and | groweth | up ;
In the evening it is cut | down and | wither- | eth.

7   So teach us to | number our | days,
That we may | get us · an | heart of | wisdom.

8   O satisfy us in the morning | with Thy | mercy ;
That we may re- | joice · and be | glad · all our | days.

9   Let Thy work appear un- | to Thy | servants,
And Thy | glory up- | on their | children.

10   And let the beauty of the Lord our | God · be up- | on us,
And establish Thou the work of our hands upon us ;
Yea, the work of our | hands e- | stablish · Thou | it.
                                                        Psalm xc.

BEATI MORTUI.

69.

A - men.

70.

1 Blessed are the dead,
Who die in the | Lord from | henceforth:

2 Yea, saith the Spirit, that they may rest from their labors;
And their | works do | follow | them.

Rev. xiv. 13.

3 Blessed and holy is he that hath part in the first resurrection:
Over these the second death | hath no | power;

4 But they shall be priests of God and of Christ,
And shall reign with | Him a | thousand | years.

Rev. xx. 6.

5 Unto Him that loveth us,
And loosed us from our sins | by His | blood,

6 And He made us to be a kingdom, to be priests unto His God
and Father;
To Him be the glory and the do- | minion · for | ever and | ever.

Rev. i. 5. f.

NOTUM FAC, DOMINE.

Lord, make me to know mine end,
And the measure of my days, | what it | is;
Let me | know how | frail I | am.

Behold, Thou hast made my days as handbreadths;
And mine age is as | nothing · before | Thee:
Surely every man at his best estate is | altogether | vani- | ty.

Hear my prayer, O Lord, and give ear | unto · my | cry;

Hold not Thy | peace | at my | tears:

For I am a | stranger · with | Thee,

A sojourner, as | all my | fathers | were.

Psalm xxxix.

I believe in God the Father Almighty, Maker of heaven and earth, and in Je - sus Christ His

on - ly Son our Lord;   { Who was conceived   { Born of the   Suffered under
               { by the Holy Ghost, { Virgin Mary ;   Pontius Pilate, Was

cru - ci - fied, dead, and bur - ied. He descend - ed in - to hell,   The

third day He rose from the dead;   He ascend - ed in-to heav'n, And sitteth on the right hand of

God the Fa-ther Al - might - y;   { From thence he shall }   quick and the dead,
                         { come to judge the }

I believe in the Ho - ly Ghost; the holy Catholic Church, the Com- munion of Saints; The for - giveness of

sins; the Resurrection of the body; And the Life ev -er - last - ing. A - men.

Sanctus I.

p

Ho - ly, ho - ly, ho - ly Lord God, Lord God of Hosts; Heaven and earth are

crescendo.

ff

full of the maj - es-ty, are full of the maj - es - ty of Thy glo-ry. Glo - - ry

be to Thee, O Lord, to Thee, O Lord most High. A - men.

Ho - ly! Ho - ly! Ho - ly! Lord God of Sabaoth! Heav'n and earth are

full, full of Thy glo - ry, Heav'n and earth are full, are full of Thy

glo - ry. Glo - ry be to Thee, Glo - ry be to Thee,
Glo - ry be to Thee, Glo - ry be to

Glo - ry be to Thee, to Thee, O Lord . . most high.
Thee,

Sentence.

Andante.

Have mercy up - on me, Have mercy, O God! Blot out my transgressions, have mercy, O God!

Cre - ate . . in me a clean heart, O God, And renew a right spir-it with - in

me. Cast me not a-way from Thy pres - ence, And take not Thy Ho - ly Spir-it from

me. Restore un - to me the joy of Thy sal - va - tion, And uphold me with a free

Spir - it, Then will I teach trans - gres - sors Thy ways: And sin - ners shall
Then will I,

be converted un - to Thee. Have mer-cy, O God! Blot out my transgres - sions!

TOPICAL INDEX.

Activity,Christian, 53–57, 413, 414, 418–421, 427.
Advent, 135–140, 143, 148, 150, 151, 154, 156.
Afflictions, 422–460.
Ascension of Christ, 152, 175, 176, 180, 184, 186.
Ashamed of Christ, 161, 398.
Atonement, 149, 154, 157, 164, 166, 209–252.
Beatitudes, 496.
Bible, 3, 16, 43, 60, 234.
Burial Hymns, 315, 462–481, 493, 495, 497.
Christ, ascended, 152, 175, 176, 180, 184, 186.
  " birth of, 135–140, 143, 148, 150, 151, 154, 156.
  cross of. 152, 153, 157, 165, 166, 211, 212.
  example of, 158, 159, 164, 191, 295, 408.
  faith in, 177, 224, 227, 264, 265, 283, 284, 288, 291–298, 341, 344, 357, 358, 371, 372, 375, 379–381, 388–390, 396, 399, 402, 404.
  future kingdom of, 214, 215, 222, 223, 225, 232, 233, 236, 237, 240, 241, 245, 247, 254, 303.
  joy in. 249, 299–406.
  the Judge, 473, 475, 476, 479, 480.
  a King, 146, 149, 150, 170, 180, 185, 214, 215, 222, 223, 237, 240, 247, 303.
  interceding, 152, 175, 176, 184, 185, 460.
  the Light of life, 70, 144, 209, 231, 344.
  love of to us, 137, 164, 106, 175, 176, 191, 217, 224, 244, 251, 202, 293, 298, 316, 320, 331.
  not ashamed of, 161, 398.
  praise to, 4, 22, 42, 46, 47, 81, 137, 140, 142, 144, 147–50, 152–154, 157, 163–166, 169–171, 173, 175–177, 184, 186, 187, 190, 191, 209–213, 216, 217, 219–221, 224, 226, 250, 251, 258, 260, 261, 263, 300, 302, 303, 306, 316, 320, 333, 334, 361.
  redemption by, 149, 154, 157, 164, 166, 200–252.
  rest in, 213, 227–229, 243, 276, 280, 285, 338, 340, 342, 368, 497, 504, 505.
  resurrection of, 29, 42, 47, 160, 171, 174, 181–183.
  a Sacrifice, 153, 164, 166, 211, 212, 217, 221, 267, 289.
  second coming of, 473, 475–481.
  sufferings of, 153, 164–166, 172, 179, 180.
  union with, 260.
  the Way, the Truth, the Life, 177.
Church, delight in the, 253–263.

Church, militant, 258.
  triumphant, 186, 214, 215, 222, 223, 287, 240, 247, 254, 261, 491, 492, 496, 499, 506, 508.
  unity of the, 255, 259–261.
Close of worship, 39, 44, 46, 48–52.
Communion hymns, 265–275.
Confession of sin, 220, 231, 277–298, 396, 404.
Conversion, 176, 205–254, 277–298.
  of the world, 205–248, 254.
Country, our, 125, 507.
Cross, Christ on the, 153, 165, 166, 211, 212.
Daily worship, 53–80.
Death, 462–481, 495.
Easter, 29, 42, 47, 160, 171, 174, 181–183.
Eternity, 97, 466, 467, 482–508.
Evening Hymns, 72–80.
Faith, 265, 291, 341, 358, 371, 372, 375, 379–381, 388, 390, 399, 402, 404.
Forgiveness, 77, 210–213, 216, 217, 219–221, 227–229, 235, 238, 243, 244, 277–298, 404.
Funeral hymns, 315, 402, 467, 471, 474, 493, 495, 497.
God, adoration of, 1–47, 82–133, 221, 299, 301, 304, 306, 314, 317, 319, 322, 324, 325, 328, 320, 331, 347, 354–356, 462.
  dependence on, 97, 100, 103, 119, 332, 357, 369, 377, 422–460.
  house of, 4–6, 8, 13, 18, 33, 41, 45.
  presence of, 93, 113.
  providence of, 58, 66, 75, 100, 103, 120, 130, 305, 332, 357, 359, 369, 377, 399.
  a Refuge, 58, 100, 213, 229, 257, 276, 312, 362–364, 378, 405, 440.
  a Sovereign, 106, 109–111, 299, 436, 452, 457.
Grace, saving. 211, 212, 216, 217, 219–221, 224, 226, 289.
Heaven, 6, 482–506.
Holy Spirit invoked, 19, 193–208, 233, 343.
Hope, Christian, 27, 209, 299–406.
House of God, 4–6, 8, 13, 18, 33, 41, 45.
Invitations of the Gospel, 210, 213, 216, 219, 226–228, 235, 238, 243, 244.
Invocations, 4, 7, 11, 17, 19, 26, 27, 35, 37, 45, 245.
Joy, Christian, 249, 299–406.
Judgment Day, 283, 473, 475–481.
Life, uncertainty of, 463–467, 469, 477, 494, 495, 500.
Lord's Day, 1–52.

280

INDEX OF FIRST LINES.

282

INDEX OF CHANTS AND OCCASIONAL PIECES.

287

INDEX OF TUNES.

METRICAL INDEX.

L. M.

Abraham, 63.
All Saints, 25.
Anvern, 118, 142.
Ascension, 117.
Ashford, 24, 103, 140.
Battell's Choral, 219.
Beethoven, 150.
Bera, 221.
Burney, 8, 26.
Cathedral, 43.
Choral, 160.
Cramer. 78.
Credo. 187.
Dedication, 32.
Deux Points, 222.
Duke St., 58, 92, 144.
Dykes. 80.
Effen, 2.
Elysium, 214, 226.
Ernan, 23, 28, 182.
Eton. 133.
Excelsis. 3.
Federal St., 77, 110, 131.
Germany, 58, 90, 191.
German Te Deum, 42.
Gloria, 41.
Hamburg, 141, 196.
Harmony Grove, 64.
Hartel, 168.
Haven, 114.
Hebron, 37.
Hochgesang, 4, 41.
Homage, 2, 41.
Loving Kindness, 152.
Malvern, 44, 73.
Mendon, 147.
Migdol, 7.
Missionary Chant, 109, 197.
— Old Hundred, 1.
Overberg, 28.
Park St., 30, 127.
Pesaro. 50, 101.
Rest, 221.
Retreat, 5, 188.
Rothwell, 90.
Schumann, 6, 89.
Sessions, 165.
St. Alban, 40.
Uxbridge, 100.
Volkslied, 113.
Vom Himmel hoch, 233.
Ward, 124.
Ware, 208.
Wimborne, 228.

Winchester, 106.
Woodworth, 186.
York, 37.
Zephyr, 6.

L. M. 6 lines.

Hastings, 90.
Melita, 43.
Old Melody, 240.
Sanctus, 213.
Stella, 27.

L. M. D.

Creation, 45.
Star of Bethlehem, 102.

L. P. M.

Union, 20.

C. M.

Abbe Vogler, 155.
Antioch, 72.
Arlington, 176.
Avon, 10, 82.
Beatitudo, 132.
Belmont, 153.
Bradford, 174.
Cambridge, 74, 157, 195.
Canaan, 228.
Cherith. 137.
Chimes, 68.
Choral, 22.
Christmas, 236.
Cincinnati, 220.
Coronation, 71.
Cowper, 104.
Dalton, 184.
Darmstadt, 4.
Dundee, 46.
Franconia, 71.
Geer, 158.
Gluck, 8, 98, 215.
Golgotha, 134.
Heber, 142, 171.
Help, 47, 106.
Holy Trinity, 74.
Hummel, 87.
Irene, 60.
Landstuhl, 53, 235.
Latour, 10, 86.
Lützen, 51.
Malkammer, 49, 166.
Manoah, 140.
Matilda, 170.
Mear, 52, 180.
Men lelssohn. 12.

Naomi, 198.
Nimbus, 181.
Ortonville, 150.
Prayer, 175.
Phuvah, 49.
Remembrance, 31.
Rhine, 229.
Robbins, 120.
Seldon, 178.
Sharon, 172, 191.
Southport, 158.
St. Agnes, 5, 184, 203.
St. Ann's, 40.
St. George's, 11.
St. Mathias, 173.
Swanwick, 55.
Three Angels, 231.
Waldhorn, 145.
Warwick, 9.
Watch, 47, 88.
Wilmington, 148.
Woodstock, 11, 38, 92.
Zerah, 110.

C. M. D.

Brattle St., 176.
Cassel, 126.
Glad Tidings, 69, 95, 123.
Greenport, 85.
Jerusal'm, 66.
Semper fidelis, 177.
St. Matthew, 125.
Vox dilecti, 128.
Zöllner, 34.

C. P. M.

Ariel, 76.
Heavenly Love, 138.
Meribah, 161, 227, 234.

S. M.

Battell, 56.
Boylston, 22, 124, 224.
Carlton, 205.
Contentment, 149.
Dennis, 24, 211.
Detroit, 114, 136.
Eisenach, 112.
Gideon, 192.
Gorton, 111, 136.
Greenwood, 165.
Hope, 159.
Laban, 192.
Lane, 107.
Leighton, 55, 127.